Jürgen Beyerer / Fernando Puente León / Thomas Längle (eds.)

OCM 2013 – Optical Characterization of Materials

Conference Proceedings

OCM 2013
Optical Characterization of Materials

Conference Proceedings

edited by
Jürgen Beyerer / Fernando Puente León / Thomas Längle

Veranstalter

Fraunhofer Institut of Optronics,
System Technologies and Image Exploitation IOSB
c/o Karlsruhe Center for Material Signatures KCM
Fraunhoferstraße 1
76131 Karlsruhe

Dieser Tagungsband ist auch als Onlineversion abrufbar unter
http://dx.doi.org/10.5445/KSP/1000032143

Impressum

Karlsruher Institut für Technologie (KIT)
KIT Scientific Publishin
Straße am Forum 2
D-76131 Karlsruhe
www.ksp.kit.edu

KIT – Universität des Landes Baden-Württemberg und
nationales Forschungszentrum in der Helmholtz-Gemeinschaft

KIT Scientific Publishing 201
Print on Demand

ISBN 978-3-86644-956-7

Preface

The state of the art in optical characterization of materials is advancing rapidly. New insights into the theoretical foundations of this research field have been gained and exciting practical developments have taken place, both driven by novel applications that are constantly emerging. The researchers in this interdisciplinary domain definitely need a platform to present, discuss and evaluate their latest research results. Due to that fact, the international conference on Optical Characterization of Materials (OCM) was founded in the year 2013 and will now take place every two years.

The OCM 2013 was organized by the Karlsruhe Center for Spectral Signatures of Materials (KCM) in cooperation with the German Chapter of the Instrumentation & Measurement Society of IEEE. The Karlsruhe Center for Spectral Signatures of Materials is an association of institutes of Karlsruhe Institute of Technology (KIT) and the business unit Automated Visual Inspection of the Fraunhofer Institute of Optronics, System Technologies and Image Exploitation IOSB.

Although the conference was organized for the first time, the organizing committee has had the pleasure to evaluate a large amount of abstracts. Based on the submissions, we selected 21 papers as talks complemented by 10 poster presentations and several practical demonstrations.

The present book is based on the conference held in Karlsruhe, Germany from March 6–7, 2013. The aim of this conference was to bring together leading researchers in the domain of Characterization of Materials by spectral characteristics from UV (240 nm) to IR (14 µm), multispectral image analysis, X-ray methods, polarimetry, and microscopy. Typical application areas for these techniques cover the fields of, e.g., food industry, recycling of waste materials, detection of contaminated materials, mining, process industry, and raw materials.

The editors would like to thank all of the authors that have contributed to these proceedings as well as the reviewers, who have invested a generous amount of their time to suggest possible improvements of the papers. The help of Henning Schulte and Dennis Heddendorp in the preparation of this book is greatly appreciated. Last but not least, we thank the organizing committee of the conference, led by Britta Ost, for their effort in organizing this event. The excellent technical facilities and the friendly staff of the Fraunhofer IOSB greatly contributed to the success of the meeting.

March 2013

Jürgen Beyerer
Fernando Puente León
Thomas Längle

General Chairs

Prof. Dr.-Ing. habil. J. Beyerer	Fraunhofer IOSB Karlsruhe
Prof. Dr.-Ing. F. Puente León	Karlsruhe Institute of Technology

Program Chair

apl. Prof. Dr.-Ing. T. Längle	Karlsruhe

Program Committee

Dr. M. Bücking	Schmallenberg
PD Dr. rer. nat. J.-D. Eckhardt	Karlsruhe
Dr.-Ing. M. Heizmann	Karlsruhe
Prof. Dr.-Ing. O. Kanoun	Chemnitz
Prof. Dr.-Ing. habil. H. Z. Kuyumcu	Berlin
Prof. Dr.-Ing. H. S. Müller	Karlsruhe
Dipl.-Ing. D. Nüßler	Wachtberg
Dr. R. Ostertag	Würzburg
Prof. Dr.-Ing. T. Pretz	Aachen
Prof. Dr. F. Salazar Bloise	Madrid
Dipl.-Ing. Dipl.-Wirt.-Ing. H. Schulte	Karlsruhe
Prof. Dr. G. Sextl	Würzburg
Dipl.-Ing. M. Taphanel	Karlsruhe
Dr. oec. troph. M. Wenning	München
Prof. Dr.-Ing. H. Wotruba	Aachen

Contents

Preface v

Contents vii

Measurement Principles

Spectral imaging in process analytics using chemometrics and
first principles 1
    S. Luckow-Markward, E. Ostertag, B. Boldrini, W. Kessler and
    R. W. Kessler

MEMS based systems and their applications in NIR spectroscopy
for materials analysis 15
    H. Grüger, T. Pügner, J. Knobbe and H. Schenk

Characterisation and identification of plastics through microwave
treatment and temperature measurement 29
    M. Labbert, T. A. Baloun, J. I. Schoenherr and
    H. Z. Kuyumcu

Optical properties of Al_2O_3/Al cermets obtained by plasma
spraying: role of composition and microstructure 41
    D. Toru, K. Wittmann-Ténèze, A. Quet, D. Damiani, H. Piombini,
    D. De Sousa Meneses, L. Del Campo and P. Echegut

Improved fault detection for inline optical inspections by
evaluation of NIR images 55
    H. Eigenbrod

Spectroscopy

Reflection and transmission Raman spectroscopy for the chemical
characterization of solid materials 65
  E. Ostertag, D. Oelkrug and R. W. Kessler

Hydrogen content of CeCl₃-doped sodium alanate powder
samples measured in-situ by ATR-FTIR-spectroscopy and
gravimetry during desorption 77
  I. Franke, H. D. Bauer and B. Scheppat

Infrared reflection absorption spectroscopy for characterization
of alkylsilane monolayers on silicon nitride surfaces 89
  X. Stammer and S. Heißler

Multispectral imaging: Development and applications for
snapshot MSI instrumentation 95
  J. Dougherty, S. Smith and O. Lischtschenko

Food Inspection

Comprehensive, non-invasive, and quantitative monitoring
of the health and nutrition state of crop plants by means of
hyperspectral imaging and computational intelligence based
analysis 103
  A. Backhaus and U. Seiffert

Improving optical fruit sorting by non-destructive determination
of quality parameters affecting wine quality 115
  M. Lafontaine and M. Freund

Active infrared thermography as a tool for quality control in the
food industry 127
  J. Aderhold, P. Meinlschmidt and V. Märgner

Inline HSI food inspection and concentration measurements of
pharmaceuticals – a report from an industrial environment 137
  M. Kerschhaggl, W. Märzinger, E. Leitner, N. Haar, M. Zangl,
  M. Jeindl and P. Kerschhaggl

Detection of non-metallic impurities and defects through radar
measurements. 151
    D. Nüßler, C. Krebs and R. Brauns

Image analysis of natural products. 157
    D. Garten, K. Anding, S. Lerm, G. Linß and P. Brückner

Spectral Data Processing

Evaluation of spectral unmixing using nonnegative matrix
factorization on stationary hyperspectral sensor data of
specifically prepared rock and mineral mixtures 169
    W. Gross, S. Borchardt and W. Middelmann

Spectral and spatial unmixing for material recognition in sorting
plants 179
    M. Michelsburg and F. Puente León

Understanding multi-spectral images of wood particles with
matrix factorization 191
    M. Asbach, D. Mauruschat and B. Plinke

A framework for storage, visualization and analysis of
multispectral data 203
    S. Irgenfried and C. Negara

Mineral Characterisation

Potential of NIR hyperspectral imaging in the minerals industry . . 215
    C. Schropp, H. Knapp and K. Neubert

Luminescence- and reflection spectroscopy for automatic
classification of various minerals 227
    J. Hofer, R. Huber, G. Weingrill and K. Gatterer

X-Ray

X-ray transmission sorting of tungsten ore 245
    M. R. Robben, H. Knapp, M. Dehler and H. Wotruba

Quantitative sorting using dual energy X-ray transmission imaging 259
*M. Firsching, J. Mühlbauer, A. Mäurer, F. Nachtrab and
N. Uhlmann*

Recycling

Polymer identification with terahertz technology 265
A. Maul and M. Nagel

Characterisation of materials in the millimeter wave frequency
region for industrial applications 275
M. Demming, D. Nüßler, C. Krebs and J. Klimek

Spectral imaging in process analytics using chemometrics and first principles

S. Luckow-Markward, E. Ostertag, B. Boldrini,
W. Kessler and R. W. Kessler*

Reutlingen Research Institute, Process Analysis and Technology,
Reutlingen University, Alteburgstr. 150, 72762 Reutlingen
*corresponding author: rudolf.kessler@reutlingen-university.de

Abstract Optical spectroscopy is able to detect not only the chemical composition of the species by their wavelength specific absorption k but also the morphological feature through their wavelength dependent scattering s. In standard multivariate data analysis in hyperspectral imaging, the focus of the chemometric treatment of the data cube is given on the suppression of the unwanted perturbation of multiple scatter of photons. This paper describes an approach how to separate the morphological information s (scatter) from the chemical information k (absorption) using the radiative transfer equation or Kubelka Munk theory. When this "first principle spectroscopy" is integrated into most modern multivariate data analysis like multivariate curve resolution (MCR), causality is obtained between the spectral data and response variables like the concentration of an active pharmaceutical ingredient in a tablet. With this approach, the spatially resolved calculated k- and s-distribution of an aspirin particle in cellactose is shown. The optical set up for real life spectral imaging in industry is discussed and examples of spectral images to control the thickness of thin films on metals, the distribution of a resin on a wood chip and the differentiation of hard and soft maize kernels are shown.

1 Introduction

Spectral imaging or chemical imaging is the determination of the chemical identity of species and the visualization of their distribution. Optical spectroscopy is able to detect not only the chemical composition of the species by their wavelength specific absorption but also the morphological feature through their wavelength dependent scattering [1]. Figure 1.1 visualizes the integration of the chemical and morphological information into an image. The most common tool to measure the distribution of components in a solid particulate system is spectroscopy, thus chemical imaging is also labeled as spectral or hyperspectral imaging [2].

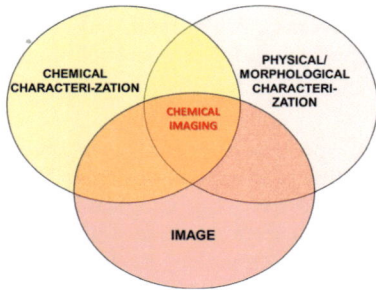

Figure 1.1: Visualization of spectral imaging.

The laterally resolved spectroscopy produces a three-dimensional data cube with two local axes, x and y, and a spectral z-axis with usually the intensity of the reflectance at different wavelengths λ. Figure 1.2 illustrates the essential differences of the techniques used to measure spectral images.

In the so-called whiskbroom imaging (= mapping), defined object areas or the entire object is measured point-by-point. This type of imaging is very flexible in relation to the object and the grid size and generally requires only a single detector; such as a monochromating element with a photomultiplier tube or a diode array. A staring imager (= imaging) takes two-dimensional images in a series at different wavelengths. A prerequisite for this technique is that the object must remain stationary during the measurement ("stop motion"), thus only atline applications can be realized [3].

In pushbroom imaging (= line scanning) the object is imaged along the y-axis using the line-scan method and is recorded in full through the movement of the object in the y-direction. Through an entrance gap in the spectrograph (x-spatial dimension), the light is routed usually into a prism-grating-prism optical arrangement and then spectrally resolved onto the second dimension of the camera. The second spatial dimension (y) is achieved through the movement of the object. In contrast to whiskbroom and staring imaging, the pushbroom system is fully on-line/inline capable, where for each line, under time-defined conditions, images can be generated and evaluated.

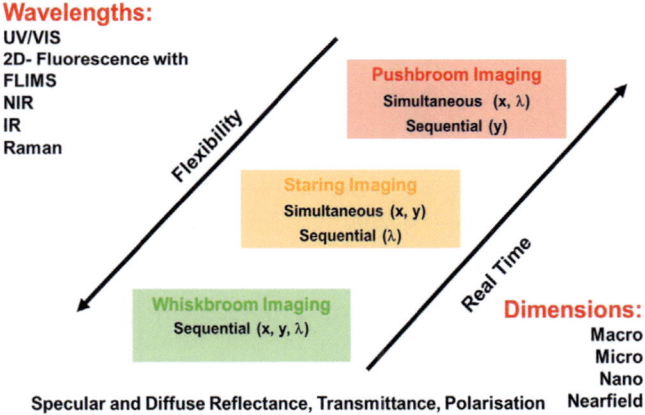

Figure 1.2: Taxonomy of spectral imaging techniques [1,3].

The objective of this paper is first to introduce fundamental principles into the evaluation of spectral imaging data with the objective to separate the chemical information from the morphology of the scattering system and then to show how this improves the robustness of the multivariate data analysis. Finally some examples of the optical setup of spectral imaging devices for inline control will be presented.

2 Integrating "first principles" into spectral imaging: separate absorption from scatter

Dispersions, emulsions or solids like powders show the wavelength dependent superposition of the scatter (s) and absorption (k) of light. In standard multivariate data analysis in process analytical technology, the focus of the chemometric treatment of the spectroscopic data is given on the suppression of the unwanted perturbation of multiple scatter of photons. A better approach may be to extract not only the chemical information but also to use the morphological information from the spectra. This approach using first principles exploits the full potential of the spectral information rather than to eliminate the morphological features. One of the most appropriate theories to describe multiple scattering and absorption in opaque systems is the radiative transfer equation (RTE). The s- and the k-spectrum can be calculated using the (inverse) Monte Carlo simulation from the superposed spectra. The approach of Kubelka and Munk (K-M) is the simplified solution of the radiative transfer theory. In this case the diffuse reflectance and transmittance of a sample with defined thickness is described by the scattering effect s and and the absorption effect k. Thus at least two independent measurements are needed to separate s and k from the measured spectra [1, 3, 4]. S and k can be determined independently measuring just spectra in diffuse reflectance of two samples with known different layer thicknesses, or measuring one sample in diffuse reflectance and diffuse transmittance. After solving the equations, two spectra are obtained which more or less solely represent the spectrum of scatter and the unperturbed absorption spectrum of the component [3].

Figure 1.3 shows as an example the spectra of an Aspirin tablet measured in transmittance and reflectance and the calculated scatter and absorption spectra using the Kubelka Munk theory.

The scatter and absorption cross sections determine the penetration depth of the photons and therefore the information depth ("scale of scrutiny") [5]. Specular reflected light of the surface may produce also spectral artefacts [3]. However, these artifacts can easily be removed using parallel and crossed polarizer during measurement. For inline applications, in most cases diffuse illumination of the object is sufficient to minimize specular reflected light.

3 Integrating "chemometrics" into spectral imaging: reduce the data cube

Principle component analysis and data pretreatment   For analysts used to interpret a single spectrum or a few averaged spectra for each

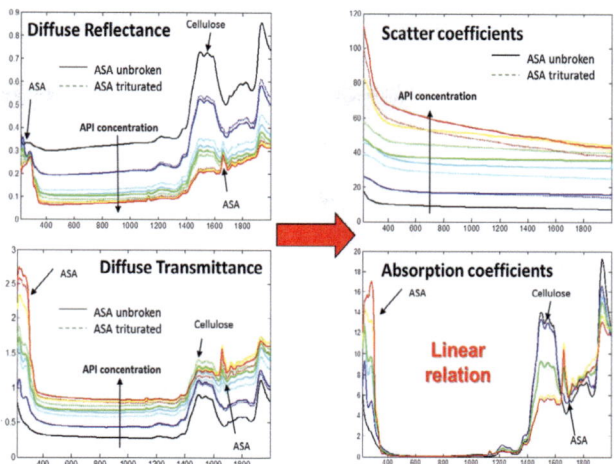

Figure 1.3: Spectra of Aspirin (ASA) tablets measured in diffuse reflectance and diffuse transmittance (left) as well as the resulting calculated scatter and absorption spectra using Kubelka Munk theory. The ASA particles show different particle size distribution (unbroken app. 80 μm, triturated app. 40 μm).

sample, the idea of getting hundreds or thousands of spectra which are spatially resolved, is confusing and may be even hindering to use spectral imaging for quality or process control. Therefore the implementation of chemometric tools is very advisable when analyzing such large amounts of data. Chemometrics offers the possibility to extract the relevant information from the full chemical imaging data set instead of using single-wavelength channels only. And additionally, chemometrics reduces this relevant information into one or a few quality defining parameters by applying either multivariate classification or regression models to the hyperspectral data.

A very effective data reduction is achieved with the principal component analysis. The PCA gives a compressed representation of the image that retains all of the relevant information in the spectral dimension [6,7]. Often three to five principal components capture most of the relevant information of several hundred spectral pixels. The principal components are linear combinations of the original spectral variables.

PCA is a chemometric method, which decomposes a two- or multi-dimensional data table $\mathbf{X}$ into a bilinear model of latent variables, the so-called principal components, according to the following expression:

$$\mathbf{X} = \mathbf{TP}^T + \mathbf{E}$$

where $\mathbf{T}$ is the scores matrix and $\mathbf{P}^T$ the transposed loadings matrix. The matrix $\mathbf{E}$ is the residual matrix and accounts for the experimental error (noise), which is not part of the model. The principal components are calculated so that they explain as much variance of the data as possible. The first principal component captures most of the variance in the data set. This information is then removed from the data and the next principal component is calculated, which again captures most of the remaining variance, this continues until a predefined stopping criteria of too little variance explained by a new component is fulfilled. All principal components are linearly independent, that means there is no correlation among them and they can therefore serve as a new coordinate system with reduced dimensions. An image spectrum can have hundreds or even thousands of pixels, but the relevant information can be contained in a very small number of principal components and each spectrum can be described by the first few scores of the principal component model. A picture of 256 lateral pixels in x- and y- direction and 1000 pixels in the spectral dimension is then reduced from to e.g. 3 latent variables: from $256 \times 256 \times 1000$ down to $256 \times 256 \times 3$, more than 300 times less.

The state of the art approach in chemometrics of spectroscopic data from particulate systems is to exclude the scattering information from the spectral features by data pre-treatment procedures like standard normal variate (SNV), multiplicative scattering correction ((extended) MSC) or orthogonal signal correction (OSC) to obtain unperturbed quantitative information [3, 6, 7]. In this case, the information scatter is often regarded as unwanted and therefore eliminated instead of being used as supplementary information on the morphology of the substrate. A better approach is to integrate the information morphology into the model as described in the previous chapter.

Multivariate curve resolution   A more advanced technique in comparison to PCA is multivariate curve resolution (MCR). The major reason of an increasing interest in multivariate curve resolution (MCR) solved by alternating least squares (MCR-ALS) is its ability to extract from a complex spectral feature a) the number of involved components b) to attribute the resulting spectra to chemical compounds and c) to quantify the individuel spectral contributions. Thus interpretable loadings which represent spectra are obtained. In addition, MCR provides a perfect means to integrate knowledge into the chemometric approach. E.g., known spectra of the components can be integrated into the model or e.g. the s- and k- "pure" spectra of the system under investigation [8].

Example   Figure 1.4 shows the results using the unperturbed k - absorption spectra from figure 1.3 for a quantitative calculation based on Lambert-Beer's law with a single wavelength or using multivariate partial least square analysis (PLS).

The separated k-spectrum shown in the centre of the chart is comparable to the spectrum in solution. In the visible range no absorption is measured as it should be the case for transparent materials. It is important to emphasize that the absorbance of aspirin is more pronounced in the UV than in the NIR region and increases with increasing concentration. The spectral features from 1400nm – 1600nm in the NIR spectra can be attributed to the excipient cellulose and decreases with increasing API content. It is remarkable that only one latent variable is necessary in PLS calculations to quantify the API content due to the "first principle" separation of the scatter from the spectrum. This increases the robustness of the chemometric model. Standard procedures in NIR spectroscopy often need many more principal components to adjust for the nonlinearity of the scatter in the spectral information. Alternatively, single wavelengths can be used to calculate the concentration of aspirin in a tablet just by Lambert-Beer's law.

The same approach can be applied in the multidimensional space of spectral imaging. Figure 1.4 also shows the spatially resolved calculated k- and s-distribution of an aspirin particle in cellactose in the UV and NIR using the Kubelka Munk approach. As can be seen, the main scatter is observed directly at the phase boundary of the particle and is much higher at shorter wavelengths. The combined effect of scatter and absorption may even hinder the penetration of the photons into the particle. In this case quantitative analysis of the composition is a challenge.

When this "first principle spectroscopy" is integrated into most mod-

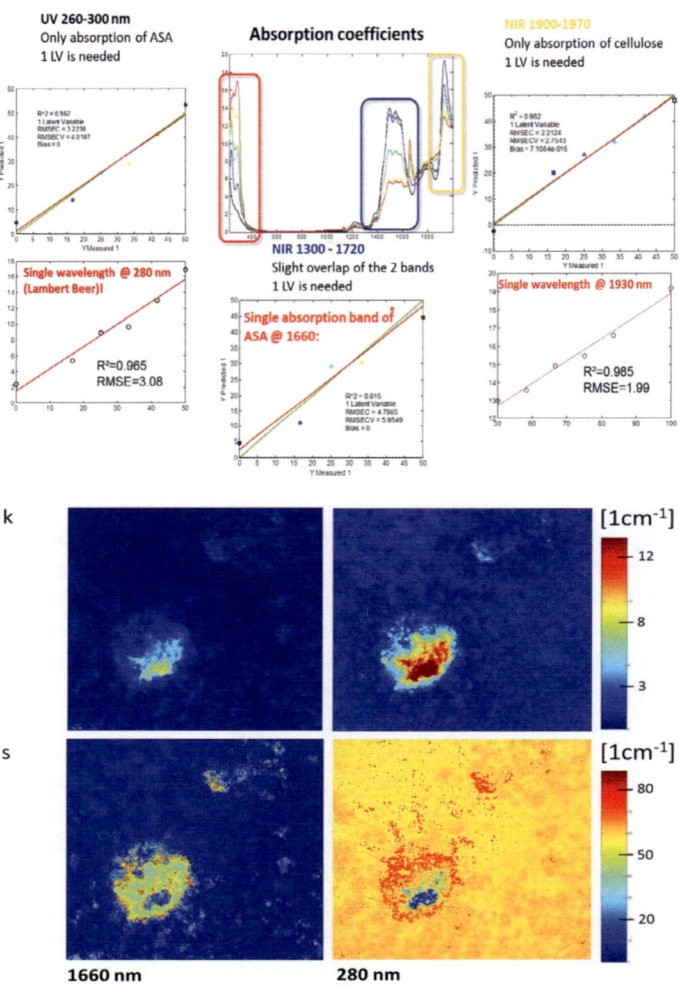

Figure 1.4: Top: quantitative calculation of the API concentration of an aspirin (ASA) tablet using the unperturbed absorption spectra (details see text), lower part: calculated s- and k- spatial distribution of an aspirin particle in cellactose measured at 1600nm and 280nm. The data are extracted from transmittance and reflectance measurements using the Kubelka Munk approach.

ern MVA methods like Multivariate Curve Resolution (MCR), causality is obtained between the data and response variables. This closes the gap between empirical correlative and first principle process information [6, 8, 9].

4 Inline control optical set up: some selected examples

Since 2002, the food and drug administration (FDA) has strongly encouraged the process analytical technique (PAT) for a better understanding of the process and to achieve a higher control of the pharmaceutical manufacturing process [9–11]. An ideal situation would be to control inline 100% of the tablet and the particle size as well as the homogeneous distribution of the active ingredient in the excipient. In the literature, there are numerous methods which use NIR, IR, Terahertz and Raman spectroscopic imaging [1–3, 11]. Figure 1.5a shows the sketch of a pushbroom imaging device as described in the previous chapters and a set of optical arrangements for inline process control (figure 1.5).

Illumination e.g. at 45° (with respect to the macroscopic surface) and detection of the reflected light at 45° (45R45) measures mainly the specular reflected light. With this arrangement the spectral interference pattern is measured and from these measurements the thickness of e.g. an oxide film on a glass or metal substrate can be calculated using the Fresnel equations [1, 12]. When pushbroom imagers with a high pixel number are used, the film thickness along the imaging line can be detected. An example how different the distribution of the oxide film thickness on aluminium can be is shown in figure 1.5c (left).

Particulate systems are commonly measured in diffuse reflectance. Here an optical arrangement with an illumination at 45° (may be from both sides) and detection at 0° (45R0) is favorable. The example in figure 1.5c (middle) shows the PCA analysis of the distribution of a resin on a wood chip [3]. However, when high specular reflectance of the object is observed together with a curvature, strong specular reflectance often superposes the diffuse reflectance with an optical setup 45R0. These spectral artifacts can hardly be mathematically eliminated. A solution is to illuminate the object with diffuse light (e.g. dR0) or a more complex arrangement by illumination with diffuse light and detection with an integrating sphere. Some possible set ups are explained in [3]. An

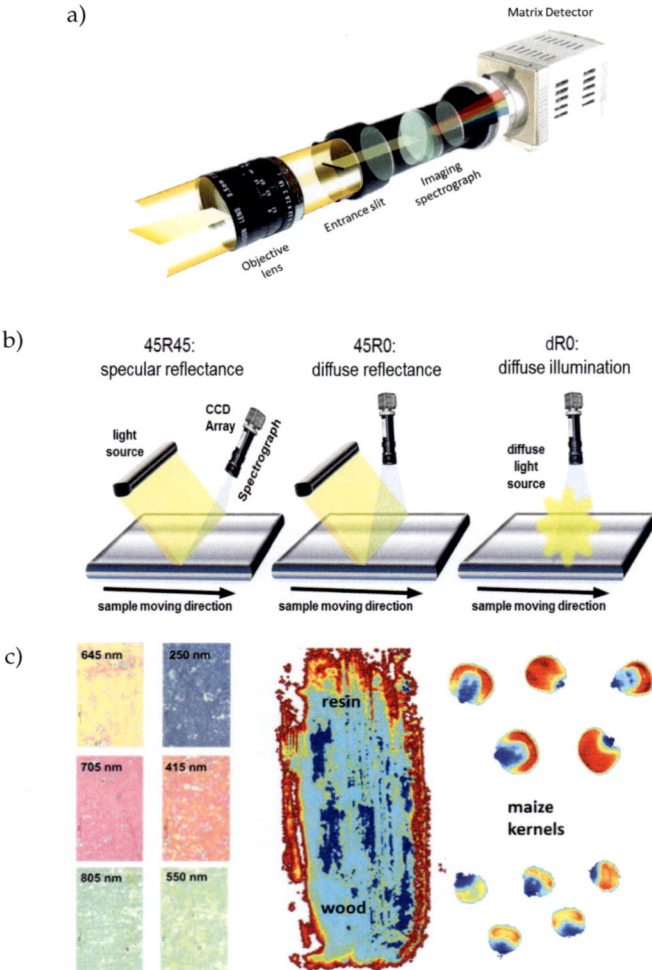

Figure 1.5: Sketch of a pushbroom imaging device (a) and a set of optical arrangements for inline process control (b). Bottom (c): examples of spectral images to control the thickness of thin films (left), the distribution of a resin on a wood chip (middle) and the differentiation of hard (bottom) and soft (top) maize kernels.

example for a typical application for dR0 is shown in figure 1.5c (right) where maize kernels of different origin are measured with a pushbroom imager. The figure shows the result of a PCA and false color representation.

5 Outlook

Focus in the pharmaceutical industry is given mainly on three different uses: blend uniformity of powders and tablets, composition and morphological features of coated tablets and granules, spatial changes during hydration, degradation and active release. Counterfeit pharmaceutical products are a real threat to the health of the patients. NIR chemical imaging provides a rapid method for detecting and comparing suspected counterfeit products without sample preparation. The advantage of imaging is that the discrimination of the tablets is not only caused by changes in the chemical composition, but also from its spatial distribution and texture of the tablet.

Online chemical imaging in agriculture is mainly remote sensing. Satellite or aerial remote sensing (RS) technology uses nowadays Pushbroom Imaging Technology in the Vis, s-NIR and NIR-range. Vegetation images show crop growth from planting through to harvest, changes as the season progresses and abnormalities such as weed patches, soil compaction, watering problems etc. This information can help the farmer make informed decisions about the most feasible solution. In food industry, numerous online controls are still made by human vision, especially for sorting bad looking products. Chemical imaging in food and agriculture can also be used to identify diseases, rot and contaminations by insects e.g. larvae.

Instead of using at each individual production step a single spectrometer, a pushbroom imager with attached fiber bundles on its slit allows individual control of the quality at every intermediate and final step. In this case, the pushbroom imager is used as a multipoint information source and can substitute a moving multiplexer.

Diffuse optical imaging (DOI) is a new emerging technique for functional imaging of biological tissues. It involves generating images using measurements in the visible or s-NIR-light scattered across large and thick tissues for e.g. detecting cancer.

A detailed description of the future trends in chemical imaging is given in [3, 11, 12].

References

1. R. W. Kessler, *Prozessanalytik: Strategien und Fallbeispiele aus der industriellen Praxis.* Wiley-VCH Weinheim, 2006.

2. R. Salzer and H. W. Siesler, *Infrared and Raman Spectroscopic Imaging.* Wiley-VCH Weinheim, 2009.

3. B. Boldrini, W. Kessler, K. Rebner, and R. W. Kessler, "Hyperspectral imaging: a review of best practice, performance and pitfalls for inline and online applications," *Journal of Near Infrared Spectroscopy,* vol. 20, pp. 438–508, 2012.

4. Z. Shi and C. A. Anderson, "Pharmaceutical applications of separation of absorption and scattering in near-infrared spectroscopy (NIRS)," *Journal of Pharmaceutical Sciences,* vol. 99, no. 12, pp. 4766–4783, 2010.

5. D. Oelkrug, M. Brun, K. Rebner, B. Boldrini, and R. W. Kessler, "Penetration of light into multiple scattering media: Model calculations and reflectance experiments. Part I: The axial transfer," *Appl Spectrosc,* vol. 66, pp. 934–943, 2012.

6. S. D. Brown, R. Tauler, and B. Walczak, *Comprehensive Chemometrics: Chemical and Biochemical Data Analysis.* Elsevier, Amsterdam, 2009.

7. W. Kessler, *Multivariate Datenanalyse: Für die Pharma-, Bio- und Prozessanalytik.* Wiley-VCH Weinheim, 2006.

8. W. Kessler, D. Oelkrug, and R. W. Kessler, "Using scattering and absorption spectra as MCR-hard model constraints for diffuse reflectance measurements of tablets," *Analytica Chimica Acta,* vol. 642, pp. 127–134, 2009.

9. U.S. Department of Health and Human Services, Food and Drug Administration, Guidance for Industry, "Process validation: General principles and practices," (Revison January 2011).

10. A. Bogomolov, "Multivariate process trajectories: Capture, resolution and analysis," *Chemometrics and Intelligent Laboratory Systems,* vol. 108, no. 1, pp. 49–63, 2011.

11. E. N. Lewis, J. W. Schoppelrei, L. Makein, L. H. Kidder, and E. Lee, "Near-infrared chemical imaging for product and process understanding," in *Process Analytical Technology,* K. Bakeev, Ed.   Wiley, 2010, pp. 245–279.

12. A. Kandelbauer, M. Rahe, and R. W. Kessler, "Process control and quality assurance – industrial perspectives," in *Handbook of Biophotonics, Vol. 3: Photonics in Pharmaceutics, Bioanalysis and Environmental Research.*   Wiley, 2012, pp. 1–69.

MEMS based systems and their applications in NIR spectroscopy for materials analysis

Heinrich Grüger, Tino Pügner, Jens Knobbe and Harald Schenk

Fraunhofer Institute for Photonic Microsystems (IPMS),
Maria-Reiche-Str. 2, 01109 Dresden, Germany

Abstract Spectrometers and spectrographs based on scanning grating monochromators are well-established tools for various applications, for example analysis of organic matter. As new applications came into focus in the last few years, there is a demand for more miniaturized systems. The future spectroscopic devices should exhibit very small dimensions and low power consumption. A spectroscopic system with a volume of only $(15 \times 10 \times 14) \ mm^3$ and a few milliwatts of power consumption, that has the potential to fulfill the demands of the upcoming mobile applications, has been developed. The approach is based on two major improvements. First, resonantly driven MEMS (micro electro mechanical systems) scanning grating chip, which provides also two integrated optical, slits and piezoresistive position detection has been used. Second, hybrid integration of optical components by highly sophisticated manufacturing technologies was applied. One objective is the combination of MEMS technology and a planar mounting approach, which potentially facilitate the mass production of spectroscopic systems and a significant reduction of cost per unit. The optical system design as well as the realization of a miniaturized scanning grating spectrometer for the near infrared (NIR) range between 950 nm and 1900 nm with a spectral resolution of 10 nm is presented. The MEMS devices as well as the optical components have been manufactured and first samples of the spectroscopic measurement device have been mounted by an automated die bonder. First application close measurements on organic matter have been performed and will be discussed.

1 Introduction

In the fields of medical analysis, food chain management, industrial measurement technology, many others Spectrometers and Spectrographs are well-established measurement devices. They facilitate a nondestructive quantitative and qualitative analysis of various kinds of substances, especially organic matter. Classical spectrometers and even modern compact systems exhibit a volume of a few hundred cubic centimeters and a few watt of power consumption [1–4]. In contrast, there is an increasing demand for miniaturized, potentially portable spectroscopic measurement systems. The design and manufacturing approach is based on two different strategies, miniaturization and hybrid integration. Key component of the spectrometer is a MEMS grating, which is based on a resonant electrostatic driving principle developed at Fraunhofer Institute for Photonic Microsystems (IPMS) [5]. In the latest generation, those MEMS contain not only a 1-d scanning grating plate and its electrostatic driving mechanism but also two additional optical slits and piezoresistive position detection. However, the task of miniaturizing the whole MEMS based system cannot be solved by simply increasing the functionality of the MEMS chip alone. Thus, hybrid integration of optical components by highly sophisticated manufacturing and assembly processes have been applied in a planar mounting approach using state of the art automated micro assembly production platforms [6]. The prototype of the miniaturized scanning grating spectrometer presented here has a volume of only $(15 \times 10 \times 14)$ mm^3, a very low power consumption and a measurement range in the near infrared (NIR) between 950 nm and 1900 nm at a spectral resolution of 10 nm. Application close measurements have been performed in the area of plastic material selection, where different kinds of plastic waste can easily be discriminated by NIR spectroscopy. Further measurements were made in the food quality business. For water, sugar and alcohol a more sophisticated chemometric model has been implemented. The analysis of honey samples showed not only the quantitative estimation of the water content but also insight to the sugar matrix (glucose, fructose, sucrose). On samples of spirits, the alcohol content has been measured. Here, the measurement accuracy was only affected by temperature, as is well known for the water-ethanol system. Other applications have been considered but not yet evaluated in detail, e.g. fruit freshness, meat watercontent, etc.

2 Optical systems design

Starting point of the optical design was the well-known Czerny-Turner setup which features two separate mirrors for collimating and refocusing, respectively while the Fastie-Ebert monochromator has only one large single spherical mirror [7–12]. The Czerny-Turner configuration offers more degrees of freedom for aberration correction, since the surface shapes and positions of the two mirrors can be chosen independently. An exemplary Czerny-Turner Monochromator is illustrated in its original version in fig. 2.1 (a). The electromagnetic radiation entering through an entrance slit (S_1) is collimated by a mirror (M_1) and subsequently impinges on a rotatable diffraction grating (G). The polychromatic radiation is spectrally dispersed by the grating and then refocused on an exit slit (S_2) by a second mirror (M_2). The exit slit cuts out a narrow part of whole spectrum. As the grating rotates, the spectrum is scanned across the slit.

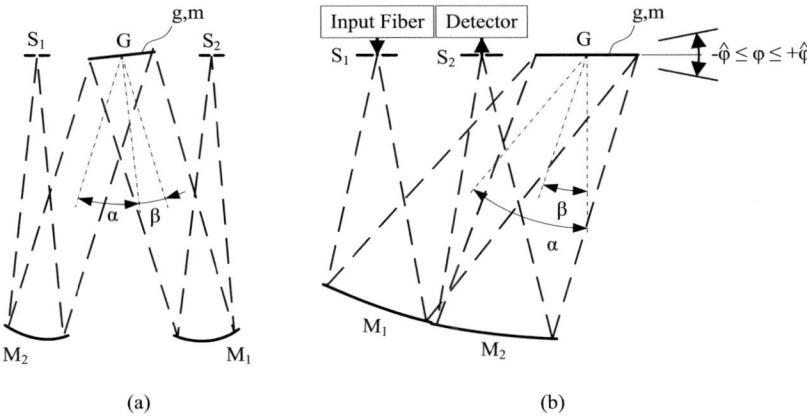

Figure 2.1: A Czerny-Turner monochromator illustrated in the historical, symmetrically arranged version (a) and a planar, unsymmetrical version (b) where the slits and the grating are located in a common plane. The planar version is well suited for a planar mounting approach. An input fiber and an integrated detector are part of this advanced system [13].

The basic grating equation gives the directions of constructive interference for light with the wavelength λ, that impinges on a grating with the grating constant g under the angle of incidence α and is diffracted in the m-th diffraction order under the angle of diffraction β. There are many publications that deal with different optical aspects, like the resolution and imaging properties of scanning grating spectrometers [14–19]. The major concern is the most favorable arrangement of the components for hybrid integration and planar mounting strategies. A suitable modification of the classical Czerny-Turner setup is needed, that allows for an assembly procedure, where all quasi-planar components are stacked on top of each other. In this way, the assembly can be done with modern pick and place die bonding machines. To find an appropriate concept the Czerny-Turner configuration is divided into three main parts. As can be seen in fig. 2.1 (a), the grating and the slits can be grouped together as the first part. The two mirrors are combined to the second part. Both are assembled with a spacer to adjust the correct focal length of the monochromator.

The basic idea is to integrate the group of grating and slits into one MEMS Substrate. This has several advantages. Thus, slits and their position relative to the grating and to each other can be controlled precisely. That means that some of the alignment procedures that are common practice in ordinary spectrometers are obsolete. They are replaced by lithographic pattern accuracy. However, one issue arises with the integration of the slits into the MEMS substrate. The result of a common substrate is an in plane configuration of the grating in rest position. In the classical Czerny-Turner spectrometer, the entrance and exit slit are located on opposite side of the grating. That is why in the originally Czerny-Turner setup illustrated in fig. 2.1 (a), the grating is tilted to yield different angles α and β. This difficulty can be overcome by placing both slits on the same side of the grating [16, 20]. That implies that the two mirrors have to be positioned on one side of the grating, too. In this approach, illustrated in fig. 2.1 (b), the angles α and β are different due to the asymmetric arrangement of the slits. Therefore, the grating can be used in first diffraction order without any problem. This arrangement is appropriate for planar manufacturing and assembly. As far as optics substrates along with the two mirrors are concerned, modern manufacturing methods like single point diamond turning can be used to generate off-axis and highly unsymmetrical surfaces within one piece of metal. An additional design constraint is that the grating plate moves symmetrically within $-\hat{\varphi} \leq \varphi \leq +\hat{\varphi}$, where φ is the detection angle. The substrate normal coincide with the rest position at $\varphi = 0°$. All in all these restrictions lead to a limited solution space for the relevant design parameters λ, g, m and $\hat{\varphi}$. The reduced solution space simply arises from the fact, that the boundaries of the wavelength range at λ_{min} and λ_{max} are assumed to coincide with the detection amplitudes of the grating at $\pm\hat{\varphi}$. With the analytical expressions for the solution space derived by Puegner et. al. [21], the values of the design parameters for a certain spectral range, the NIR in the present case, have been determined. The grating properties are given by the technology available at Fraunhofer IPMS. A summary of the resulting specifications of the miniaturized scanning grating spectrometer are given in table 2.1.

Table 2.1: Characteristics of the miniaturized MEMS scanning grating spectrometer [13].

Parameter	Form	Typ	Unit
Grating constant	g	1600	nm
Diffraction order	m	-1	
Deviation angle	$\|\hat{\varphi}\|$	9.5	$°$
Spectral Range	$\Delta\lambda$	950	nm
Minimum Wavelength	λ_{min}	950	nm
Maximum Wavelength	λ_{max}	1900	nm
Spectral resolution	$d\lambda$	10	nm
Outer Dimensions	$L \times B \times H$	$15 \times 10 \times 14$	mm^3

The specifications of table 2.1 have been used as input for a first order optical system layout and a subsequent optic design process with commercially available optical design software. In order to minimize aberrations, the mirrors are designed as off-axis aspherical surface. The resulting optical path is illustrated in fig. 2.2 in a sectional representation.

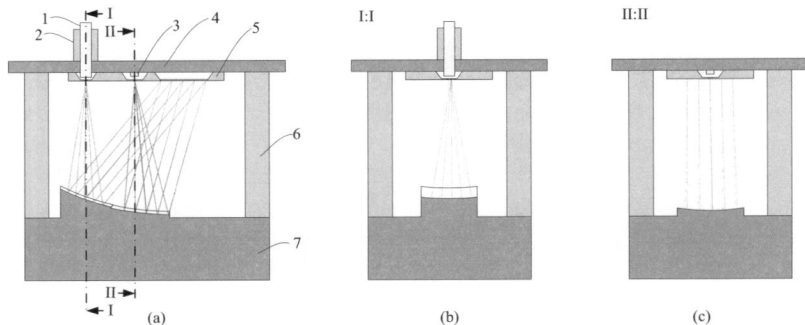

Figure 2.2: Sectional representations and optical path of the miniaturized scanning grating spectrometer for the near infrared between 950 *nm* and 1900 *nm*. The spectrometer consists of the following components: input fiber (1), ferrule (2), InGaAs photo detector (3), MEMS Grating with integrated slits (5), spacer (6) and optic substrate (7) containing two aspheric tilted mirrors. The whole set-up has a volume of $(15 \times 10 \times 14)$ mm^3 [13].

3 Spectrometer realization

According to fig. 2.2 the miniaturized MEMS scanning grating spectrometer consists of seven separate parts which are arranged as a stack. The individual components are made of different materials applying special technologies. The first one makes use of semiconductor technologies and is employed for the MEMS device. The second is the fabrication of metallic parts by machining, especially single point diamond turning for the optical substrate with its mirrors. In order to illustrate the arrangement of the parts inside the spectrometer and clarify the planar stacked mounting, fig. 2.3 illustrates two exploded views of 3-d CAD model.

The printed circuit board serving as carrier substrate has a size of (17×12) mm^2. The gold metalization is suited for wire bonding and conductive adhesive bonding, as well. On top of the carrier substrate the InGaAs photo diode with the physical dimensions of about $(0.49 \times 0.49 \times 0.2)$ mm^3 is mounted. The photo diode has a spectral range of 900 *nm* to 1900 *nm* with a peak sensitivity at 1750 *nm*. In the

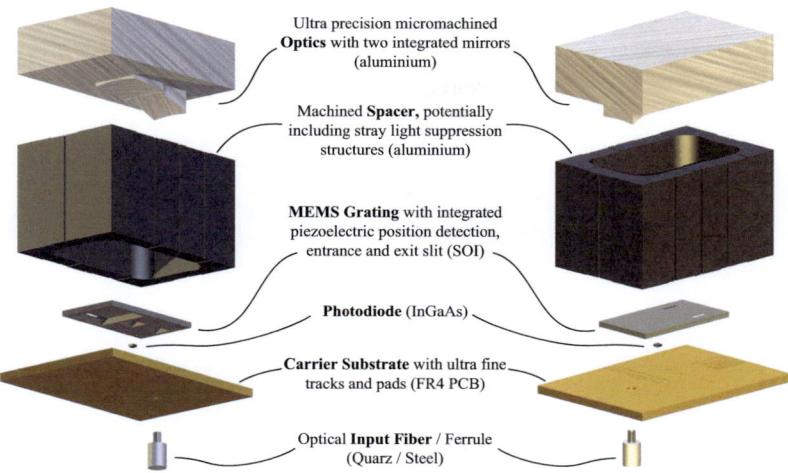

Ultra precision micromachined
Optics with two integrated mirrors
(aluminium)

Machined **Spacer**, potentially
including stray light suppression
structures (aluminium)

MEMS Grating with integrated
piezoelectric position detection,
entrance and exit slit (SOI)

Photodiode (InGaAs)

Carrier Substrate with ultra fine
tracks and pads (FR4 PCB)

Optical **Input Fiber** / Ferrule
(Quarz / Steel)

Figure 2.3: Exploded views from bottom to top (a) and from top to bottom (b) of the miniaturized scanning grating spectrometer. The ultra precision machined optical substrate and machined spacer of the prototype made from aluminum can be replaced by plastic parts, microinjection embossing or shiny pressing, respectively [13].

next step, the MEMS device is mounted to the PCB and electrically connected by wire bonding. It is positioned in such a way, that the photo diode previously bonded to the same PCB is enclosed in one of two cavities that defines the exit slit. The MEMS grating, which is the key component of the miniaturized spectrometer, contains a 1-d scanning trapezoidal grating with grating constant of $g = 1600$ nm and a size of (3×3) mm^2 [22, 23]. The MEMS chip (9.6×5.3) mm^2 wide not only carries the rotatable grating plate, but also features a piezoresistive position detectors and the two optical slits. Fabrication and test of the MEMS device were performed in the IPMS clean room facility on 6" silicon on insulator (SOI) substrates. For better stray light suppression, the spacer with dimensions of $(15 \times 10 \times 9.1)$ mm^3 is black anodized. The spacer is mounted on the optics substrate by the same conductive adhesive used in the previous assembly steps. Although electrical conductivity is not necessary at this point, the thermal conductivity of the applied adhesive might be advantageous. Optics (a), spacer (b) and the corresponding subassembly (c) are illustrated in fig. 2.4.

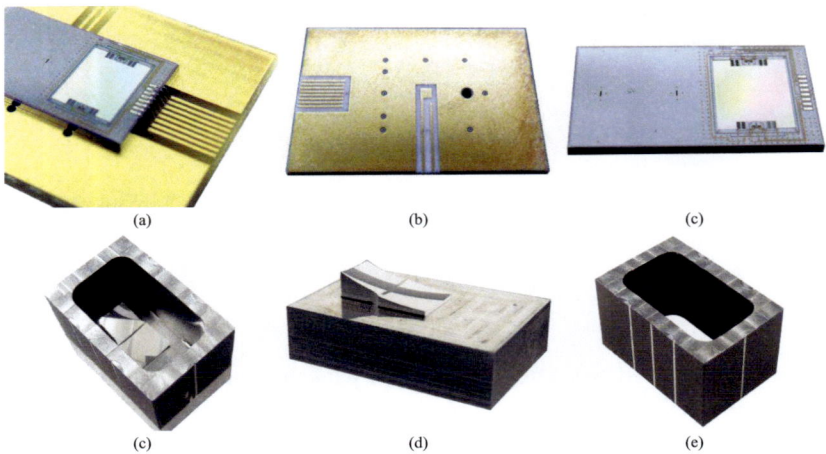

Figure 2.4: The lower subassembly (a) consisting of carrier substrate (b), MEMS device (c) and buried InGaAs photo detector as well as the upper subassembly consisting of ultra precision-machined optics substrate (d) and precision milled spacer (e) are the component parts of miniaturized MEMS scanning grating spectrometer [13].

Finally, the upper and the lower subassemblies are joined together by adhesive bonding. The assembly process is completed by mounting the optical fiber to the carrier substrate. To this end, the ferrule of the fiber is inserted into the carrier substrate from the backside through a matching hole. Afterwards the polished surface of the fiber is located in close proximity the entrance slit. The second end of the fiber is customized with a SMA fiber connector. The alignment and assembly of whole system is performed by a fully automated micro assembly production platform. An illustration of the complete MEMS spectrometer is shown in fig 2.5.

Figure 2.5: Hybrid-integrated MEMS scanning grating spectrometer for the near infrared between 950 *nm* and 1900 *nm* with a volume of only $(15 \times 10 \times 14)$ *mm*^{3}. The spectrometer is nearly as small as the corresponding SMA fiber connector [13].

4 Measurement results

The hybrid-integrated spectrometer has been connected to a system electronic for readout and drive. This board is controlled by a digital platform that computes final spectra by unfolding the sinusoidal movement of the grating and transfers data as a table of measured intensities for well-defined wavelength to the host computer. The complete spectroscopic measurement system consisting of microspectrometer and the corresponding electronic is illustrated in fig. 2.6. On the host computer spectral evaluation software was implemented for the scanning grating spectrometer SGS 1900. The digital platform of the hybrid-integrated spectrometer has been realized in a way, that the application software remains compatible. Thus, applications served before can easily be transferred to the hybrid spectrometer system. Examples for materials analysis have been evaluated in different context. For recycling issues, the selection of different kinds of plastics has been demonstrated. Pharmaceutical products were analyzed and different examples

Figure 2.6: The complete USB-powered miniaturized spectroscopic measurement system consisting of microspectrometer and the corresponding electronic [24].

in the area of food analysis have been considered. The water content and the sugar matrix (glucose, fructose, sucrose) of honey samples were analyzed quantitatively. For the water-ethanol system, a chemometric model was implemented based on synthetic mixtures. Using this model the alcohol content of spirits could be measured. A demo setup used for the presentation of the scanning grating spectrometer SGS 1900 is illustrated in fig. 2.7.

5 Discussion and summary

The miniaturization of scanning grating spectrometer has been a challenging task. The Czerny-Turner setup has been found a particularly suitable starting point for miniaturization. The reduction of system dimensions affects all the major parts of a spectrometer. The MEMS scanning grating developed at Fraunhofer IPMS is a small robust device, which might enable the use of spectrometers in harsh environments. The integration of entrance and exit slit into the MEMS chip leads to a significant reduction of the spectrometers outline. In addition, the numbers of components that have to be adjusted in the spectrometer is reduced. The use of aspheric, off-axis surfaces for the collimating and focusing mirror, fabricated by single point diamond turning, ensures good optical system performance. Due to the small size of components and their asymmetrical shape, some manufacturing tolerances are rather tight. Modern die bonding machines can provide the means

Figure 2.7: Exemplary demo setup used for the presentation of the scanning grating spectrometer SGS 1900. The measurement result displayed on the screen is the alcohol concentrations liquid sample.

for highly accurate fully automated assembly processes needed. Today the first prototype is working already but the aims for the spectrometer resolution have not yet been met. First simple applications could be served even with the limited performance but more sophisticated examples requiring the same optical performance that has been achieved for the larger SGS 1900 scanning grating spectrometer. Active assembly is the next step planned to increase accuracy during the realization of the hybrid-integrated spectrometer. Achieving the resolution the spectrometer was design for, interesting applications in the field of food analysis or medical will be addressed.

References

1. H. Grüger, A. Wolter, T. Schuster, H. Schenk, and H. Lakner, "Realization of a spectrometer with micromachined scanning grating," in *Proc. SPIE*, vol. 4945, 2003, pp. 46–53.

2. *NIR Spectrometer SGS1900, Data Sheet*, August ed., HiperScan GmbH, Maria-

Reiche-Str. 2, 01109 Dresden, Deutschland, 2011, www.hiperscan.com, last donloaded am 2012-03-07.

3. A. Kenda, W. Scherf, R. Hauser, H. Grüger, and H. Schenk, "A compact spectromter based on a micromachined torsional mirror device," in *Sensors, 2004, Proc. of IEEE*, vol. 3, 2004, pp. 1312–1315.

4. H. Schenk and H. Grüger, "Spektrometer," Patent WO 002003069289 A1, 2003.

5. H. Schenk, P. Dürr, D. Kunze, and H. Kück, "A new driving principle for micromechanical torsional actuators," in *Proc. Int. Mech. Eng. Cong. & Exh.*, vol. 1999, 1999, pp. 333–338.

6. T. Egloff, J. Knobbe, and H. Grüger, "Optische Vorrichtung in gestapelter Bauweise und Verfahren zur Herstellung derselben," Patent DE 102008019600 A1, 2008.

7. M. Czerny and A. F. Turner, "Über den Astigmatimus bei Spiegelspektrometern," *Zeit. f. Phys.*, vol. 61, pp. 792–797, 1930.

8. M. Czerny and V. Pletti, "Über den Astigmatimus bei Spiegelspektrometern II," *Zeit. f. Phys.*, vol. 63, pp. 590–595, 1930.

9. H. Ebert, "Zwei Formen von Spectrographen," *Ann. d. Phys.*, vol. 274, pp. 489–493, 1889.

10. W. G. Fastie, "A small plane grating monochromator," *J. Opt. Soc. Am.*, vol. 42, pp. 641–647, 1952.

11. A. H. C. P. Gillieson, "A new spectrographic diffraction grating monochromator," *J. Sci. Instr.*, vol. 26, pp. 334–339, 1949.

12. G. S. Monk, "A mounting for the plane grating," *J. Opt. Soc. Am.*, vol. 17, pp. 358–362, 1928.

13. T. Pügner, H. Grüger, J. Knobbe, and H. Schenk, "Realization of a hybrid-integrated mems scanning grating spectrometer," in *Proc. SPIE*, vol. 8374, 2012, pp. 8374–32.

14. B. Bates, M. McDowell, and A. C. Newton, "Correction of astigmatism in a czerny-turner spectrograph using a plane grating in divergent illumination," *J. Phys. E: Sci. Instrum.*, vol. 3, pp. 206–210, 1970.

15. G. T. Best, "Dispersion of plane grating spectrometers," *Appl. Opt.*, vol. 12, pp. 1751–1752, 1973.

16. V. L. Chupp and P. C. Grantz, "Coma canceling monochromator with no slit mismatc," *Appl. Opt.*, vol. 9, pp. 925–929, 1969.

17. W. G. Fastie, "Image forming properties of the ebert monochromator," *J. Opt. Soc. Am.*, vol. 42, pp. 647–650, 1952.

18. J. K. Pribram and C. M. Penchina, "Stray light in czerny-turner and ebert spectrometers," *Appl. Opt.*, vol. 7, pp. 2005–2014, 1968.

19. A. B. Shafer, L. R. Megill, and L. Droppleman, "Optimization of the czerny-turner spectrometer," *J. Opt. Soc. Am.*, vol. 54, pp. 879–887, 1964.

20. T. Pügner, J. Knobbe, H. Grüger, and H. Schenk, "Design of a hybrid-integrated mems scanning grating spectrometer," in *Proc. SPIE*, vol. 8167, 2011, p. 816718.

21. T. Puegner, J. Knobbe, and H. Lakner, "Basic angles in microelectromechanical system scanning grating spectrometers," *Appl. Opt.*, vol. 50, pp. 4894–4902, 2011.

22. F. Zimmer, A. Heberer, T. Sandner, H. Grüger, H. Schenk, H. Lakner, A. Kenda, and W. Scherf, "Investigation and characterization of high-efficient nir-scanning gratings used in nir micro-spectrometer," in *Proc. SPIE*, vol. 6466, 2007, p. 646605.

23. F. Zimmer, A. Heberer, H. Grüger, and H. Schenk, "Investigation and characterization of highly efficient near-infrared scanning gratings used in near-infrared microspectrometers," *J. Micro/Nanolith. MEMS MOEMS*, vol. 7, pp. 021 005–1–10, 2008.

24. H. Grüger, J. Knobbe, T. Pügner, and H. Schenk, "Design and characterization of a hybrid-integrated mems scanning grating spectrometer," to be published in Proc. SPIE, vol. 8616, 2013.

Characterisation and identification of plastics through microwave treatment and temperature measurement

M. Labbert[1], T. A. Baloun[1], J. I. Schoenherr[1] and H. Z. Kuyumcu[2]

[1] Hochschule Zittau/Görlitz, Institut für Verfahrensentwicklung, Torf- und Naturstoff-Forschung (iTN),
Friedrich-Schneider-Str. 26, D-02763 Zittau
[2] Technische Universität Berlin, Institut für Prozess- und Verfahrenstechnik,
Straße des 17. Juni 135, D-10623 Berlin

Abstract A research project on a thermo-sensitive sorting process was carried out at the Institute of Process Development, Peat and Natural Matter Research (iTN) of the Zittau/Goerlitz University of Applied Sciences to show a new way of recycling of plastics. The aim of the research is to evaluate the separability of plastics with a new sorting process and to clarify relevant influencing parameters. The laboratory tests involve microwave heating of plastic specimens in a cavity resonator at a frequency of 2.45 GHz and a non-contact temperature measurement by means of infrared detection. The results confirm the suitability of the thermo-sensitive sorting process to distinguish many different types of plastics and reveal the significant influence of parameters such as microwave heating time, microwave power, particle size, and water content on the differentiation of plastics on the basis of microwave heating.

1 Introduction

Plastics are organic polymers with excellent properties so that they are used in many applications today. Their production has increased steadily since the 1950s, leading to an equally steady rise of the amount of plastics waste [1]. To protect the environment and to conserve natural resources it is useful and desired by society and government in general that plastics waste is recycled as much as possible. For reuse, the quality of recycling products should be almost equivalent to virgin materials [2]. With today's sorting processes for plastics waste, for example gravity separation and near-infrared spectroscopy, many recycling tasks are being performed, but due to various problems such as overlapping property values and compounds, they are not yet capable to reach maximum recycling rates and product qualities. Therefore, it is necessary to optimise plastics recycling by utilising other separation characteristics of the materials.

2 Basic idea of the thermo-sensitive sorting process

In the thermo-sensitive sorting process, plastics are heated selectively according to their dielectric properties in a microwave oven followed by non-contact measurement of the thermal radiation emitted from the particles' surface by infrared detection [3, 4]. The tailor-made control software converts the measured irradiation values into temperature values. By means of temperature differences the materials can be identified and differentiated from each other. The separation of particles meeting the separating criterion can be realised by air nozzles.

3 Experimental

The employed materials, the test specimen, and the materials preparation as well as the performance of microwave heating and cooling experiments are described below.

3.1 Materials

Research was carried out with 9 different types of plastics (cf. Table 3.1). These are semi-finished products obtained from REIFF Technische Produkte GmbH, Reutlingen, Germany. Some of the plastics are available in various colours. In the following, the sample materials used are characterised by the abbreviation of the plastics type and the colour. The colour abbreviations are (according to [5]): BK black, GN green, GY grey, RD red, TR transparent, WH white, lBN light brown, dBN dark brown. Red polyvinyl chloride, for example, will be referred to as PVC_RD.

Table 3.1: Employed plastics, their colours and related cooling constants a.

Abbreviation	Name	Colour	a in s^{-1}
PTFE	Polytetrafluoroethylene	WH	0.0036
PE	Polyethylene	WH/GN/BK	0.0039/0.0043/0.0041
PP	Polypropylene	WH/GY	0.0044/0.0046
PMMA	Poly (methyl methacrylate)	TR	0.0043
PC	Polycarbonate	TR	0.0050
PVC	Polyvinyl chloride	RD/GY/BK	0.0047/0.0049/0.0047
PA 6	Polyamide 6	WH/BK	0.0039/0.0040
POM	Polyoxymethylene	WH/BK	0.0037/0.0036
PUR	Polyurethane	lBN/dBN	0.0037/0.0037

The cooling constant a of a sample depends on the thermal properties of the material, the sample volume, and the sample surface. Values listed in Table 3.1 are determined by cooling experiments. The specimens employed are cylindrically shaped with a height of 5 mm and a diameter of 5, 10, 15, or 20 mm. For sample preparation, the polymers were dried at 50 °C in a drying oven (according to [6]). To evaluate the influence of different materials' water content on microwave heating, specimens of selected plastics were placed in deionised water for different periods of dwelling.

3.2 Procedures

Microwave tests were carried out in a resonant cavity developed in-house at a frequency of 2.45 GHz. The plastic specimens were placed on a carrier made of PTFE in the range of the largest field strength in the resonator. During microwave heating, the temperatures were directly measured at the centre of the samples' surfaces by an infrared camera (detection wavelength λ: 8-14 μm). The microwave power, the specimen diameter, and the water content were altered. In addition to microwave heating tests, cooling experiments were carried out as well using a temperature chamber. The plastic specimens with diameters of 20 mm were heated to a temperature of 50 °C and the surface temperature was measured during the cooling process by an infrared camera. On the basis of these experiments, the cooling constants a of the individual plastics types are determined. Cooling constants are used to calculate the cooling rates.

4 Results and discussion

Experimental results show that there is an influence of individual materials' characteristics on microwave heating which can be used in thermo-sensitive sorting processes. Thereafter the procedure in differentiating plastics using their remaining temperatures is explained.

4.1 Microwave heating behaviour and influence of the microwave heating time

The plastics exhibit different temperature increases in microwave heating, as seen in Figure 3.1. This behaviour is a result of different dielectric properties of the plastics, which are defined by their chemical structure [7]. Non-polar materials such as PTFE, PE and PP show no significant warming. In contrast, polar materials such as PA 6 and POM heat up fast and to a considerable degree.

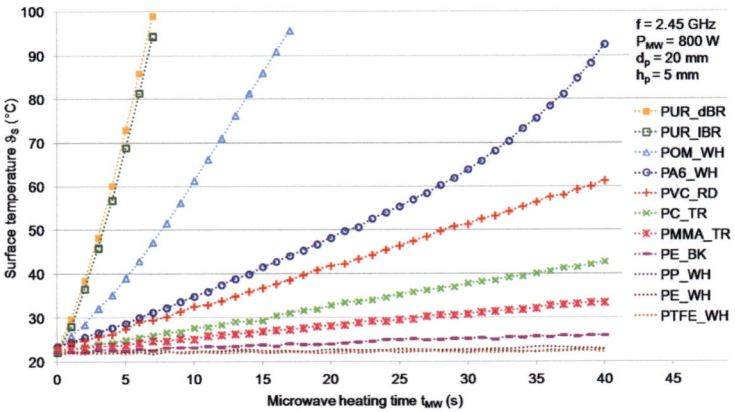

Figure 3.1: Surface temperatures during microwave heating.

However, all plastics show a significant dependence on the residence time t_{MW} within the microwave field. A longer microwave heating time was found to cause higher measured surface temperatures and larger temperature differences between the plastics types. Most of the plastics variants show nearly the same heating profiles, with the exception of polyethylene. PE_WH heats up only slightly, which can be explained by its basis of non-polar chemical structure. In contrast, PE_BK shows a much larger change in temperature, an effect which might be caused by additives contained in PE_BK which lead to a stronger microwave heating. A well-known example of a substance which improves the heatability of non-polar plastics is carbon black [8, 9]. The slopes of the heating or temperature curves are not constant. This is due to the change in dielectric materials properties [10]. The cooling rate may show changes as a function of temperature.

With regard to the thermo-sensitive sorting process many plastics can be distinguished from each other due to the different dielectric properties and the associated microwave heatability. A longer microwave heating time promotes the differentiation between the plastics types. Due to strong heating of some plastics such as PUR and POM, a step-by-step identification and sorting process is required.

4.2 Influence of the specimen temperature on the microwave heating

The microwave heating rate, in this paper referred to as v_{MW}, is the change in the measured surface temperature $d\vartheta_S$ in the time period of dt. Figure 3.2 shows the microwave heating rate of selected plastics as a function of surface temperature.

The microwave heating rates of polymers, which are very strongly heated in the microwave field, such as PUR, POM, PA 6, and PVC show a significant increase in their surface temperature. This can be explained by the reduced physical bindings within the matter, e.g. between the dipoles and their improved mobility [10]. In case of plastics which are less heated by microwave irradiation, such as PC and PMMA, the heat transfer to the ambient air is larger than the increased heating due to improved dipole mobility. Therefore, the microwave heating rate rather decreases with increasing temperature. The microwave heating rate can be seen as the difference of the dielectric heating rate and the materials cooling rate. This relation is shown in Equation 3.1, Equation 3.2, and, simplified in Equation 3.3.

$$\left(\frac{d\vartheta_S}{dt} \right)_{MW} = \left(\frac{d\vartheta_S}{dt} \right)_{diel} - \left(\frac{d\vartheta_S}{dt} \right)_{cool} \tag{3.1}$$

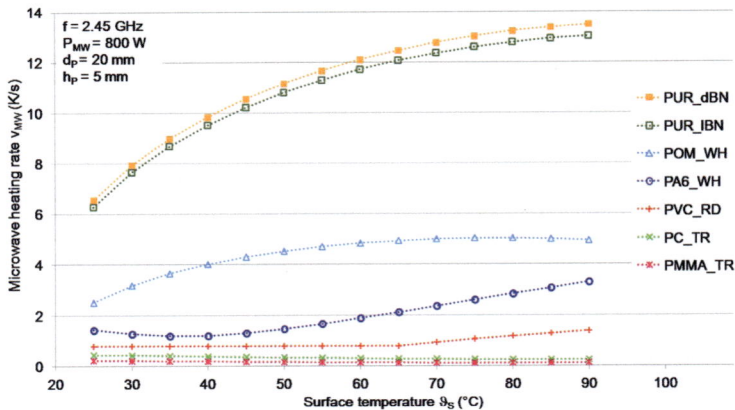

Figure 3.2: Microwave heating rate as a function of surface temperature.

$$\left(\frac{d\vartheta_S}{dt}\right)_{MW} = \left(\frac{d\vartheta_S}{dt}\right)_{diel} - a \cdot (\vartheta_S - \vartheta_U) \tag{3.2}$$

$$v_{MW} = v_{diel} - v_{cool} \tag{3.3}$$

The dielectric heating rate v_{diel} describes the temperature increase due to the interaction of the dipoles with the electric field and the cooling rate v_{cool} describes the temperature decrease due to the heat released to the ambient air. The latter results out of the fact that the ambient air is not heated by microwave radiation (ϑ_U = const.). The cooling rate can be calculated by using the cooling constants of the materials, which depend on the thermal properties of the material as well as the size and shape of the specimens. As seen in Figure 3.2, the microwave heating rate of PVC_RD rises suddenly at the temperature of 65 °C. The reason is the glass transition of the material in this temperature range. From this temperature range on the dipoles of an amorphous material have an increased mobility and can align better in the electric field. This leads to a stronger heating by the microwave irradiation.

With regards to the sorting process, it should be noted that temperature has a significant influence on the microwave heating of the plastics. However, the risk of material destruction results from an increase in microwave heating rates (thermal runaway).

4.3 Influence of the applied microwave power on the microwave heating

Tests show that the applied microwave power has a noticeable influence on the microwave heating of plastics. An increase of the microwave power leads to a more or less considerable increase in the microwave heating rate (see Figure 3.3).

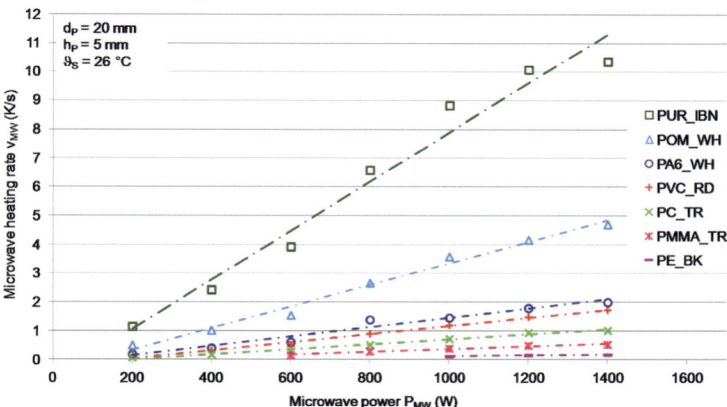

Figure 3.3: Microwave heating rate as a function of the fed microwave power.

The average power absorbed by an object in an electric field is given by Equation 3.4 [11].

$$P_{MW} = \omega \cdot \varepsilon_0 \cdot \varepsilon_r'' \cdot E^2 \cdot V \tag{3.4}$$

Absorbed power depends on the angular frequency ω, the permittivity of the vacuum ε_0, the dielectric loss ε_r'' of the material, the electric field strength E, and the volume V of the object. The increased heating rate due to increased applied power results from higher power consumption by the material. If the other parameters of Equation 3.4 are constant, an increase in the electric field strength is indicated.

With regard to the sorting process, an increase in the applied microwave power has a positive effect due to larger differences in microwave heating rates, resulting in larger temperature differences and improved differentiation between the plastics.

4.4 Influence of the sample size on the microwave heating

A closer look at Equation 3.4 shows the dependence of the absorbed power of an object in the microwave field on its volume or even size. The experiments show that a larger sample diameter, and therefore also a larger sample volume, leads to increased microwave heating rates. Figure 3.4 shows the microwave heating rates of POM_WH, PVC_RD, and PC_TR as a function of the sample volume.

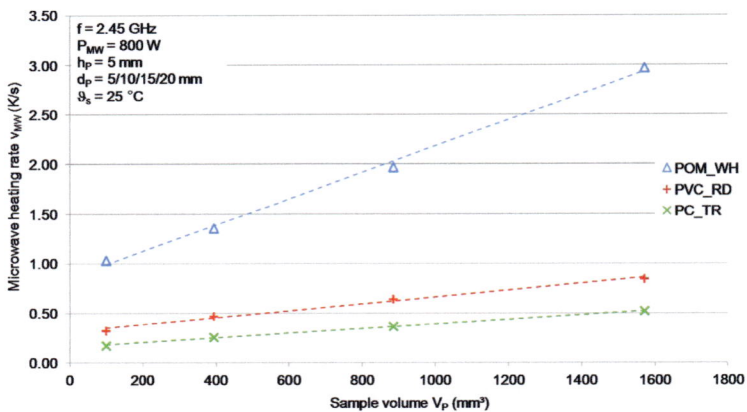

Figure 3.4: Microwave heating rates as a function of the sample volume.

In addition to higher energy absorption, the change in volume results in different cooling characteristics. Smaller particles are said to have a higher cooling rate based on their larger surface-to-volume ratio than the larger particles, since the heat loss to the environment is large if the particle surface is big.

With regard to the sorting process, the particle size, and hence the particle volume and mass, have to be known in order to distinguish the types of plastics using their individual heating behaviour. This can be implemented by the determination of the particle size during the running process or by ensuring almost the same particle sizes by a narrow screening.

4.5 Influence of the water content on the microwave heating

Plastics are able to absorb different amounts of water. Since water molecules are dipoles, their presence influences the microwave heating of the materials dramatically. The experimental results show that the more water is contained in the plastic, the larger is the microwave heating rate. Figure 3.5 shows the microwave heating rates as a function of the gravimetric water content (dry state) for selected plastics.

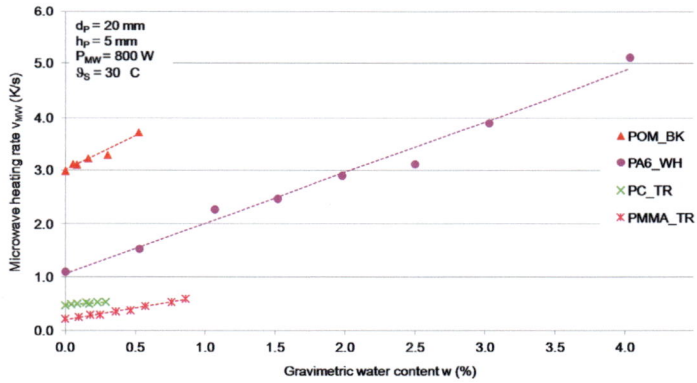

Figure 3.5: Microwave heating rates as a function of the gravimetric water content (dry state).

Under certain circumstances, the water content affects the distinguishability of the plastics. This means that several types of plastics, which undergo different temperature increases in the dried state, show in the moist state an almost identical heating behaviour. PC_TR and PMMA_TR, for example, show the same microwave heating rate if PC_TR has a water content between 0 and 0.3 % and PMMA_TR between 0.63 and 0.77 %. This means the temperature increase by microwave heating is almost the same for both plastics and differentiation between them is rather impossible.

With regards to the sorting process, water content has a significant influence on the microwave heating behaviour and the distinguishability of plastics. Therefore, it is necessary to create defined conditions in terms of water content, e.g. by pre-drying of the material.

4.6 Procedure for the distinction of plastics in the thermo-sensitive sorting process

The temperature profiles of two different plastics during the entire thermo-sensitive sorting process are shown schematically in Figure 3.6. In the microwave heating phase, between t_{in} and t_{out}, the plastics are heated selectively according to their dielectric materials properties. After leaving the microwave oven at t_{out}, there will be a gradual levelling of particle temperature to the temperature of the ambient air. The rate of cooling depends on the thermal properties of the material, the ambient temperature, the particle shape, and the particle size, and can be calculated using the cooling constant a.

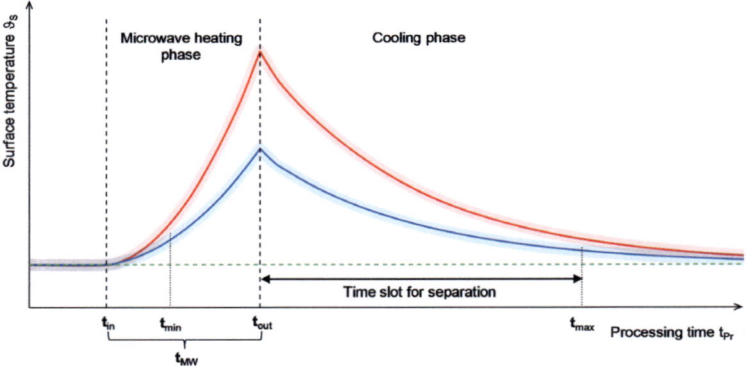

Figure 3.6: Temperature profiles of two different plastics during thermo-sensitive sorting process, schematically.

Within the thermo-sensitive sorting process, the distinction between the plastics should be made on the basis of their temperature differences. For this purpose, the temperature curves of the materials during the microwave heating and subsequent cooling stage have to be determined, applying the function of the applied microwave power, the water content, the particle size, and the particle shape. In order to take the signal noise into account, the confidence intervals around the curves are designed to include almost 95 % of the measured temperature values. Therefore, the distinction between two plastics is possible, as soon as their confidence intervals do no longer overlap (t_{min}). The larger the difference between t_{min} and t_{out}, the larger the temperature differences between the plastics and the longer the period to have their confidence intervals overlap again (t_{max}) after leaving the microwave oven. For the thermo-sensitive sorting process, infrared detection is intended to take place after leaving the microwave oven, resulting in a time slot between t_{out} and t_{max} in which the plastics can be identified and distinguished.

The described evaluation procedure was used for the differentiation of plastic specimens having the same shape (cylindrical), size ($d_P = 20\,mm$, $h_P = 5\,mm$), and water content ($w = 0\,\%$). The separation criterion is that the difference between t_{out} and t_{min} is larger than zero after 10 s microwave heating. Immediately after the microwave heating infrared detection takes place ($t_D = t_{out}$). The studies suggest that the sorting process should be done step by step. Based on the findings, the following approach is recommended. First the plastic types heated very strongly, such as POM and PUR, are distinguished and separated from the other plastics at low microwave power levels ($P_{MW} = 200\,W$). In each subsequent step, the microwave power is increased. Step by step, PA 6, PVC, PC, and PMMA can be separated from the mixture. At the end of the process, a mixture of the plastics only heated insignificantly (PMMA, PE, PP) remains. Benefits of this gradual separation are the reduction of the remaining amount of materials to be sorted and the prevention of material destruction by overheating.

5 Conclusions

Various plastics differ in their microwave heating behaviour due to different dielectric properties. That allows the identification and the differentiation between the plastics samples based on the temperatures reached. In addition to the dielectric properties, other parameters have significant impact on the microwave heating of the plastics and hence the distinction. These influencing parameters are microwave power, microwave heating time, the particle size and shape, additives, and the water content. The requirements for a successful plastic separation by a thermo-sensitive sorting process are a narrow screening to ensure almost identical particle sizes and shape, the drying of the materials, the adjustment of microwave power and microwave heating or duration time on the sorting materials, and a step-by-step separation. When meeting all requirements and employing sophisticated microwave system technology, the thermo-sensitive sorting process has great potential to run proper plastics recycling and to increase recycling rates and improved product qualities of recycled plastics.

References

1. "Plastics - the facts 2012 : An analysis of european plastics production, demand, and waste data for 2011," http://www.plasticseurope.de/, 2012.

2. H. Martens, *Recyclingtechnik: Fachbuch für Lehre und Praxis.*   Heidelberg: Spektrum Akademischer Verlag, 2011.

3. M. Labbert, "Untersuchungen zur Infrarot-Detektion von dielektrisch erwärmten Kunststoffteilchen," Zittau/Goerlitz University of Applied Sciences, diploma thesis, 2010.

4. M. Labbert, T. A. Baloun, J. I. Schoenherr, and H. Z. Kuyumcu, "Studies on thermo-senstive sorting of plastics," in *Sensor Based Sorting 2012*, vol. 128, 2012.

5. *Electronical engineering; code for designation of colours, identical with IEC 757 edition 1983*, DKE German Commission for Electrical, Electronic and Information Technologies of DIN and VDE, 1986.

6. *Plastics : Determination of water absorption (ISO 62:2008); German Version EN ISO 62:2008*, Plastics Standard Committee, 2008.

7. J. Detlefsen and U. Siart, *Grundlagen der Hochfrequenztechnik.*   Munich: Oldenbourg Wissenschaftsverlag, 2009.

8. F. Liu, X. Qian, X. Wu, C. Guo, Y. Lei, and J. Zhang, "The response of carbon black filled high-density polyethylene to microwave processing," *Materials Processing Technology*, vol. 210, no. 14, pp. 1991–1996, 2010.

9. J. A. Menéndez, A. Arenillas, B. Fidalgo, Y. Fernández, L. Zubizarreta, E. G. Calvo, and J. M. Bermúdez, "Microwave heating processes involving carbon materials," *Fuel Processing Technology*, vol. 91, no. 1, pp. 1–8, 2010.

10. A. C. Metaxas and R. J. Meredith, *Industrial Microwave Heating.*   London: Peter Pegrenius Ltd., 1993.

11. M. Rudolph and H. Schaefer, *Elektrothermische Verfahren : Grundlagen, Technologien, Anwendungen.*   Berlin: Springer-Verlag, 1989.

Optical properties of Al₂O₃/Al cermets obtained by plasma spraying: role of composition and microstructure

D. Toru[1], K. Wittmann-Ténèze[1], A. Quet[1], D. Damiani[1], H. Piombini[1], D. De Sousa Meneses[2], L. Del Campo[2] and P. Echegut[2]

[1] CEA Le Ripault
BP 16, 37 260 Monts, France
[2] CEMHTI
1 avenue de la Recherche Scientifique, 45 100 Orleans, France

Abstract *Al₂O₃/Al* cermets (ceramic/metal) have been made by plasma spraying with different metal concentration in order to study their optical properties. A metal has a high reflectivity in the visible and the IR region, but the optical behaviour of an oxide ceramic is much more complicated, mainly if synthesised by plasma spraying. Indeed, a crystallised and dense ceramic, as alumina for example, is widely transparent in the visible region up to 5 µm, whereas in the same range of wavelength a ceramic synthesised by thermal spray will be broadly reflective. Due to its specific microstructure, plasma sprayed coatings include intrinsic open and closed porosity (5 to 20%), rough surfaces and a lamellar microstructure. Plasma operating parameters have been selected during a preliminary study of pure alumina: the nature of the plasma gas, the spray distance, and the powder feed rate. Same parameters were used to realise cermet coatings, with a double injection system. Optical properties of as-sprayed and polished coatings are discussed. The reflectance rises with the aluminium concentration, but in the transparent region of alumina ($1 < \lambda < 5$ µm), we notice a remarkable behaviour for low aluminium concentration where the reflectance of a cermet is lower than pure alumina.

1 Introduction

Atmospheric plasma spraying (APS) is a process in which particles are deposited on a substrate in a molten or semi-molten state. Particles are heated in the plasma jet at very high temperature (10 000 to 15 000 K), and propelled at high velocity to impact the substrate where they flatten and rapidly solidify [1]. The great advantage of this process is its ability to spray a wide range of materials, from metals to ceramics, on a large variety of geometries and sizes of substrates. In addition, it is an inexpensive technique which enables to produce thick coatings with thicknesses ranging from 50 µm to few millimetres. Plasma sprayed coatings confer industrial solutions for heat and oxidation protection, wear and erosion resistance, high temperature applications, but few studies were carried on optical properties [2–5].

Conventional plasma sprayed coatings have a lamellar and heterogeneous microstructure, include a multi-scaled open and closed porosity (5 to 20%), and have rough surfaces. As a consequence, optical properties of plasma sprayed coatings are different compared to ones known for homogeneous materials obtained by thin film processes as PVD or sol-gel. For homogeneous materials, the knowledge of the optical complex index and the thickness are sufficient to predict the optical behaviour. The real part of the index corresponds to the ratio between the celerity of the light in the vacuum over the celerity in the material. The imaginary part corresponds to the absorption coefficient and represents the attenuation of the radiation in the material. Then Fresnel equation and Beer law enable respectively the access to the normal reflectance and the transmittance. When light proceeds from one medium into a homogeneous solid medium, a part of the radiation can be transmitted, a part can be absorbed and the other part can be reflected at the interface between the two media. The sum of the fractions of incident light that are transmitted, absorbed and reflected is equal to unity. For heterogeneous coatings, parameters such as roughness and porosity have an influence on scattering radiation. So the optical properties depend on the complex refractive index and the microstructure of the material. Studies on the optical behaviour of porous materials showed that the reflectivity is not only linked to the optical index, but also to the type of heterogeneities in the material such as porosity, roughness, grain boundaries... [4–8]. Actually, optical properties are mainly affected by the roughness and the porosity and grain boundary effects can be neglected [7].

In this study, the optical behaviour of plasma sprayed cermets (ceramic–metal materials) was investigated. Cermet materials possess the advantages of both ceramics and metals. By varying the amount of each material, cermets can be designed to obtain desired mechanical properties, thermal or electrical conductivity. In the same way, reflectivity and so emissivity could be adjusted through the use of cermet coatings. Low and high-emissivity coatings are of great interest in applications such as solar collectors, automotive or aeronautical components and a better understanding of the optical properties of plasma sprayed coatings would allow disposing alternative solutions in these fields. Here, aluminium and alumina were selected due to their well known optical properties. Aluminium is one of the best reflective metals. Ceramics such as alumina manufactured with a process like plasma spraying contain heterogeneities giving an optical behaviour different from a monocristal. By modifying the metallic charge in the cermet, the evolution of the reflectance was studied for as-sprayed and polished coatings.

2 Experimental

2.1 Material

Commercially available powders were used as the starting materials: aluminium powder (Medicoat, 45-75 µm, Amperit 740.1) and alumina powder (Metco, 22-45 µm, 54NS-1). Aluminium plates with nominal dimensions of 50 x 50 x 2 mm3 were used as substrates. Prior to spraying, the surface of the substrates was grit-blasted and degreased by heating. Plasma spraying was performed with a F4VB torch (Sulzer Metco) working under atmospheric pressure. Metallic and ceramic powders were fed radially and separately into the plasma jet using argon as carrier gas then heated and accelerated by the plasma jet towards the substrate. Metal was injected farther than the ceramic into the plasma jet because of the different thermal properties such as the melting point (Figure 4.1). In flight particle velocity and temperature were measured with a DPV2000 diagnostic system (Tecnar Automation, Qc, Canada). Plasma spraying makes intrinsically porous coatings. In order to minimise the impact of the porosity on optical properties, several conditions were tested to have the densest alumina coating as possible, by varying particle velocity (200-300 m.s-1) and temperature (2300-2600 K). Studied parameters were the spray distance, the current intensity, and the composition of the plasma gas. Selected parameters are given in Table 4.1. Mixtures of $Ar - He - H_2$ were used as plasma gas. Cermet coatings were realized with the same set of conditions. The amount of metal was adjusted ranging from $0\%_{wt}$ to $100\%_{wt}$.

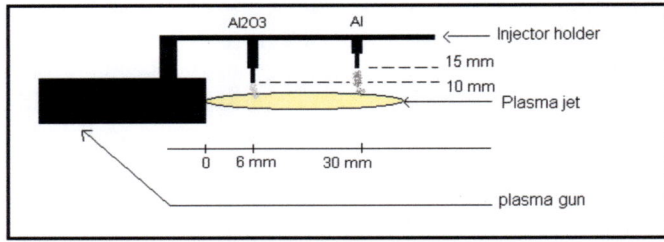

Figure 4.1: Schema of the double injection system.

Spray parameters for plasma spraying	
Arc current intensity, A	500
Argon flow rate (%)	30
Helium flow rate (%)	54
Hydrogen flow rate (%)	16
Injector diameter, mm	1.5
Spray distance, mm	140
Powder deviation angle, °	3.5

Table 4.1:

2.2 Characterisations

Coating cross sections were observed by Scanning Electron Microscopy (SEM, LEO 440). The crystalline structure was assessed with a D5000 X-Ray Diffractometer (XRD, Siemens A.G.) using Cu Kα radiation. Total reflectance and transmittance were measured between 1 and 20 μm with a Bruker IFS66 spectrometer. A 7.6-mm diameter integrating sphere with gold inner coating was used in order to collect hemispherical radiation. The porosity was estimated by Archimedean method. The roughness was measured with a Perthometer S2.

3 Results and discussion

The coatings were deposited up to around a 400 µm thickness. Open porosity measured by Archimedean method was about 10%. The roughness of the as-sprayed coatings was ranged between 5 and 10 µm because of the difference in starting particle size distribution. Surface morphology of the as-sprayed coatings is revealed in Figure 4.2(b). The roughness of the polished coatings was lower than 1 µm. XRD analysis showed both α and $\gamma - Al_2O_3$ phases in the coatings. Optical properties are discussed through the reflectivity values obtained for three wavelengths selected according to the specific optical behaviour of alumina (2, 8 and 12 µm).

3.1 As-sprayed single material coatings

Traditional characteristics of plasma sprayed coatings were identified [9], as the lamellar microstructure, unmelted particles and globular, interlamellar or intralamellar porosity (Figure 4.2(a)). The coatings resulted from spreading and solidification of liquid Al_2O_3 droplets on the substrate. Stacking defects of lamellae can be due to unmelted particles or to imperfect spreading, inducing globular pores and interlamellar flat pores along the splats which are perpendicular to the spraying direction. Intralamellar cracks occur especially in brittle ceramic due to rapid solidification. Thus porosity made of pores and cracks of various shapes and sizes, from hundred nanometres to about ten micrometers makes complicated its characterisation and its correlation to the optical behaviour. As regards to the optical properties of the alumina coating, a part of transparency of about 25% was measured for $1 < \lambda < 5$ µm linked to the 400-µm coating thickness and to the semi-transparent behavior of each alumina lamella (Figure 4.5). The first focused wavelength was 2 µm, because it matches with this semi-transparent region [8] and highlights volume phenomena. At this wavelength, phonon vibration or water absorption peak are not present, and alumina does

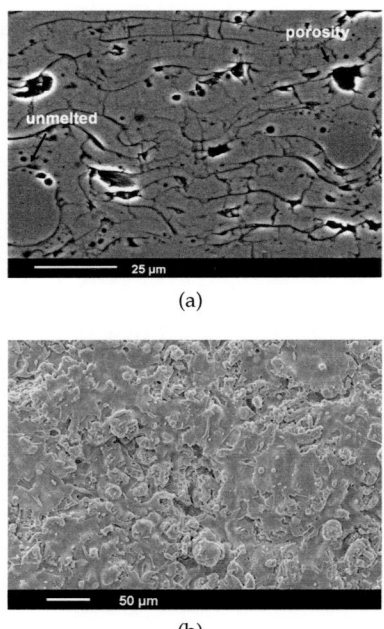

(a)

(b)

Figure 4.2: SEM of the Al_2O_3 coating: (a) polished cross section, (b) as-sprayed surface morphology.

not absorb radiation. Despite its semi-transparent behaviour, the reflectance of the alumina coating at 2 µm is very high (about 80%) because of the interactions between the electromagnetic radiation and the matter. Heterogeneities induce scattering phenomena including three types of interactions [4]: (i) diffraction which results in a modified direction of light propagation around the heterogeneity; (ii) refraction which involves penetration of light in the heterogeneity, and modification of the emerging direction; and (iii) multiple reflections at the interface between the heterogeneity and the matrix medium. These interactions between radiation and alumina matrix are summarised under the term "volume scattering" in Figure 4.6. The second wavelength chosen was 8 µm which is near to the Christiansen wavelength and characteristic of the opaque and the absorbent domain of the alumina comprised between 5 and 10 μm. As a result, the reflectance is close to zero. The last selected wavelength was 12 μm, because it matches with a domain where alumina does not only absorb but also reflects the radiation (10 < λ < 16 μm). A monocristal of alumina reflects about 80% of the radiation at 12 μm, whereas a plasma sprayed coating reflects 20% due to its microstructure. At 12 μm, the imaginary part of the alumina optical index is strong, and because the 6-μm measured roughness was high, a large part of the radiation is absorbed due to the trapping of photons on heterogeneities.

Aluminium coatings appeared more porous than alumina; the open void content was 15%. Unmelted particles and voids are shown in Figure 4.3. As expected, the reflectance of the aluminium coating was constant and high, above 80%, for the three wavelengths (Figure 4.5). The measured roughness (about 10 μm) can explain that the reflectivity is lower than one obtained for an homogeneous metal. Surface scattering inducing absorption occurs.

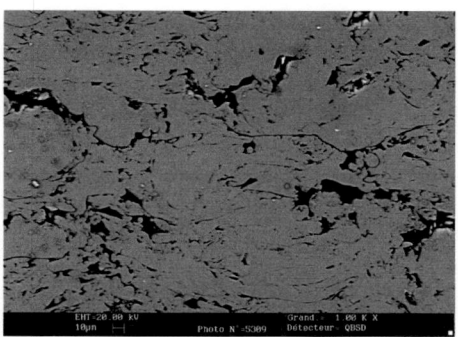

Figure 4.3: SEM polished cross section of the Al coating.

3.2 As-sprayed cermet coatings

For cermet coatings no transmittance was revealed from visible to IR region. Figure 4.4 shows that aluminium was homogeneously spread out, but splats present various shapes resulting from different spread-

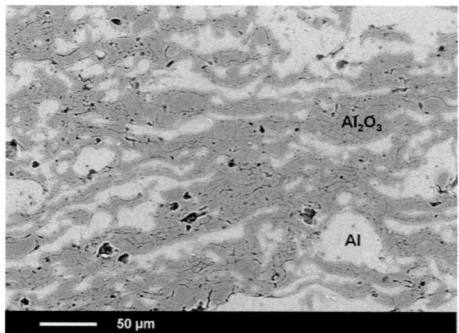

Figure 4.4: SEM polished cross section of a cermet coating with 33%$_{wt}$ Al.

ing degree. At 2 µm, for a low amount of aluminium in the cermet, the reflectance decreased compared with pure alumina. Mechanisms occurring in the low Al content cermets are proposed schematically in Figure 4.6. Aluminium lamellae do not only reflect a part of the existing radiation, extending therefore the path travelled by the photons in the material, but also absorb a small part of the radiation in the volume. Thus, reflectance linked to scattering effects and to alumina coating heterogeneities is softened. In addition, there are not enough metallic lamellae in the top of the coating to increase the reflectance by specular reflexion or surface scattering. Volume effects prevail on surface effects. When the metal amount is higher than 75%, the surface contribution of the metal is prevailing, so the reflectance increases compared with pure alumina (Figure 4.5). At 8 µm, both of the materials are opaque. Close to the Christiansen wavelength, alumina is absorbent, so the reflectance level is close to zero. In this domain, only surface effects are present; no photons can penetrate into the volume. As a result, the reflectance is directly linked to the amount of aluminium in the surface: higher the aluminium quantity is, higher the reflected radiation. The same trend is observed at 12 µm, where pure alumina is opaque as well. An additional contribution of alumina should raise the cermet reflectance values. However the reflectance appeared lower at 12 µm than at 8 µm independently of the metal amount. The part of the scattered reflectance was measured and represented by dotted lines for each wavelength in Figure 4.5. It appeared that it scattering contributes to the main part of the reflectance. The specular part corresponds to about 20 % of the total reflectance. These values are easily correlated to the coating roughness in the opaque region (8 and 12 µm) and to both volume and surface heterogeneities in the alumina semi-transparent domain (2 µm).

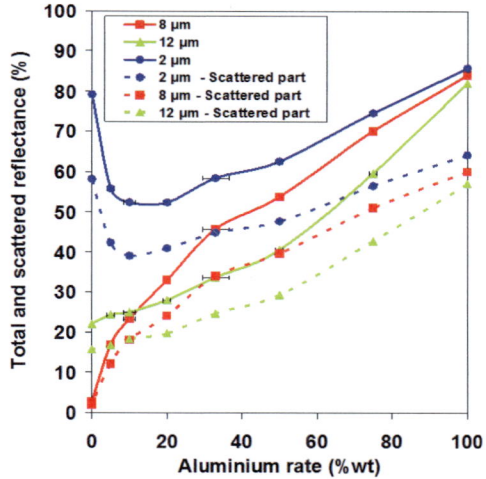

Figure 4.5: Total and scattered reflectance of the as-sprayed cermets depending on the wavelength as a function of Al rate.

3.3 Polished single material coatings

Cermets were polished to study the influence of the roughness on the optical response (Figure 4.7)

As-sprayed and polished alumina reflectance was identical except at 12 µm. At 2 µm, the reflectance of the polished specimen is still 80%, proving that the roughness has no influence at this wavelength unlike the volume heterogeneities. The scattering part is about 40%, because

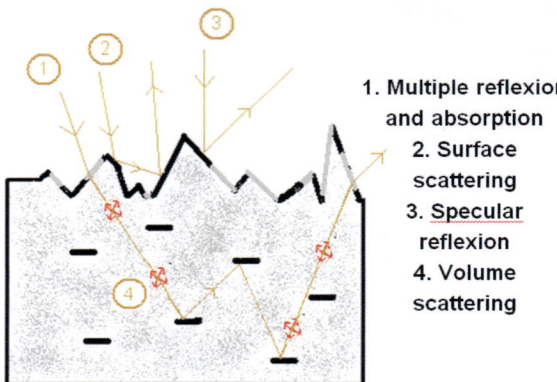

Figure 4.6: Schematic mechanisms occurring in the cermet in the transparent region.

pores scatter in the volume, as presumed. At 8 μm, alumina is almost fully absorbent. Indeed, it is characterised by none transparency and a weak reflectivity due to scattering. No roughness effect is revealed either. However, at 12 μm, the reflectivity of polished alumina increases. A part of the radiation which has been absorbed by the trapping of photons in surface heterogeneities is now reflected by specular reflexion. For the aluminium coating, the polishing rises the reflectance because smaller quantity of photons can be absorbed by heterogeneities.

3.4 Polished cermet coatings

About the cermet, the argument has been conducted considering that the composition at the as-sprayed surface is the same that a slice in the volume. At 2 μm, the reflectance decreases up to an aluminium rate of 50%. That behaviour could be explained by the fact that a larger part of the radiation can penetrate in the material compared to the rough coatings. Indeed, the light would not be scattered by the surface roughness but absorbed as a result of multi reflexion on aluminium splats (Figure 4.6). For large amount of aluminium (upper than 50%), surface effects

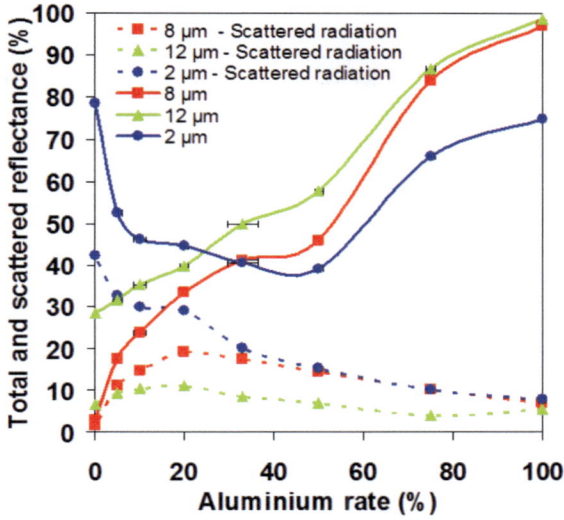

Figure 4.7: Total and scattered reflectance of the polished cermets depending on the wavelength as a function of Al rate.

are predominant, and so the reflectivity rises with aluminium content. At 8 µm, cermet reflectance does not significantly change with the aluminium rate, except for large amount of aluminium, meaning that polishing reduces the absorption part due to heterogeneities. Finally, the reflectance of a polished coating at 12 µm is higher than at 8 µm, proving that without polishing, surface scattering induces absorption.

3.5 Modeling considerations

The establishment of a model reproducing trends of the cermet reflectance is intended. In the opaque region, a rough calculation was realised. Knowing that photons can't penetrate in the volume, a possibility to predict the reflectance is therefore to assimilate the coating into a mosaic, with zones representing alumina and zones representing aluminium. The reflectance was estimated by taking into account the experimental reflectivity of each pure polished material (R), and their proportions on the surface, using a particle section (Figure 4.8). Then the following formula is used: R = p x R(*Al*) + (1-p) x R(Al_2O_3) With p the proportion of aluminium at the surface, calculated knowing the powder flow rate per second, and the surface of each particle. The spreading degree of alumina and aluminium lamellae was supposed to be equal. Calculated points are close to the experiment. However, Figure 4.8 shows the reflectance is a little underestimated at 8 µm and not proportional to the aluminium amount. Indeed, the level of scattering light is higher for polished pure alumina and aluminium coatings than for the cermets. At 12 µm, the two curves are very close because the scattering is almost constant, and so there is proportionality between the reflectance and the aluminium rate. Maxwell Garnett or Bruggeman methods are both not adapted because of the size range of lamellae. That means that the material should be more considered as a heterogeneous coating than a homogeneous one to model its optical response in the opaque region.

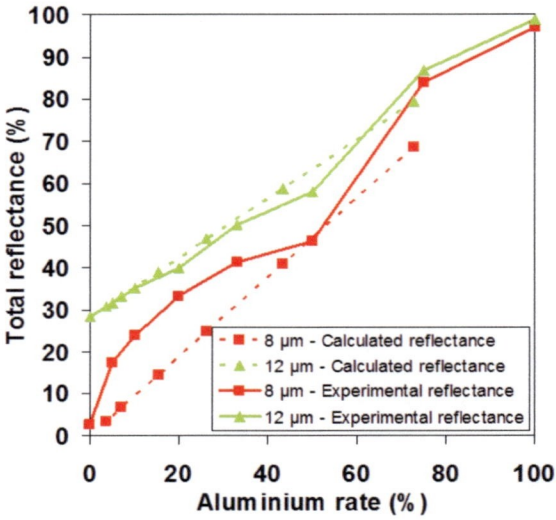

Figure 4.8: Experimental cermet reflectance and calculated reflectance depending on the wavelength as a function of Al rate.

4 Conclusion

Several Al_2O_3/Al cermets have been realised by APS, adjusting the aluminium rate to study the influence on the optical properties. Three characteristic wavelengths of specific domains of pure alumina were selected. In the transparent region, volume effects occur, and we notice that a cermet is less reflective than a pure alumina coating when the aluminium rate is low. Only surface effects occur in the opaque region, so the reflectance rises with the amount of aluminium. By changing plasma operating parameters, it will be worth investigating the impact of the total void content on the optical behaviour of plasma-sprayed cermets. Moreover, the next objective is to model the optical behaviour of plasma-sprayed cermets. A good approximation is to assimilate coatings into a mosaic of each material.

References

1. P. Fauchais, "Understanding plasma spraying," *J. Phys. D: Applied Physics*, vol. 37, pp. R86–R108, 2004.

2. V. Debout, E. Bruneton, E. Meillot, S. Schelz, P. Abelard, P. Fauchais, and A. Vardelle, "Correlation between processing parameters, microstructure and optical properties for plasma-sprayed yttria-stabilized zirconia coatings." ISPC17, 2003.

3. M. Tului, F. Arezzo, and L. Pawlowski, "Optical properties of plasma sprayed semiconducting oxides," in *Proceeding of the International Thermal Spray Conference (ITSC)*, Düsseldorf, Germany., 2004.

4. V. Debout, A. Vardelle, P. Abelard, P. Fauchais, E. Bruneton, S. Schelz, and N. Branland, "Optical properties of yttria-stabilized zirconia plasma-sprayed coatings," in *Proceeding of the International Thermal Spray Conference (ITSC)*, 2006.

5. K. S. Caruso, D. G. Drewry, and J. S. Jones, "Heat treatment of plasma sprayed alumina: evolution of microstructure and optical properties," in *Advanced Ceramic Coatings and Interface II : Ceramic and Engineering Science Proceedings*, vol. 28, 2009, pp. 177–192.

6. G. Peelen, "Relation between microstructure and optical properties of polycristalline alumina, science of ceramics," vol. 6, pp. pp.1–13, 1973.

7. O. Rozenbaum, D. S. Meneses, Y. D. Auger, S. Chermanne, and P. Echegut, "A spectroscopic method to measure the spectral emissivity of semi-transparent

materials up to high temperature," *Review of Sc. Instruments*, vol. 70, pp. 4020–4025, 1999.

8. J. Milo E. Whitson, "Handbook of the infrared optical properties of al2o3, carbon, mgo and zro2," 1975.

9. M. Vardelle, "Etude de la structure des dépôts d'alumine obtenus par projection plasma en fonction des températures et des vitesses des particules au moment de leur impact sur la cible. in french," PhD thesis, 1980.

Improved fault detection for inline optical inspections by evaluation of NIR images

Hartmut Eigenbrod

Fraunhofer Institute IPA,
Machine Vision and Data Processing Department,
Nobelstr. 12, D-70569 Stuttgart, Germany

Abstract Industrial image processing is a widespread technology to evaluate the quality of work pieces. Major advantages of this technology are its contact-free mode of operation, fast evaluation times and moderate system costs. Usually the visible part of the light spectrum is used to discriminate between good and bad work pieces. However, in several applications a combination or even a substitution with the near infrared (NIR) part of the spectrum advances the evaluation. In this paper, several real world applications are presented and the achieved improvements are summarized by showing qualitative and quantitative results.

1 Introduction

Industrial image processing in the visible spectrum has a long and successful history. One reason for the success is the imitation of human perception. Inspection tasks that otherwise would be done manually are implemented in an automatic, continuously running mode. Thereby, the influence of the human factor (e.g. exhaustion) on the classification accuracy is highly reduced. Moreover, the availability of camera chips based on silicon enables cost-effective inspection systems.

Image processing is not limited to the visible range. Advanced cost-intensive detector materials (InGaAs, InSb) allow data acquisition up to 5 μm (wavelength) and more. In combination with optics for spectroscopic imaging, a detailed characterization of surfaces is feasible [1].

Additional insight on surface properties, however, could already be achieved with moderate costs and efforts. When applying silicon based sensor chips, the available spectral information extends up to 1000 nm (and more, depending on the noise level of the chip). Commercial off-the-shelf cameras allow the simultaneous data acquisition for imaging in the visible (VIS) and near infrared (NIR) range. In several applications, the additional information improves the contrast and facilitates the discrimination between good and bad parts (see e.g. [2,3] on hyperspectral imaging applications).

In this paper, real world applications from the field of industrial inline quality inspections are presented.

2 Approach

2.1 Combined image acquisition in VIS and NIR ranges

The demonstration of improved image quality (when switching from the visible spectrum to the near infrared spectrum) requires images from the same scene in different spectral ranges. An efficient way to acquire these images is to use multichannel cameras. For the image acquisition tasks in this paper, the camera JAI AD-080 CL was employed. Its key components are two silicon chips and a wavelength sensitive prism (see Fig. 5.1). In this way two images (with a one-to-one pixel correspondence) are acquired, the first one in the range from approx. 400 – 700 nm (VIS), the second one in the range of approx. 700 – 1000 nm (NIR). The image resolution is 1024 × 768 pixels with a frame rate of 30 Hz. Depending on the requirements of inspection tasks, other multichannel cameras by JAI or other manufacturers could be used as well.

2.2 Dye-based contrast enhancement in the NIR range

Dyes are typically tailored for their intended impact on the human eye. As a result, the spectral properties of the dyes are well defined in the visible range. In the NIR range, the properties are usually of less interest (for the dye manufacturers and product designers) and therefore only rarely described. In many real world applications, dyes are often not or only slightly absorbing in the NIR range which reveals the optical properties of the substrate in captured images. For several inspection tasks this effect could be used to improve the image contrast by performing the inspection in the NIR range (instead of the VIS range). The benefit of this approach will be demonstrated in the subsequent chapters.

More rarely, dyes are jointly optimized for the VIS and NIR range. This class of dyes is exemplified by the dye "Paliogen Black L 0086" from BASF: It has been designed for surfaces that require a dark black impression in the visible range. On the other hand, the surfaces should not overheat when exposed to bright sunlight. The reflectivity of the dye is shown in Fig. 5.1. The low reflectivity in the visible range hinders surface inspection such as detection of scratches, holes, etc. In this case, an evaluation of NIR images leads to more accurate and robust results.

2.3 Quantification of detection capability for surface flaws

In the subsequent chapters different fault detection applications will be shown. The detection will be done in the VIS and NIR range. In order to quantify the improvement, a defect signal to background signal ratio (DBR) will be calculated based on the standard signal to noise ratio (SNR) in optical inspection:

$$\text{DBR} = \frac{E_D(I) - E_{BG}(I)}{\sigma_{BG}(I)} \tag{5.1}$$

The difference between the average defect intensity $E_D(I)$ and the average intensity of the background structure $E_{BG}(I)$ is calculated in the numerator. The denominator $\sigma_{BG}(I)$ contains the standard deviation of the background structure. The capability for detecting flaws depends on many factors, mainly on the statistics of the background structure (incl.

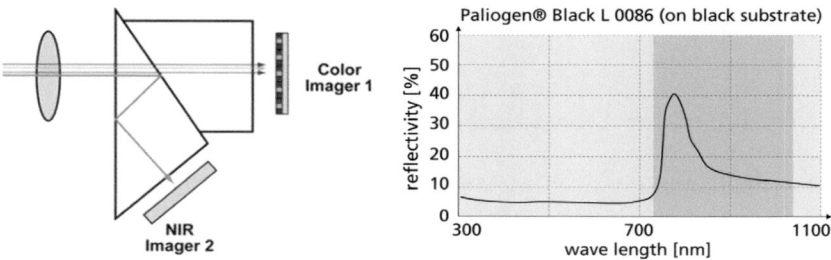

Figure 5.1: Optical path for the 2-CCD-camera JAI AD-080 CL [4] (left). Reflectivity of Paliogen Black L 0086, based on [5] (right).

spatial correlations) and the evaluation algorithms. However, higher DBR values usually indicate a higher probability for detecting flaws.

3 Application: Inspection of dyed polyester fabrics

Fault detection in polyester fabrics has several objectives: A key aspect is the identification of grease based contaminations, but also scratches and different foreign objects should be identified. The inspection task is especially difficult for black polyester fabrics: The contrast between unaffected fabric and grease based contaminations is very low. In this case, it is useful to switch to the NIR range. There are two reasons for this approach: (1) Polyester is highly transparent in the NIR range and (2) polyester dyes are usually optimized for the visible spectrum.

This is illustrated in Fig. 5.2: In the left image, the scratch and the contamination (red arrows) are nearly invisible on the black polyester fabric. The same scene recorded in the NIR range, however, shows excellent contrast: The DBR value increases from 0.7 to 30.3 (for the scratch) and from 2.1 to 19.7 (for the contamination). For the polyester fabrics, the flaws are already detectable by simple thresholding methods in the NIR range. Please note that a white layer was placed behind the fabric which reflects the illumination in the NIR range (originating from next to the camera). By a combined evaluation of both VIS and NIR images the probability of detection is highly improved when compared the VIS range only.

Moreover, as polyester is transparent in the NIR range, one could also detect flaws on the carrier or other subsurface structures when required (see Fig. 5.3).

4 Application: Detection of misssing threads in textiles

Flaw detection in woven material is a key task in textile industry. Fig. 5.4 shows a typical example for a missing thread that has to be identified during production. The inspection task is complicated by the existence of yarns in different colors, at least when evaluating images in the visible spectrum. An image in the NIR range from 700 – 1000 nm, however, reveals that the different dyes are only active in the visible range. In

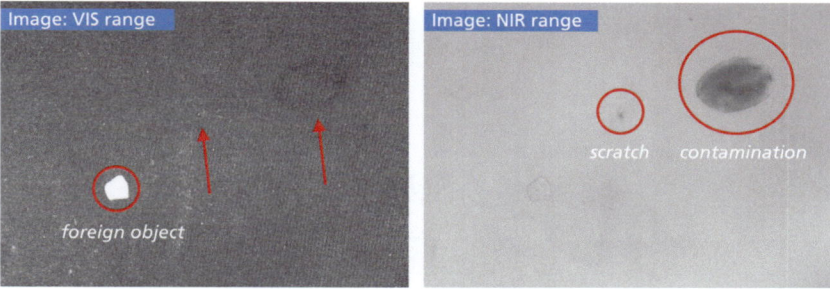

Figure 5.2: Quality inspection for a black polyester fabric using different spectral ranges. Only the combined evaluation of the VIS and NIR images reliably reveals all flaws.

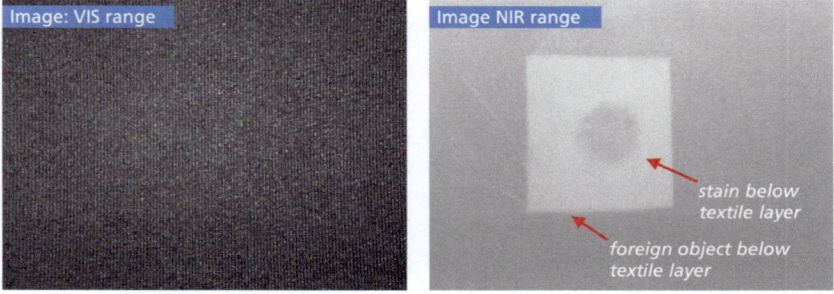

Figure 5.3: Subsurface inspection for black polyester fabrics. The left image was captured in the VIS range, the right image in the NIR range.

this case, using the NIR image decreases the contrast within the desired textile structures and increases the contrast of the faults.

The DBR value increases from 2.4 to 5.6 when switching from the VIS range to the NIR range. Depending on the detailed optical structure of the textile, the contrast may already be sufficient for thresholding algorithms. One may also apply more complex algorithms that reveal statistical anomalies in the image. As an example, Fig. 5.4 shows the evaluation results of the DefDetect algorithm [6]. Again the inspection task is highly facilitated in the NIR range.

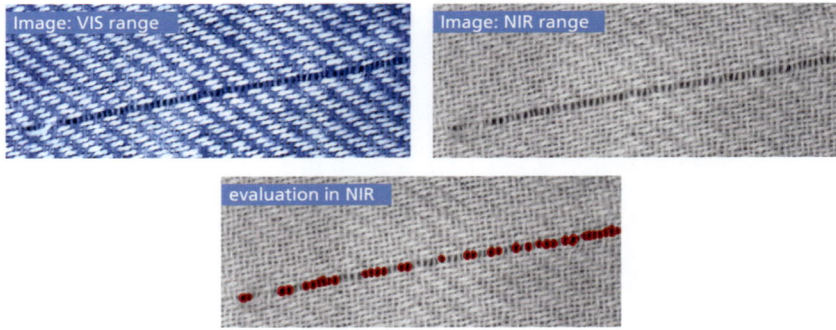

Figure 5.4: Missing thread in a woven material in the VIS and NIR range (top). Classification results based on statistical image analysis (bottom).

5 Application: Inspection of threads in textile seams

In textile industry, connecting different textile layers is usually done by making seams. The quality inspection of seams is rather difficult when the textile layers and the thread have similar colors. An example is shown in Fig. 5.5: Two sheets of black leather are interconnected by a black synthetic thread. In the VIS range, the contrast between the layers and the thread is relatively low. Inspecting the NIR image, however, is much easier as the black thread is highly reflective in this spectral range. The segmentation of the thread is easily done by thresholding methods and the regularity of the stitches is later evaluated by blob analysis methods. In this example, the DBR value increases from 3.5 to 5.5 when switching from the VIS range to the NIR range.

6 Application: Detection of surface contaminations on printed surfaces

Small surface contaminations (small particles or small patches of viscous fluids) are difficult to detect when they are located on printed surfaces with comparable colors. A good example is that of extruded window profiles covered with a wood imitating foil. Small particles from the production environment might be located directly on the foil which is undesirable for subsequent processing steps. In standard bright field

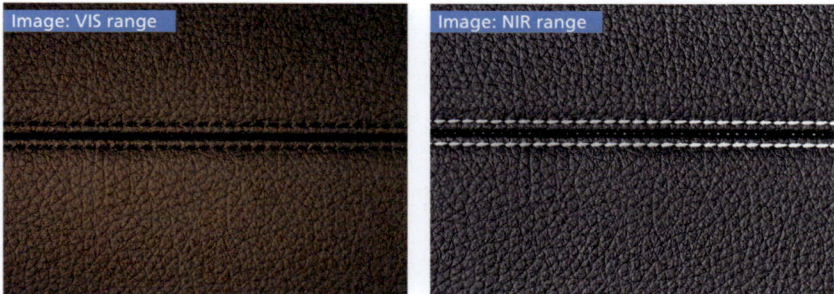

Figure 5.5: Black leather connected by black synthetic yarn. Low contrast in the VIS range (left), improved contrast in the NIR range (right).

illumination, see Fig. 5.6, the particles are hardly visible in the VIS range. Yet different other techniques from machine vision are available for detecting these kinds of particles: Dark field image acquisition typically reveals the defects although illumination needs additional efforts for big areas. The particles could also be detected by 3D imaging when their diameter is above the detection level of the imaging system.

Fig. 5.6 demonstrates that quality inspection is also feasible in bright field NIR imaging. On the left side, the image is shown in the visible range. It is difficult to identify the contaminations on top as they are constituted by small rusty iron fragments. On the right side, the image is shown in the NIR range. The different printing dyes are again optimized for the visible range showing only minimum NIR absorbance. The contaminations however are also highly absorbing in the NIR, leading to good contrast. In this application, the DBR value increases from 4.4 to 19.7 when switching from the VIS range to the NIR range.

7 Improvement of DBR values

The DBR values are a first indicator whether an inspection task is facilitated in the NIR range or not. The DBR values for the presented inspection tasks are summarized in Tab. 5.1. For these applications, the value typically increases by a factor 2 – 50 when switching to the NIR range. Assuming a Gaussion distribution for the background intensities, DBR

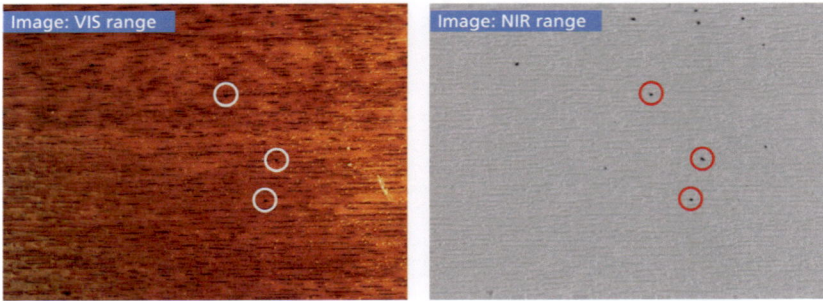

Figure 5.6: VIS and NIR image for a printed plastic foil covered with small metallic fragments, recorded in bright field illumination.

values greater than five should lead to good sensitivities/ specificities of subsequent binary classifiers. However, the requirement of a Gaussion distribution is seldom fullfilled in real word applications. Therefore, the final assessment of the improved detection capability requires the application of the full image processing chain.

Table 5.1: Summary on DBR values for the applications in this paper.

Inspection task	DBR value	
	VIS range	NIR range
Polyester fabrics inspection – scratch	0.7	30.3
Polyester fabrics inspection – contamination	2.1	19.7
Missing thread detection	2.4	5.6
Thread inspection in textile seams	3.5	5.5
Contamination detection on printed surfaces	4.4	19.7

8 Summary

Quality inspection tasks are usually performed in the visible spectrum imitating human inspection capabilities. It has been demonstrated for different applications that inspection tasks could be facilitated by switching from the VIS range to the NIR range. In this way one takes advantage that dyes are often not active in the NIR range. A noticable improvement of the image quality has already been achieved in the range from 700 nm – 1000 nm. Silicon based CCD camera chips could be used in this range which enables cost sensitive inspection solutions.

References

1. R. Bhargava and I. W. Levin, Eds., *Spectrochemical Analysis Using Infrared Multichannel Detectors*. Wiley-Blackwell, 2005.

2. H. Eigenbrod, "Surface Inspection with Non-Visible Technologies: Process Integration with Low-Cost Sensors and Spectral Imaging Devices," In: Automated Imaging Association: Machine Vision Online - The Vision Show East / CD-ROM : Technical Conference Proceedings, May 9-11, 2006, Boston, MA, U.S.A., 2006.

3. A. Gowen, C. O'Donnell, P. Cullen, G. Downey, and J. Frias, "Hyperspectral imaging – an emerging process analytical tool for food quality and safety control," *Trends in Food Science & Technology*, vol. 18, no. 12, pp. 590–598, 2007.

4. JAI, "JAI's new 2-CCD camera AD-080 CL." URL: http://www.jai.com/ SiteCollectionDocuments/Camera_Solutions_Other_Documents/AD-080CL _Article.pdf, 2008, promotional brochure.

5. BASF, "Paint it cool! Pigments for solar heat management in paints." URL: http://www.dispersions-pigments.basf.com/portal/streamer?fid=560474, 2009, promotional brochure.

6. J. Pannekamp, "Adaptive Verfahren zur Bewertung texturierter Oberflächen." Ph.D. dissertation, Stuttgart, Univ., Fak. Maschinenbau, Inst. für Industrielle Fertigung und Fabrikbetrieb, 2005.

Reflection and transmission Raman spectroscopy for the chemical characterization of solid materials

E. Ostertag[1], D. Oelkrug[2] and R. W. Kessler[1]

[1] Process Analysis and Technology, Reutlingen Research Institute,
Reutlingen University, D-72762 Reutlingen
[2] Institute of Physical and Theoretical Chemistry,
University of Tübingen, D-72076 Tübingen

Abstract This paper compares Raman intensities from reflection (X_R) and transmission (X_T) setups for the chemical characterization of solid materials. The suitability of measuring the Raman radiation for deep probing of the inner volume of turbid matter is discussed from a theoretical and an experimental point of view.

1 Introduction to Raman spectroscopy in turbid matter

Raman radiation (RR) originates in the volume of a material mainly from multiple scattered primary radiation, and the Raman signal itself is also elastically scattered many times before it leaves the sample. Figure 6.1 illustrates the generation of RR: A laser irradiates the scattering sample. Photons migrate into the sample and move within the sample a short or long way depending on the scattering and absorption properties of the material. Photons leave the sample with the same wavelength like the laser source as reflected or transmitted primary light. In the case of a Raman scattering event, the RR can be collected in reflection or transmission. RR is a volume effect, where the light is generated in the sample as follow-up process: the longer the light lasts in the sample, the more Raman scattering is generated. Thus even in thick samples measurable Raman transmission intensities can be achieved in a conventional setup.

There is a rising demand for optical analytical techniques which allow a deep probing of solid matter [1, 2]. Transmission Raman spectroscopy has been presented as an emerging tool to gather information

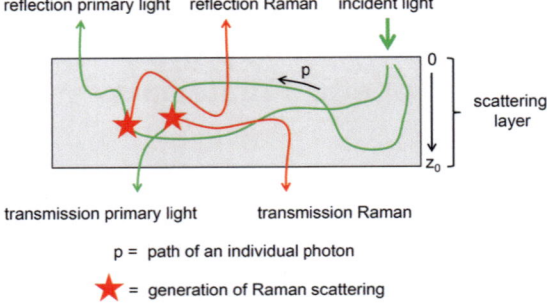

Figure 6.1: Generation of Raman radiation in reflection (X_R) and in transmission (X_T) in a scattering solid sample of layer thickness z_0. A laser irradiates the sample with a certain number of photons which migrate through the sample, generating Raman photons or leaving the sample as primary light in reflection or transmission.

from the inner volume of solid samples including a quantitative analysis [3,4]. Application examples are in-line process monitoring, fast quality control in pharmaceutical production, counterfeit detection of tablets through the packaging, in-situ characterization of surface reactions on supported catalysts or medical screenings like the noninvasive characterization of tissues and bones. Transmission Raman spectroscopy has already been shown in combination with multivariate data analysis for the quantification of active pharmaceutical ingredients (API) in pharmaceutical mixtures.

Conventional backscattering (= reflection) Raman spectroscopy of opaque media with a low absorption ($\kappa = 0.1$) is strongly biased to the surface layers of the sample from some micrometers up to several millimeters depth [3].

Spatially offset Raman spectroscopy (SORS) marks an approach to overcome the sub-sampling restrictions of conventional backscattering Raman spectroscopy and provides an access to deeper volumes of the sample. Here, the detection is laterally separated with an offset to the laser excitation. Raman spectra can be extracted in combination with multivariate data analysis from different depths of turbid samples [5].

In thin samples with typical thicknesses of $z_0 \leq 1$ cm, the backscattering mode can be expanded by forward scattering (= transmission) Raman spectroscopy. This type of detection was worked out already in 1967 by Schrader and Bergmann [6] and received its revival in 2006 by Matousek and Parker [7]. Hence, transmission Raman spectroscopy represents a special case of SORS for deep Raman probing. Matousek et al [7]. showed for the first time with numerical simulations and experimentally that the depth of impurities in tablets plays a minor role in Raman transmission spectroscopy compared to a Raman backscattering setup, where they are not detected.

2 Model calculation

2.1 Mean path lengths of radiation in a non-absorbing scattering layer

Figure 6.2 depicts the calculated mean path lengths of radiation until reflection $<p_R>$ (left) and until transmission $<p_T>$ (right) under the assumption of a non-absorbing sample. The calculations are performed with the help of a random walk approach. For the reflection case

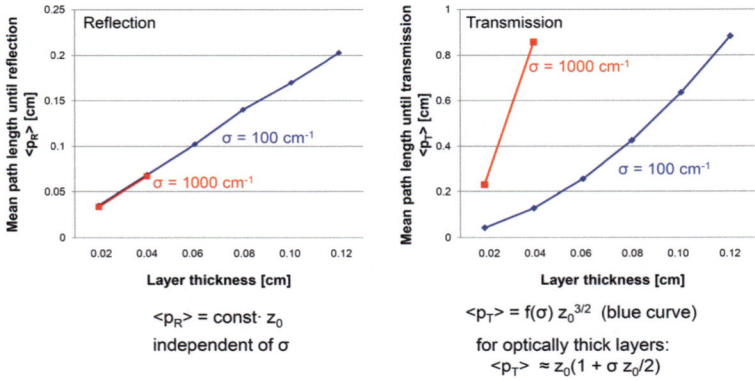

Figure 6.2: Mean path lengths of radiation in a non-absorbing scattering layer calculated by the random walk approach for a reflection (left) and a transmission setup (right).

$<p_R>$ is linearly dependent on the layer thickness z_0 and independent of the scattering coefficient σ. For the transmission case the right graph of Fig. 6.2 shows clearly the influence of the scattering coefficient on the mean path length. The figure also indicates the equations for the scattering coefficient $\sigma = 100$ cm^{-1} and for optically thick layers.

2.2 Reflection Raman versus transmission Raman: Monte Carlo simulations

Monte Carlo simulations for calculating the reflected and transmitted Raman intensities of non absorbing and absorbing materials as function of the layer thickness are performed. Figure 6.3 (left) shows, that in strongly scattering media with no absorption the Raman intensity increases with the layer thickness. The reflected Raman intensity is twice the transmitted Raman intensity. In strongly scattering media with absorption (Fig. 6.3, right) Raman backscattering setups yield higher intensities and smaller signal variations due to the smaller Raman active volume element. The presence of sample absorption leads to a decay of the Raman intensities, which is more pronounced in the transmission setup.

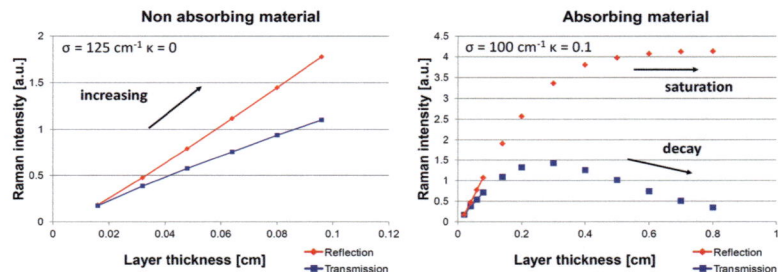

Figure 6.3: Monte Carlo simulations calculate the reflected and transmitted Raman intensities of stronlgy scattering materials for the cases with no absorption (left) and absorption (right).

3 Measurement setup

The reflection and transmission Raman measurements are carried out with a RamanRXN1™ analyzer from Kaiser Optical Systems, Ann Arbor, USA equipped with an Invictus™ 785 nm NIR diode laser specified for a maximum output power of 450 mW. The spectral resolution is 0.3 cm^{-1}. The laser irradiates the sample via an optical fiber with additional optics. Figure 6.4 illustrates the reflection and transmission setups. For the reflection setup a PhAT™ probe is attached to the optical fiber to illuminate the sample with a spot diameter of 0.6 cm. For the transmission setup a transmission illuminator is coupled to the optical fiber for the excitation of the sample with an irradiation diameter of 0.1 cm. The detection is realized for both the reflection and transmission setups with the PhAT™ probe with a collection spot diameter of 0.6 cm. The collected Raman and primary radiation passes a further optical fiber and filter elements on the way to the volume phase transmission grating and the Peltier cooled CCD matrix detector to generate the Raman spectra. The Raman intensities X_R and X_T in reflection and transmission are calibrated with liquid cyclohexane in a thin optical cuvette. PTFE as optical diffuse material for thickness dependent investigations is supplied by Gigahertz-Optik, Türkenfeld, Germany in thicknesses of 0.02 and 0.15 cm. Additional thicknesses up to 0.5 cm were cut from a PTFE block or prepared as stacks from the 0.02 cm layer. Cellulose is purchased as filters type MN 615 from Macherey-Nagel, Düren, Germany with 0.016 cm thickness. Acetylsalicylic acid (ASA), product no. 158185000 from Acros Organics, Geel, Belgium is used to press a cylindrical disc with 2 cm diameter and 0.425 cm thickness as inner layer of a composite triple layer. The upper and the lower layer consists of a PTFE layer.

4 Results and discussion

Raman emission in a scattering layer system originates from different depths depending on the reflection or transmission setup. Experiments with multiple, double and triple layer systems illustrate the behavior in z-axis.

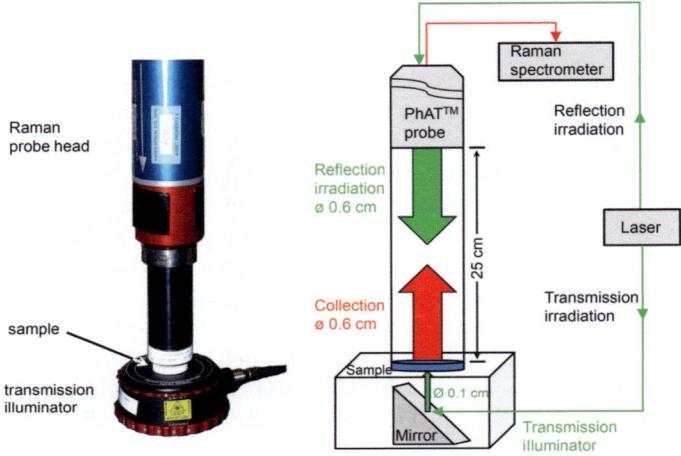

Figure 6.4: Setups for reflection and transmission Raman spectroscopy. In the reflection mode the sample is irradiated from top with a diameter of 0.6 cm (wide area illumination). In the transmission setup the sample is irradiated from the bottom side via the transmission illuminator which generates a spot size diameter of 0.1 cm. The Raman probe head (PhAT™) collects the Raman radiation in both setups with a diameter of 0.6 cm and routes it to the spectrometer. Left: photograph, right: schematic diagram.

4.1 Multiple layer system

Multiple layers with 1 to 5 layers of cellulose and PTFE with both low absorption coefficients are investigated in the reflection and transmission mode (Fig. 6.5). For cellulose the intensities of the Raman band at $\Delta v = 1095$ cm^{-1} are recorded at layer thicknesses from 0.016 cm to 0.08 cm in reflection and transmission. The Raman band belongs to several closely spaced intense bands in the region between $\Delta v = 950$ cm^{-1} to 1180 cm^{-1}. For PTFE the intensities of the Raman band at $\Delta v = 1382$ cm^{-1} are recorded at layer thicknesses from 0.15 cm to 0.5 cm in reflection and transmission. The Raman band at $\Delta v = 1382$ cm^{-1} is the most intense sub-band of the characteristic PTFE-triplet. The measured Raman intensities in reflection and transmission of the cellulose multilayer system confirm the Monte Carlo model calculations:

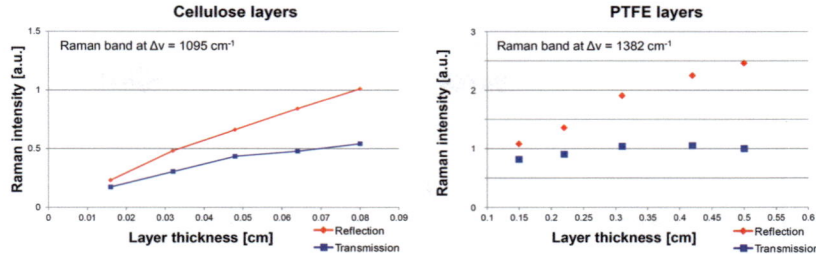

Figure 6.5: Raman intensities in the reflection and the transmission mode from a multilayer system of 1-5 layers of cellulose with low absorption coefficients. The experimental data confirm the results from the Monte Carlo simulations (left). Raman intensities in the reflection and the transmission mode of PTFE with low absorption coefficients at 5 different layer thicknesses show deviations to the model (right).

In strongly scattering media with negligible background absorption the Raman intensity increases with the layer thickness. Here the reflected Raman intensity is twice the transmitted Raman intensity.

In the case of the PTFE system the experimental data show deviations to the model: With a layer thickness above 0.3 cm the transmitted Raman intensity reaches a maximum and then slowly decreases. This behavior may be caused by an unexpected absorption of the layers due to contamination, a too simple model or a limited detection aperture. If a specific layer thickness is reached the Raman photons laterally spread wider than the diameter of the detection area. In the experiments the maximum thickness of the PTFE layers with 0.5 cm exceeds the maximum thickness of the cellulose layers with 0.08 cm by a factor of approximately 6.

4.2 Double layer system

A double layer with two axially separated different Raman emitters A and B produce signals that do not depend only on the thickness of the emitting layer but also on the thickness and position of the co-layer. The reflected Raman intensity X_R of the front layer increases strongly with the thickness of the back layer because part of the initially transmitted

Raman signal is now reflected, but mainly because the density of the primary radiation becomes higher. The reflected intensity of the back layer behaves in the opposite way.

In the experiment in reflection geometry (Fig. 6.6, left) a double layer of cellulose and PTFE is irradiated alternatively from one of the two sides. The PTFE signal from the front side is approximately four times as high as from the back side (see e.g. the Raman band of PTFE at $\Delta v = 1382$ cm^{-1}).

Contrary to X_R, transmission Raman spectra are expected to be independent of the side of irradiation. The spectra of Fig. 6.6 prove experimentally the independency of the side of irradiation in transmission geometry with a double layer of PTFE and cellulose.

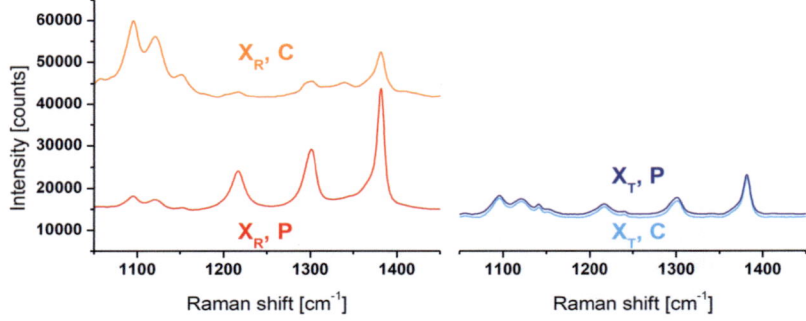

Figure 6.6: Raman reflection and transmission intensities X_R (left) and X_T (right) of a double layer of 0.020 cm PTFE and 0.016 cm cellulose with P = orientation of PTFE to the detector and C = orientation of cellulose to the detector. The spectra are fluorescence corrected. In reflection the measured spectra depend strongly on the upper material. The spectral influence of the subjacent material is lower. In transmission the spectra are independent from the orientation of the layers.

4.3 Triple layer system

A triple layer A/B/A simulates coated tablets or encapsulated powders, and is expected to behave as follows: The reflection mode highlights the spectrum of A, whereas the transmission mode highlights the spectrum of B since the generation probability of the central layer is much higher than of the border layers.

Figure 6.7 shows experimental data for a triple layer arrangement of PTFE (0.15 cm) / acetylsalicylic acid (ASA, 0.425 cm) / PTFE (0.15 cm). The Raman band at $\Delta v = 733$ cm^{-1} originates from PTFE, the three other bands from ASA. The Raman reflection setup emphasizes clearly the spectrum of PTFE, the transmission setup the spectrum of ASA.

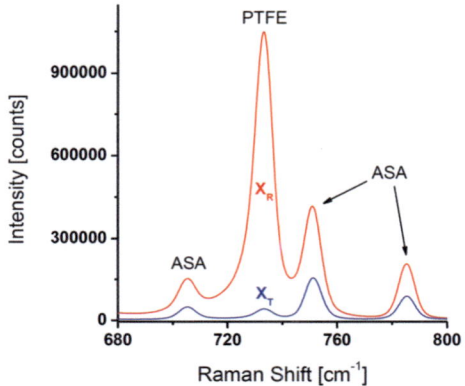

Figure 6.7: Raman reflection (X_R) and transmission intensities (X_T) from a model system of a coated tablet with excess coating thickness (PTFE 0.15 cm / ASA 0.425 cm / PTFE 0.15 cm). In Raman transmission the main spectral information is generated in the inner medium. The band at 733 cm^{-1} Raman shift results from PTFE. The remaining bands are assigned to acetylsalicylic acid. The Raman spectrum of ASA does not comprise a band at $\Delta v = 733$ cm^{-1}.

5 Conclusions and outlook

Reflection Raman spectroscopy yields higher signal intensities than transmission, but is limited in conventional spectroscopy setups to the material located in vicinity to the surface. Nevertheless, the transmission Raman intensities are higher than expected as long as the sample is not absorbing (X_T is at least half as intense as X_R). In transmission Raman spectroscopy of absorbing samples, the intensity firstly reaches a maximum with increasing layer thickness and then decays. The strong decrease of X_T with absorption is a consequence of the long path length of the transmitted radiation. In those cases the reflection mode is superior to the transmission mode. In solid samples with axial concentration the mean reflected signal originates from the first quarter of the layer depth, whereas the mean transmitted signal originates predominantly from the central regions. Here, for probing the inner volume of a sample the T-mode is superior to the R-mode. As a consequence it must be carefully considered which multilayer systems are measured.

A possible limitation of the detector aperture has to be taken into account as the radial expansion of the signals increases linearly with the layer thickness, where X_T spreads wider than X_R. Especially quantitative transmission Raman spectroscopy requires diameters of the detected sample areas that are adopted thoroughly to the sample thickness.

For an improved detection of buried layers the weak signal strength of transmitted Raman radiation can be enhanced by a dielectric mirror system [8]. In future work the authors will present a modified approach for enhanced reflection Raman spectroscopy, where it is possible to monitor the whole depth of a multiple scattering sample with equal statistical weight. The authors consider an enhanced reflection setup as a favorable approach for inline Raman spectroscopy in process analytical technology.

Acknowledgement

We acknowledge the support of Kaiser Optical Systems Inc. for the allocation of an RXN1™ system.

References

1. R. W. Kessler, *Prozessanalytik - Strategien und Fallbeispiele aus der industriellen Praxis*.   Weinheim: Wiley-VCH, 2006.

2. K. A. Bakeev, *Process Analytical Technology - Spectroscopic Tools and Implemen-*

tation Strategies for the Chemical and Pharmaceutical Industries, second edition. 2. ed.   Chichester: John Wiley and Sons, 2010.

3. K. Buckley and P. Matousek, "Non-invasive analysis of turbid samples using deep Raman spectroscopy," *Analyst*, vol. 136, pp. 3039–3050, 2011.

4. M. D. Hargreaves, N. A. MacLeod, M. R. Smith, D. Andrews, S. V. Hammond, and P. Matousek, "Characterization of transmission Raman spectroscopy for rapid quantitative analysis of intact multi-component pharmaceutical capsules," *Journal of Pharmaceutical and Biomedical Analysis*, vol. 54, pp. 463–468, 2011.

5. P. Matousek, I. P. Clark, E. R. C. Draper, M. D. Morris, A. E. Goodship, N. Everall, M. Towrie, W. F. Finney, and A. W. Parker, "Subsurface probing in diffusely scattering media using spatially offset Raman spectroscopy," *Applied Spectroscopy*, vol. 59, pp. 393–400, 2005.

6. G. Schrader, B.; Bergmann, "Die Intensität des Ramanspektrums polykristalliner Substanzen," *Fresenius' Journal of Analytical Chemistry*, vol. 225, pp. 230–247, 1967.

7. A. W. Matousek, P.; Parker, "Bulk Raman analysis of pharmaceutical tablets," *Applied Spectroscopy*, vol. 60, pp. 1353–1357, 2006.

8. P. Matousek, "Raman signal enhancement in deep spectroscopy of turbid media," *Applied Spectroscopy*, vol. 60, pp. 845–854, 2007.

Hydrogen content of CeCl$_3$-doped sodium alanate powder samples measured in-situ by ATR-FTIR-spectroscopy and gravimetry during desorption

Ingo Franke, Hans-Dieter Bauer and Birgit Scheppat

RheinMain University of Applied Sciences, Dept. of Engineering, D-65428 Rüsselsheim, Am Brückweg 26, Germany

Abstract For future applications of solid-state hydrogen tanks a reliable method for hydrogen content monitoring is necessary. The chemical reactions of a sodium hydride/alanate system during hydrogen desorption were followed in-situ using two methods in parallel: First, changes of the FTIR spectra due to the crystal structure phase changes were recorded. Second, precision weight measurements were carried out. To do so, a set-up consisting of a FTIR spectrometer, equipped with a special sample chamber for ATR measurements, combined with a high precision balance was developed. The results presented in this paper were obtained on a self-prepared CeCl$_3$-doped sodium alanatesample. Absorbed weight percentage of hydrogen and spectroscopic data correspond to each other in a reproducible way. Moreover, activated and non-activated materials show very similar behavior.

1 Introduction

Metal hydrides, in combination with a second metal, are capable of forming complex compounds with gaseous hydrogen, i.e. they are able to absorb hydrogen in the solid state. The bonds formed may be of more covalent or more ionic character, respectively [1]. Because this type of reaction is very often fully reversible and absorption/desorption cycles may be performed under rather moderate pressure and temperature conditions many times, it is considered as a promising storage concept in hydrogen technology [2]. Depending on the specific type of hydride / metal system up to 10 wt.% of hydrogen could be stored [3], which is a remarkable value also compared with liquid hydrogen storage or pressure storage concepts, especially for small and mobile tank applications [4].

The system under investigation in this research project is sodium hydride (NaH). It shows a chemical reaction with hydrogen in the presence of aluminum (Al) and the catalyst (CeCl$_3$) to form different types of alanates [5]. Because of their nanoporous crystal lattice morphology, hydrogen molecules are able to diffuse easily into the material and are going to be absorbed within the lattice. In a first reaction step of the hydrogenation an octahedral phase is formed:

$$6\,NaH + 2\,Al + 3\,H_2 \rightleftharpoons 2\,Na_3\,AlH_6 + E_{th} \tag{7.1}$$

In this phase, the Al atoms are symmetrically surrounded by six hydrogen atoms, forming an octahedron. The second hydrogenation step is the formation of a tetrahedral phase [6]:

$$2\,Na_3\,AlH_6 + 4\,Al + 6\,H_2 \rightleftharpoons 6\,NaAlH_4 + E_{th} \tag{7.2}$$

Here, Al and the four H atoms form a symmetric tetrahedron. Theoretically, the "fully loaded" tetrahedral phase may contain up to 7.4 wt.% of hydrogen. Catalysts, that are usually added to the hydride / alanate system, allow the reduction of the activation barrier, which has to be overcome for a fast de- and rehydrogenation reaction. The experiments presented in this paper have been carried out with CeCl$_3$ as a catalyst. Other possible catalysts are TiCl$_4$, carbon nanotubes [7] or metal nanoparticles [8].

For storage applications it is essential to know about the instant hydrogen content of the tank, especially while hydrogen is being desorbed to be used in fuel cells to power an electric vehicle, e.g. A gravimetrical measurement of the remaining hydrogen content, like it is possible in laboratory use, is not applicable for such a mobile application because of shock and vibration effects. Optical measurements, like spectrophotometry, have non-contact character and seem to be more promising than mechanic or electric measurement principles. The main reason to use optical spectrometry for this problem, is the fact that the absorption and desorption of hydrogen goes along with a structural change in chemical conformation: The hydride, the octahedral phase and the tetrahedral phase should show different spectroscopic "fingerprints," especially in the IR region, i.e. in the region of vibrational transitions.

To investigate the IR spectra of the sodium hydride / alanate system the FTIR (Fourier Transform Infrared) spectroscopy was chosen. Transmission measurements on thin alanate layers were done. However, it was shown that these layers were not suitable for different reasons: First, the preparation of thin layers of the granular powder material with well-defined thickness was difficult. Second, the material is highly scattering. During absorption / desorption cycles the material increases and decreases its volume, causing the granularity and the arrangement of the grains to change and the thickness to change dramatically. Therefore, it was decided to use an ATR (attenuated total reflection) assembly in addition to the FTIR spectrometer. This kind of measurement does not depend on sample thickness. Moreover, one had to find a way to establish a relation between optical signal and weight percentage of the absorbed hydrogen. To solve this problem a parallel measurement of FTIR-ATR spectrum and weight was done.

2 Experimental

2.1 Set-up

For spectroscopy on highly absorbing media attenuated total reflection (ATR) spectroscopy is often used. ATR takes place at the interface between a material of high index of refraction and the sample, which has to have a lower index of refraction. Light is guided inside the high-n material and when hitting the interface under an angle higher than the critical angle of total internal reflection, it is reflected. Before, an evanescent wave is penetrating into the medium with the lower index of refraction and "senses" the material's absorption [9]. That means, the totally reflected light in principle carries the same spectroscopic information as a transmission spectrum does. Of course, the information is obtained from the surface of the sample only.

The experimental set-up primarily consists of a commercial Perkin Elmer Spectrum65® FTIR spectrometer, which was equipped with a Harrick Seagull® ATR unit. Its central part is a high-index material hemisphere made of ZnSe, 25 mm in diameter. To avoid corrosive effects that would destroy the polished surface of the ZnSe element, a 100 μm thin diamond platelet was placed between the ZnSe and the sample.

The housing of the sample is a gas-tight chamber with a hydrogen inlet/outlet and with an inductive heating system realized in the course of the project. The sample itself is formed into a pellet of 10 mm in diameter and with a maximum thickness of 5 mm, corresponding to a mass of approximately 500 mg of alanate. The alanate sample can be heated now up to a maximum temperature of 200 °C, and the hydrogen absorption can be carried out with a maximum applicable pressure of 11 MPa. The sample is pressed against the flat surface of the diamond platelet with a constant force to provide good optical contact throughout the measurement, which is a very prerequisite for ATR measurements. The sample chamber can be weighted during the desorption process, therefore this component is decoupled mechanically from the spectrometer unit to make it force-free.

A Pinnacle® PI-314 precision balance has been applied for the weight measurements. The mass precision reached by using this set-up is estimated to be better than 0.05 wt.%, i.e. 0.1 mg precision and 0.3 mg linearity with a 500 mg sample at a full balance load of 300 g. Figure 7.1 shows a scheme of the central sample chamber.

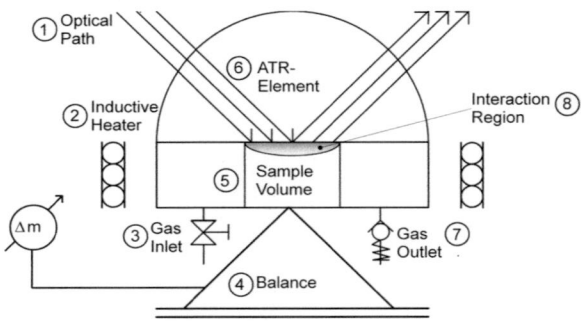

Figure 7.1: Schematic diagram of the measurement scheme.

2.2 Sample preparation

Because its sensitivity to oxygen the powder samples have to be handled under dry nitrogen or argon atmosphere in a glove box. For material preparation, 1.5 g of $NaAlH_4$, 2 mol% of $CeCl_3$ and 18 balls (Ø 10 mm) made of the identical material as the milling pot are filled into a planetary ball-mill "Pulverisette 5" and milled for 15 h at 360 rpm. Every 30 min, a milling break of 30 min was made, to exclude an overheating of the milling pot and thus to avoid a partial hydrogen desorption of the powder sample during the milling process. Before in-situ measurements on the powder samples were performed, two sample pellets were pressed. The pellets were compacted with a force of up to 10 kN. The press shoes consist of polished steel to allow a good optical contact between the the powder sample and the diamond platelet. The first "non-activated" pellet was made of a "freshly" synthesized material. The second sample was first pressed to a pellet, then cycled three times in a Sieverts apparatus that is described elsewhere [10]. Typical pressure and temperature conditions for desorption were 140 °C against a backpressure of 7-30 kPa. Absorption was performed at 120 °C and 90 bar. After cycling, the "fully loaded" sample was evacuated from the Sieverts apparatus and milled for a short time in a mortar. Thereafter the second "activated" sample was pressed.

2.3 Measurements

For the hydrogenation of the $CeCl_3$-doped alanate powder sample the typical conditions used were 9 MPa of pressure and a temperature of 120 °C, which resulted in a load duration of about six hours and "pure" tetrahedral $NaAlH_4$. The desorption was done against atmospheric pressure and a control valve allowed the hydrogen to leave the cuvette as soon as a threshold pressure of 7 kPa above ambient pressure was reached. Different from our earlier experiments [11] not a single temperature for the whole desorption process was chosen, but a stepwise procedure:
The tetrahedral phase is known to desorb hydrogen at 30 °C, whereas the usual temperature for desorption is 80 °C [12]. During heating the sample to 80 °C, a counterpressure of 4 MPa was applied. After reaching the constant temperature of 80 °C, the pressure was reduced to the

atmospheric value and the desorption started. In an identical way the desorption of the octahedral phase was initiated: After completion of the first desorption step, the same counterpressure was applied during heating to 140 °C to avoid desorption of hydrogen, which otherwise would have started at 110 °C already. Reducing the pressure to atmospheric level caused the desorption to start. This stepwise procedure allows to clearly distinguish between the two desorption processes. As a first step of the experiment, a FTIR spectrum and the weight of the cuvette were measured without the sample. After that the cuvette was loaded with the alanate pellet and re-inserted into the setup. First, the mass of the sample was measured as a weight reference. Weight and spectral data acquisition were then carried out simultaneously during the desorption, every 270 s, using a software routine based on PYTHON®.

3 Results and Discussion

3.1 In-situ measurements on non-activated CeCl$_3$-doped NaAlH$_4$ powder samples

The FTIR-ATR-spectra were monitored in-situ during the hydrogen desorption of a CeCl$_3$-doped NaAlH$_4$ pellet in the MIR-region of 650 to 1900 cm^{-1}. The most prominent vibrational absorption bands, observable in this region, could be attributed to the Al-H stretch modes of the tetrahedral phase (1620-1680 cm^{-1}) and octahedral phase (1250-1330 cm^{-1}), respectively, following [13, 14], e.g.

In Fig. 7.2, the result of the gravimetrical measurement during the hydrogen desorption of the NaAlH$_4$ phase is shown. A total amount of 3.4 ± 0.1 wt.% of hydrogen were desorbed within 600 min. In comparison to the calculated theoretical value of 3.4 wt.% in the first phase, both result are consistent. It can be seen, that up to a amount of 3.1 wt.%, an almost linear relation between desorbed hydrogen and time was observed. Afterwards, a much slower kinetic of the pellet was measured [15].

Figure 7.3 shows the FTIR-ATR spectra during the hydrogen desorption reaction of the CeCl$_3$-doped NaAlH$_4$ powder sample. The peak around 1654 cm^{-1}, characteristic for the antisymmetric stretch vibration of the AlH$_4$ molecule, vanished during transformation to the octahedral phase. In addition to that, at the beginning of the desorption of the tetrahedral phase, two more peaks at 891 cm^{-1} and 704 cm^{-1} were

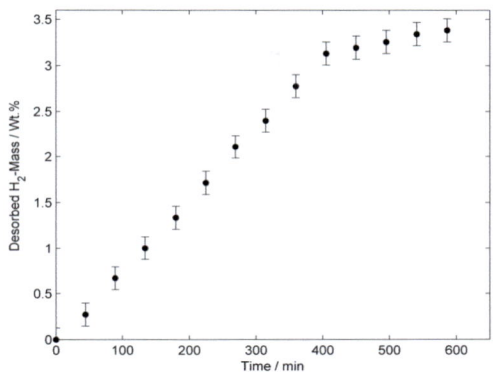

Figure 7.2: Desorption of hydrogen from CeCl$_3$-doped NaAlH$_4$ at 80 °C and a backpressure of 7 kPa. Every measurement point represents a spectrum in Fig. 7.3.

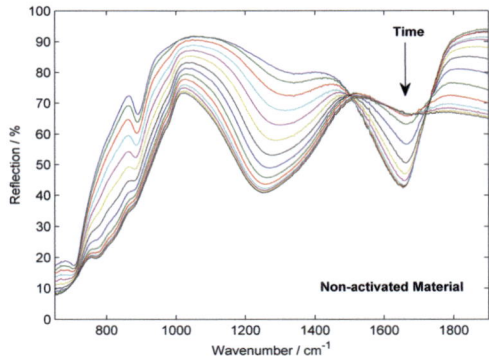

Figure 7.3: Time sequence of ATR spectra of CeCl$_3$-doped NaAlH$_4$, measured in-situ, showing the transformation to the Na$_3$AlH$_6$ phase at 80 °C and at a backpressure of 7 kPa. Time interval between two subsequent spectra is 45 min.

detected, also attributed to the vibrations of the AlH_4 molecule [16]. In parallel, a broad peak around 1254 cm^{-1} appears that could be attributed to the Na_3AlH_6 phase. Furthermore a shoulder around 790 cm^{-1} was detected.

In Fig. 7.4, the ongoing ATR spectra of the hydrogen desorption of the octahedral phase to the sodium hydride phase can be seen. The peak at 1254 cm^{-1} decreases, and forms a shoulder between 1254 cm^{-1} and 900 cm^{-1}. The shoulder at 790 cm^{-1} also vanishes.

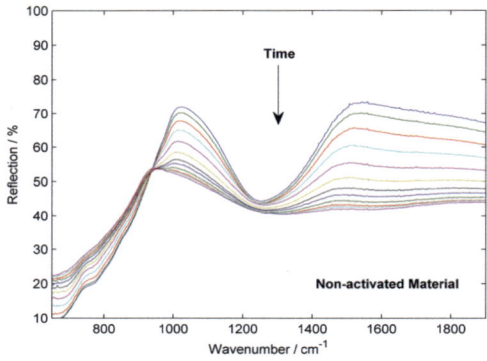

Figure 7.4: Hydrogen desorption of $CeCl_3$-doped Na_3AlH_6, at 140 °C and a backpressure of 7 kPa. Time interval between two subsequent spectra is 45 min.

3.2 In-situ measurements on activated $CeCl_3$-doped $NaAlH_4$ powder samples

The measurement of the activated $CeCl_3$-doped powder sample followed the identical procedure as described in the previous chapter. Figure 7.5 shows the gravimetrical data during the hydrogen desorption measurement of the $CeCl_3$-doped $NaAlH_4$ phase. The hydrogen desorption up to 3.1 wt.% shows the same linear relation between desorbed hydrogen mass and time, like the non-activated sample in the previous chapter. Thereafter a much slower hydrogen desorption, for the last 0.3 wt.% of desorbed hydrogen follows. Finally a total amount of 3.4 wt.% of hydrogen were desorbed from the $NaAlH_4$ phase within 600 min.

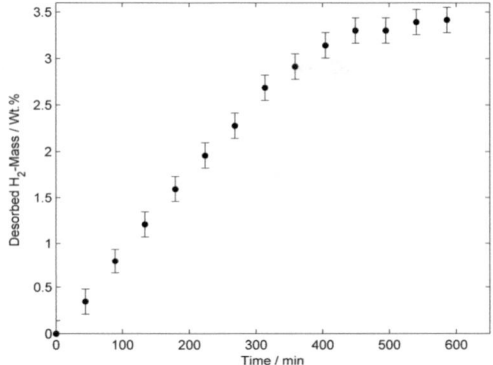

Figure 7.5: Gravimetrical data during the hydrogen desorption measurement of CeCl$_3$-doped NaAlH$_4$ at 80 °C and a backpressure of 7 kPa. Every measurement point represents a spectrum in Fig. 7.6.

Therefore, the results of the gravimetrical measurement of the activated and non-activated sample are consistent.

Figure 7.6 shows the ATR spectra during the hydrogen desorption of the activated CeCl$_3$-doped NaAlH$_4$ pellet. The broad peak at 1654 cm^{-1}, characteristic for antisymmetric stretching vibration of the AlH$_4$ molecule decreases during the hydrogen desorption reaction. In addition to that, the peak at 704 cm^{-1}, existent for the non-activated sample, shows only a weak shoulder during the measurement of the activated sample. Furthermore, it is remarkable that the peak height, especially for the AlH$_4$ peak at 1654 cm^{-1}, has an up to 10 % lower intensity than for the non-activated sample. Further measurements should show, whether this is a degradation effect, due to side reactions with air or moisture, or a result of crystallographic changes within the material. However, the spectral and gravimetrical data of the activated and non-activated pellet are nearly identical, related to peak position, peak shape and peak change during the hydrogen desorption experiments. Thus, spectral and gravimetrical data could be correlated to each other, to calibrate the ATR signal, for using it as a charging level signal for the NaAlH$_4$ pellet.

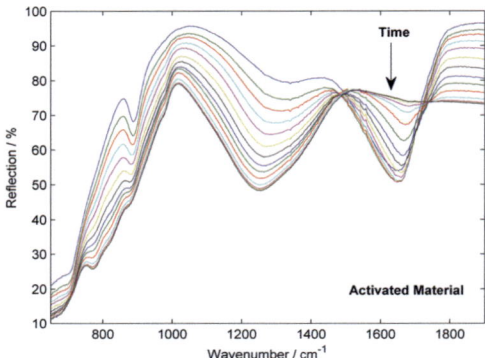

Figure 7.6: ATR-spectra during hydrogen desorption of the CeCl$_3$-doped NaAlH$_4$ phase to the Na$_3$AlH$_6$ phase, at 80 °C and a backpressure of 7 kPa. Time interval between two subsequent spectra is 45 min.

4 Conclusion

It could be shown that the measurements, FTIR-ATR-spectroscopy and gravimetry, reflect the 2-phase-hydrogenation mechanism regarded as typical for this class of hydrogen storage materials. The results further show that both measurements correlate to each other in a reproducible way, i.e. an optical signal represents the hydrogen content of a sodium alanate sample in a quantitative way. Therefore, the measurements show that FTIR-ATR signals can be used for monitoring the absorbed absolute hydrogen level in alanate powder tanks and may be regarded as the starting point for further work on hydrogen level sensors, especially because the whole set-up necessary for the measurements discussed has remarkable potential for miniaturization. Ongoing measurements on powder pellets should show, which external or internal influences affect the peak height of the non-activated and activated powder sample. Furthermore, a detailed peak analysis and theoretical calculation of the vibrational frequencies should be done. Thus, more detailed explanations to the measured data could be achieved.

Acknowledgement

This work has been supported by the German Ministry of Education and Research (ProfUnt grant no. 177X09). In addition to that, we want to thank C. Hess and his group at the Technical University of Darmstadt for using the milling equipment.

References

1. A. Léon, *Hydrogen Technology Mobile and Portable Applications.* Berlin, Heidelberg: Springer, 2008.

2. I. P. Jain, P. Jain, and A. Jain, "A review of lightweight complex hydrides," *Journal of Alloys and Compounds*, vol. 503, pp. 303–309, 2010.

3. L. George and S. K. Saxena, "Structural stability of metal hydrides, alanates and borohydrides of alkali and alkali- earth elements: A review," *International Journal of Hydrogen Energy*, vol. 35, pp. 5454–5470, 2010.

4. A. Züttel, A. Borgschulte, and L. Schlappach, Eds., *Hydrogen as a Future Energy Carrier.* Weinheim: Wiley-VCH, 2009.

5. X. Fan, X. Xiao, L. Chen, K. Yu, Z. Wu, S. Li, and Q. Wang, "Active species of $ceal_4$ in the $cecl_3$-doped sodium aluminium hydride and its enhancement on reversible hydrogen storage performance," *Chemical Communications*, vol. 44, pp. 6857–6859, 2009.

6. K. J. Gross, G. J. Thomas, and C. M. Jensen, "Catalyzed alanates for hydrogen storage," *Journal of Alloys and Compounds*, vol. 330-332, pp. 683–690, 2002.

7. M. Sterlin, L. Hudson, R. Himanshu, D. Pukazhselvan, and O. N. Srivastava, "Carbon nanostructures as catalyst for improving the hydrogen storage behavior of sodium aluminum hydride," *International Journal of Hydrogen Energy*, vol. 37, pp. 2750–2755, 2012.

8. M. Fichtner, J. Engel, O. Fuhr, O. Kircher, and O. Rubner, "Nanocrystalline aluminum hydrides for hydrogen storage," *Material Science and Engineering*, vol. B108, pp. 42–47, 2004.

9. F. M. Mirabella, *Internal Reflection Spectroscopy Theory and Applications.* New York: Marcel Dekker Inc., 1993.

10. R. Checchetto, G. Trettel, and A. Miotello, "Sievert-type apparatus for the study of hydrogen storage in solids," *Measurement Science and Technology*, vol. 15, pp. 127–130, 2004.

11. I. Franke, O. Henschel, D. Nitsche, M. Stops, H. D. Bauer, and B. Scheppat, "Parallel ftir-atr and gravimetrical in-situ measurements on sodium alanate powder samples during hydrogen desorption," *International Journal of Hydrogen Energy*, 2013.

12. G. Sandrock, K. Gross, G. Thomas, C. Jensen, D. Meeker, and S. Takara, "Engineering considerations in the use of catalyzed sodium alanates for hydrogen storage," *Journal of Alloys and Compounds*, vol. 330-332, pp. 696–701, 2002.

13. S. Gomes, G. Renaudin, H. Hagemann, K. Yvon, M. P. Sulic, and C. M. Jensen, "Effects of milling, doping and cycling of *naalh*$_4$ studied by vibrational spectroscopy and x-ray diffraction," *Journal of Alloys and Compounds*, vol. 390, pp. 305–313, 2005.

14. S. F. Parker, "Spectroscopy and bonding in ternary metal hydride complexes-potential hydrogen storage media," *Coordination Chemistry Reviews*, vol. 254, pp. 215–234, 2010.

15. G. Lozano, J. M. Bellosta von Colbe, R. Bormann, T. Klassen, and M. Dornheim, "Enhanced volumetric hydrogen density in sodium alanate by compaction," *Journal of Power Sources*, vol. 196, pp. 9254–9259, 2011.

16. A. E. Shirk and D. F. Shriver, "Raman and infrared spectra of tetrahydroaluminate, *alh*$_4$-, and tetrahydrogallate, *gah*$_4$-, salts," *Journal of the American Chemical Society*, vol. 95, pp. 5904–5912, 1973.

Infrared reflection absorption spectroscopy for characterization of alkylsilane monolayers on silicon nitride surfaces

Xia Stammer[1], Stefan Heißler[2] and Christof Wöll[2]

1 Bruker Optics GmbH, Ettlingen, Germany
2 Institute of Functional Interfaces (IFG), Karlsruhe Institute for Technology
(KIT), Eggenstein-Leopoldshafen, Germany

1 Introduction

Infrared reflection absorption spectroscopy (IRRAS) is a well-established technique for the characterization of surfaces and adsorbate films, which provides specific information on the chemical composition and structure of thin surface layers and adsorbed molecules. Most of the investigations have been carried out on metal substrates due to the high reflectivity and the ease of the spectra interpretation. Only since the 1980s the method has also been used for dielectric substrates with high refractive index, weakly reflection and vanishingly small absorption in the mid-IR region [1].

The formation of silane-based self-assembled monolayers (SAMs) on silicon oxide surfaces has attracted an increasing amount of interest since three decades. A number of previous works have focused on the formation mechanism, the thermal, mechanical and chemical stability of the silane-based adlayers [2,3]. Silicon nitride is one of the most common materials used in semiconductor industry and has been due to its unique biocompatibility the topic of a few studies and applications in biotechnology. In comparison to silicon oxide the formation process of silane-based SAMs is not completely understood [4,5].

2 Results

In the present work, we used IRRAS to determine the film quality of SAMs formed on antireflective coated silicon nitride substrates

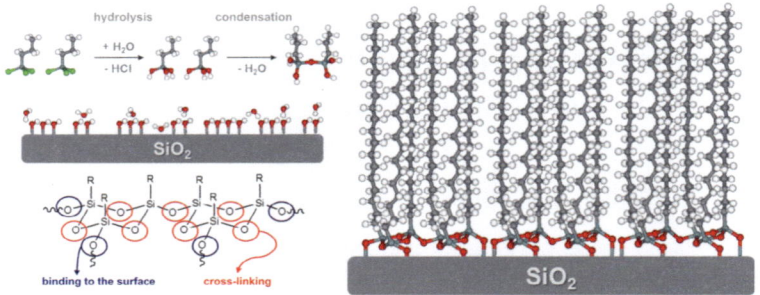

Figure 8.1: Formation of the silane film on the SiO$_2$ surface.

for state-of-the-art applications in industry. The formation of SAMs made of n-alkylsilanes (n-octadecyltrichlorosilane $\mathbf{C_{18}SiCl_3}$, n-dodecyltrichlorosilane $\mathbf{C_{12}SiCl_3}$ and n-dodecyltriethoxysilane $\mathbf{C_{12}Si(OEt)_3}$) on silicon oxide and silicon nitride surfaces has been investigated. The resulting films were characterized with IRRAS to improve the detailed parameters for the preparation. The IRRA spectra have been taken with polarized light using a Bruker Optics VERTEX 80 FT-IR spectrometer in combination with an optimized variable angle reflection sample accessory (A513) equipped with an automated polarizer rotation unit (A121). All IRRAS data were recorded with a resolution of 2 cm^{-1} using p- or s-polarized radiation with different incidence angles. All data were normalized by subtracting a spectrum recorded for the same substrate (clean Si$_3$N$_4$ or SiO$_2$). The substrates have been pretreated with ethanol and chloroform in an initial wet cleaning step. Subsequently, they were placed in an UV/Ozone chamber (λ=185 and 254 nm) for 30 min to remove residual organic contaminations. In our studies we realized the most important treatment to be the following, final step, wet chemical oxidation with piranha solution. This step consists of immersing the SiO$_2$ or Si$_3$N$_4$ substrate in a freshly prepared piranha solution (H$_2$SO$_4$/H$_2$O$_2$ 4:1) for 30 min at 70 °C, followed by rinsing with deionized water (Caution! Piranha solution should always be handled with great care and can react explosive with organic solvents). This preparation process fabricates hydroxylated and highly hydrophilic substrate surfaces.

The silane-based SAMs were prepared generally by immersing the pretreated Si_3N_4 or SiO_2 substrate in the corresponding silane solutions. For the formation of the silane-based SAMs not only reactions between the silane monomers and the surface but also reactions occurring within the solution have to be considered, as schematically depicted in Fig. 8.1. The velocity of the hydrolysis reaction depends strongly on the leaving group. In the next step, the silanols formed in the hydrolysis reaction will either react with each other to form polysiloxanes or bind to surface OH-groups. These two reactions, condensation in the solvent and binding to the surface compete with each other. In principle, for the formation of well-defined silane-based SAMs on the surface the condensation reaction between silanol molecules in solution leading to oligomerization, polymerization and deformation of siloxane patches is unwanted. Different preparation parameters, such as the temperature, the water content in the solution, the concentration of the silane solution, the solvent, the immersion time and the pretreatment of the substrate, have been shown to be critical for the kinetics of the SAM formation process and for the quality of the final SAM. As shown in Fig. 8.1, the silanol molecules condensed on the silicon surface are not only covalent bonded to the substrate, but also lateral linked to each other within the monolayer. This covalent cross-linking is characteristic for silane films and determines the stability and toughness of the formed silane-based SAMs.

With the help of the achieved IRRA spectra (see Fig. 8.2) we could make a statement for the ordering, the density and even for the orientation of the adsorbed molecules on the substrate surface and hence optimize the preparation conditions. The asymmetric (ν_{as} CH_2) and the symmetric stretching modes (ν_s CH_2) of the CH_2 groups in the alkyl chain are located at 2918 cm^{-1} and 2850 cm^{-1}. The position and the intensity ratio of the both vibrational bands are in good agreement with those reported in the literature [1]. The band positions and shapes demonstrate the presence of well-ordered, densely packed with the alkyl chains mostly in an all-trans conformation. Since the position of ν_{as} CH_2 vibrational mode is very sensitive to the ordering of the alkyl chains or rather of the monolayer, we use it as an indication of the film quality. According to previous work the presence of a highly ordered densely packed n-alkylsilane SAM with the alkyl chains in an all-trans conformation is indicated by a CH_2 vibrational frequency of

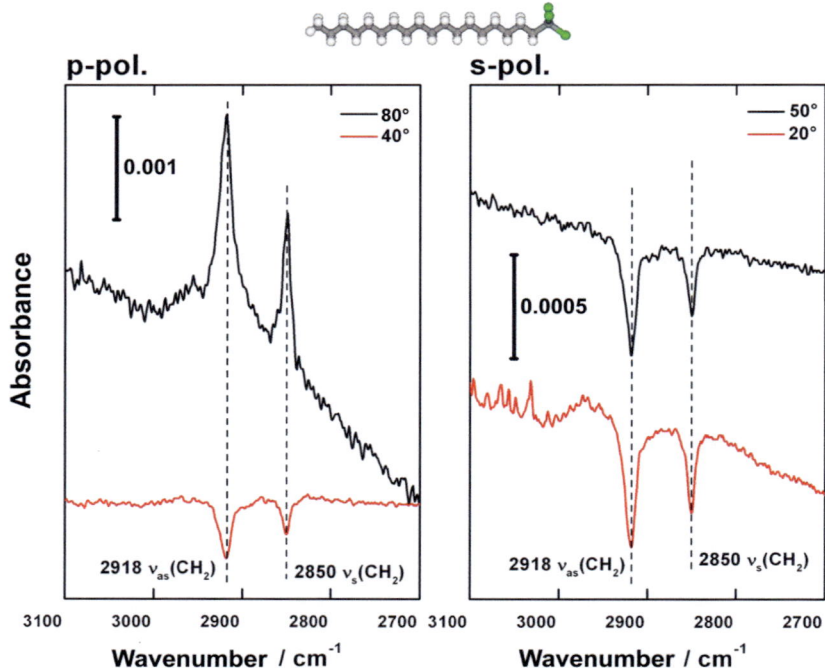

Figure 8.2: IRRA spectra of *n*-octadecyltrichlorosilane (structure shown above)-based SAM on silicon oxide surface measured with p- (left) and s-polarized light (right) each with two different incident angles using a Bruker Optics FT-IR VERTEX 80 spectrometer. The region of the CH_2 stretching modes is presented.

2919 cm^{-1}. As a consequence of a less dense packing, where the alkyl chains are disordered and exhibit high density of Gauche defects, the ν_{as} CH_2 band will be shifted towards higher energies (blue-shifted) by a few wavenumbers. The data shown in Fig. 8.2 reveal that there is a pronounced dependence of both band intensity and polarity, on IR-light incidence angle. With s-polarized light only negative absorption bands are observed with higher intensity at lower incident angle, whereas with p-polarized light an inversion of the absorbance from negative to positive at incident angles higher than 75° is characteristic for these ab-

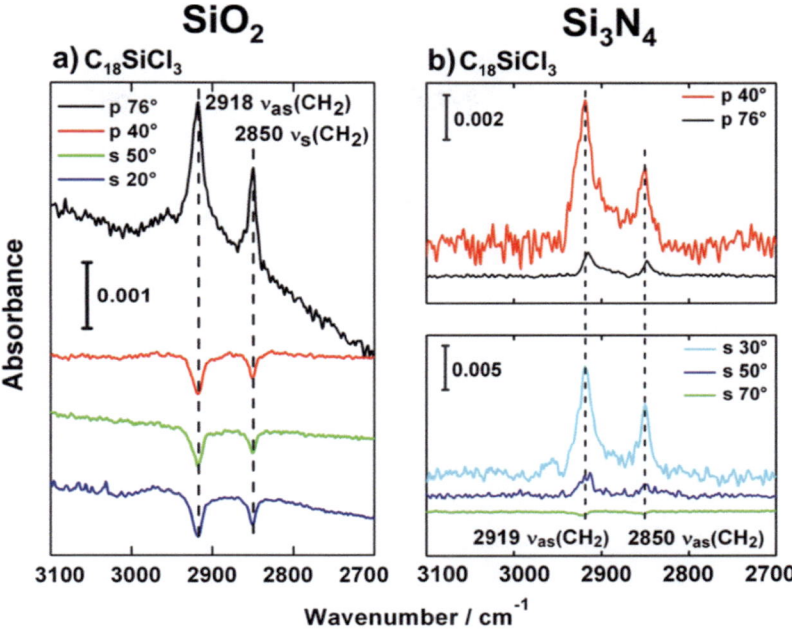

Figure 8.3: IRRA spectra of $C_{18}SiCl_3$ SAM a) on silicon oxide and b) on silicon nitride with p- and s-polarized light and different incident angles using a Bruker Optics FT-IR VERTEX 80 spectrometer.

sorption modes in a well-ordered anisotropic silane based monolayer on silicon oxide. A successful coupling of n-alkyltrichlorosilane on the rarely passive silicon nitride surface and the optimized preparation parameters of a well-defined silane-based SAM on this substrate could be achieved (see Fig. 8.3).

3 Summary

In our application of the IRRAS method using the novel setup provided by the Bruker Optics FT-IR spectrometer technology, highest sensitivity in combination with detailed structural information also on weakly reflecting, nonmetal surfaces was demonstrated. IRRAS was proved to be a steady, reliable and effective technique to control the quality of ultra-thin films on dielectric surfaces.

References

1. J. Kattner and H. Hoffmann, *Handbook of Vibrational Spectroscopy*. Chichester: Wiley, 2002.

2. K. Bierbaum and H. Fuchs, *Langmuir*, vol. 11, p. 2143, 1995.

3. S. R. Wasserman and J. D. Axe, *Journal of American Chemical Society*, vol. 111, p. 5852, 1989.

4. A. Arafat and H. Zuilhof, *Langmuir*, vol. 23, p. 6233, 2007.

5. C. A. E. Hamlett and J. A. Preece, *Surface Science*, vol. 602, p. 2724, 2008.

Multispectral imaging: Development and applications for snapshot MSI instrumentation

John Dougherty[1] and Steve Smith[1] and Oliver Lischtschenko[2]

[1] Ocean Thin Films,
16080 Table Mountain Pkwy, Golden, CO 80403, United States of America
[2] Ocean Optics BV,
Geograaf 24, 6921 EW Duiven, The Netherlands

Abstract While there are a wide variety of commercially available MSI imaging techniques and instruments, the community has long desired a simultaneous multichannel imaging sensor. We will describe the design and utility of exactly such a system as there has recently been a snapshot multispectral imaging system released to the market. Here, we will focus on the development path from standard research-grade spectrometer to filter wheel-based multispectral imager leading to the simultaneous multichannel "snapshot" MSI camera. Representative data from each modality will be presented to illustrate the progression of instrumentation. For the purposes of this paper, two similar looking samples, one biological in nature and one synthetic in nature will provide suitable objects for illustration.

1 Introduction

Every multispectral imaging application is unique and the wavelength ranges of interest run from the UV through short-wave infra red (SWIR). The particular regions that will be useful for one application will be dictated by the material properties of the components that will be used for imaging. The first step to successful multispectral imaging will always be accurate identification of relevant wavelengths to utilize for imaging. For many applications, these proof of concept parameters are already known or are proprietary knowledge. Filters to be utilized in either a wheel camera or on a patterned dichroic filter array sensor can

typically be designed with 5nm to 100nm FWHM bandpasses. Therefore, the approach described here utilizing three different instruments
in the experimental pathway is a valid one for commercial, industrial
and academic applications.

2 A non-imaging start

For initial studies to better define wavelengths of interest for a system,
a research spectrometer can be a very useful tool. As mentioned above,
we will present data from two samples, one biological and one synthetic. The initial measurements on these roses are shown in Fig. 9.1,
done with an Ocean Optics NIRQuest IR spectrometer. The differences
in the reflectance measurements obtained from the roses are significant,
though perhaps not what one would consider diagnostic. However, as
you see from the data obtained in the NIRQuest, it hints at the fact there
will be some interesting spectral differences between the two samples.

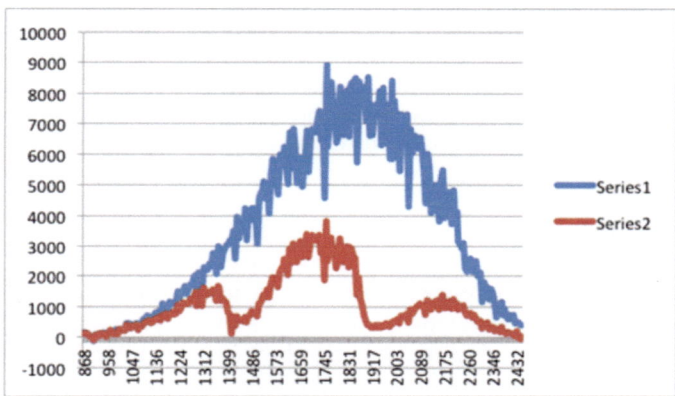

Figure 9.1: Raw spectral traces obtained from Ocean Optics NIRQuest IR spectrometer operating in reflectance mode, 400nm-2200nm data. Series 1 represents
reflectance data from synthetic flower, Series 2 is from a natural flower.

3 Seeing multispectrally

With spectral data now in hand, we can move on to an imaging method that will utilize the information obtained on the two samples in the NIRQuest. The spectrometer data shows some potentially significant differences in the spectral behavior of the two samples and we will attempt to use that in the next step on our pathway. The SpectroCam from PIXELTEQ (Fig. 9.2) is a multispectral imaging system with sensitivity from the UV through the SWIR regions. A SWIR camera was utilized here with six filters in order to take the next steps towards a snapshot MSI system. The screenshot in Fig. 9.3 below demonstrates the raw image output from SpectroCam.

Figure 9.2: The PIXELTEQ SpectroCam design.

Spectrally specific image data can be very powerful information and provide essential proof-of-concept data before progressing to a snapshot MSI system. In this example, you can see clear visual differences in the two samples. Contrast between the biological sample as compared to the non-biological are clearly shown in filters 3-5, especially filter 5. Filter 5 here corresponds to a wavelength range of approximately 1500nm–1600nm, which matches an area of the spectral reflectance data (Fig. 9.4) indicating significant differences between the real and synthetic flowers. A larger image from filter 5 is shown below and demonstrates how an imaging system perceives the spectral differences in the 1500nm wavelength range. Important for next section to note that in a wheel-based camera, each image is collected sequentially as the filters move and cover the sensor in succession.

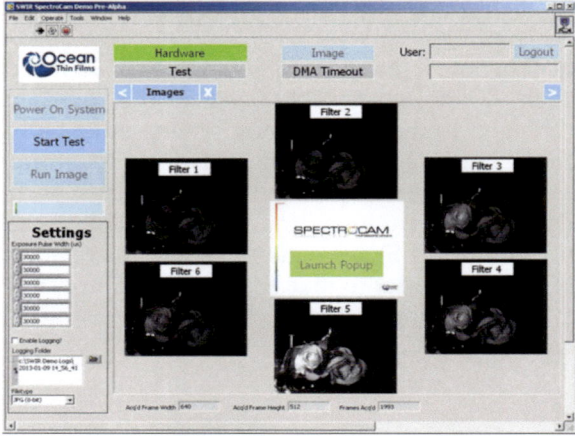

Figure 9.3: SpectroCam by PIXELTEQ live view screenshot. The six channels refresh constantly to provide a live view of the samples. Filters with approximately 100nm bandwidths spanning from 1050nm to 1700nm were utilized.

Figure 9.4: Image from filter 5 in PIXELTEQ SpectroCam MSI camera, corresponding to 1500nm-1600nm. Note the real rose on the left shows stronger signal (indicated by greater pixel intensities) in the 1500-1600nm range.

4 Real-time snapshot multispectral imaging system

After proving concept and imaging criteria for the system, it may be advantageous to migrate to a real-time snapshot MSI system. The primary advantage of a snapshot multispectral system is that all spectral channels are imaged simultaneously and therefore, imaging can be close to video rate in all channels. For this method, a custom sensor is created using proprietary technology [1–3]. However, the classic Bayer pattern sensor is a good illustration here to recall how typical imaging sensors are created.

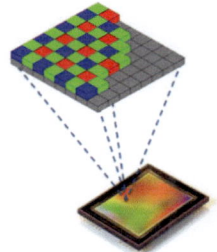

Figure 9.5: Classic Bayer pattern RGB sensor. Illustrative of how a dichroic filter array can be created directly on an imaging sensor.

With a custom patterned dichroic filter array sensor in place, integrated in an instrument called PixelCam, we were then able to produce the images shown below in representative screen shot, Fig. 9.6. Three channels were utilized in this demonstration camera, however, the biological matter clearly shows distinctive spectral properties when compared to the synthetic rose. That channel includes the 1500nm-1600nm range that was illustrated in the SpectroCam data. It is important to note the individual spectral channels are successfully de-mosaiced in the software and each channel provides an image of the subject matter. The images can be assigned a pseudo-color as well and reassembled into the image shown in the lower right panel of the software screen shot.

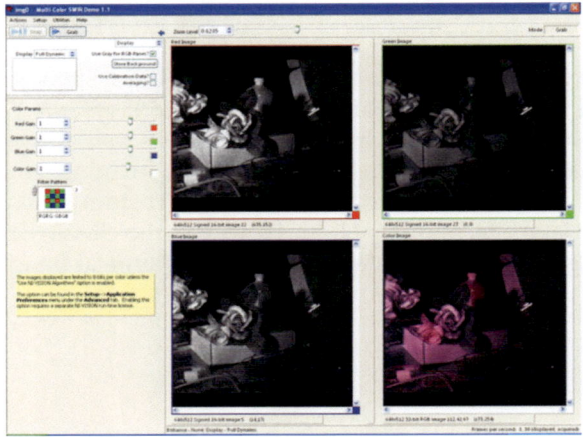

Figure 9.6: Snapshot multispectral imaging data, screen capture.

Figure 9.7: Pseudo-color combination image representing three channels obtained from snapshot MSI camera, PixelCam. Real rose on left.

5 Downstream applications

The true utility and power of multispectral imaging systems is best illustrated by the wide range of applications already successfully implemented or are currently under development. To mention just a few here,
MSI imaging has been a very powerful tool for: art and archaeology
analysis, forensics, industrial inspection, agricultural analysis and water quality monitoring. Perhaps the most interesting however, are the
potential applications for MSI systems in the biomedical sciences. As
a case study in the biomedical world, consider the emerging applications both in research and in clinical use for indocyanine green (ICG) as
a contrast agent for imaging. Currently growing in popularity, ICG is
FDA approved for use in humans and research animals and specifically
labels vascular tissues: arteries and veins. It has been successfully used
for retinal angiography (Fig. 9.8) as well as in-vivo animal research.

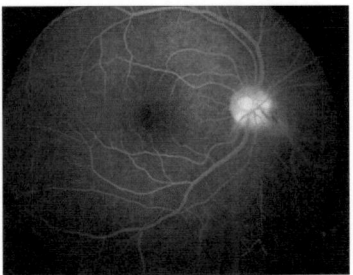

Figure 9.8: Retinal angiography.

A SpectroCam wheel camera or perhaps even better yet, a PixelCam
can be very useful tools for this type of imaging. The specific fluorescence emission from the ICG can be shown along with other channels
(such as RGB) in order to better analyze and present image data. This
particular application could be relevant for imaging during surgery, to
analyze wound healing after surgery or to assess hepatic function or
other circulatory system functioning in real-time. Applications are currently under development for this type of imaging and provide just one
example of the potential for MSI imaging in the biomedical sciences.

References

1. J. D. Jason M. Eichenholz, "Ultracompact fully integrated megapixel multi-spectral imager," ser. SPIE Proceedings, vol. 7218, 2009.

2. G. Overton, "Multispectral imaging: Filter-based multispectral imager has low complexity and cost," *Laser Focus World*, 2009.

3. J. D. Jason M. Eichenholz, "From science experiments to commercial products," *Advanced Imaging Magazine*, 2011.

Comprehensive, non-invasive, and quantitative monitoring of the health and nutrition state of crop plants by means of hyperspectral imaging and computational intelligence based analysis

Andreas Backhaus and Udo Seiffert

Fraunhofer Institute for Factory Operation and Automation IFF
Sandtorstr. 22, 39106 Magdeburg, Germany

Abstract Against the background of hyperspectral imaging this paper evaluates a number of different machine learning based classification methods in terms of their performance. All considered methods offer relevance profiles that additionally provide valuable information about the relevance of all acquired wavelengths to get the obtained classification. This relevance profile can be used to select appropriate wavelengths or wavelength bands to customize data acquisition and analysis tailored to the specific application at hand.

1 Introduction

Quantitative assessment of phenotypic properties of crop plants in relation to different genotypes, nutrition, stress tolerance, and fruit quality has become increasingly important in crop plant research, modern plant breeding, and particularly in precision agriculture / smart farming. The required assessment can generally be based either on morphological features, such as plant height, leaf shape, root structure etc., or on biomolecular/biochemical analyses. While the latter one is typically invasive and destroys the intact biological structure, morphological features are often not sufficient to unravel all relevant information at the required level of detail. Moreover, wet lab analyses typically assess only a more or less small number of samples and are not suitable to monitor crop plants in productive operation on the field or for large-scale (high-throughput) phenotyping of many genotypes in plant breeding. The results of wet lab analyses typically cannot be incorporated into on-line monitoring systems.

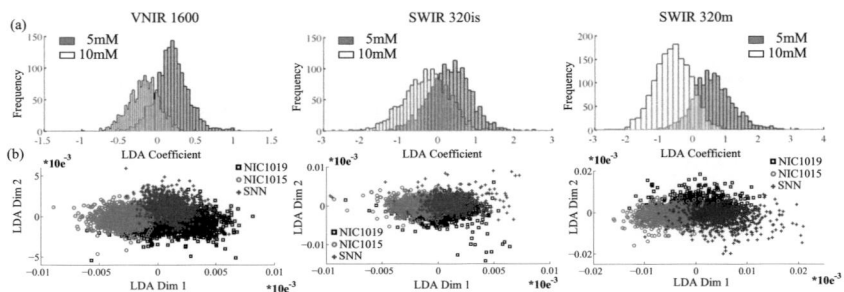

Figure 10.1: (a) Histogram of LDA coefficient for the two class problem of nutrition state; (b) Scatter plot of the LDA coeffcients for the three class problem of genotype classification.

There are several non-invasive systems currently available on the market. Typical applications are ground-based or airborne data acquisition for precision agriculture / smart farming as well as automated greenhouses in crop plant research and plant breeding. Technically these systems are based on broadband or selective color imaging (ca. 400-800 nm) that is sometimes accompanied by a few selected spectral bands in IR (>800 nm) or UV (<400 nm) range. From the application's perspective these systems can only monitor for example the level of green color (chlorophyll) of the plants (leaves) as indicator of nitrogen nutrition (e.g. Yara N-Sensor), the water content, or some particular biochemical compounds. Monitoring of a comprehensive health and nutrition state of crop plants is currently not commercially available.

Hyperspectral imaging linked to subsequent computational intelligence based analysis has proven its suitability to unravel complex information in a number of different application areas, such as geology, defense, etc. The extension of this approach to crop plant research, plant breeding, agriculture, and food processing has started just quite recently. Here, the image acquisition ranges from airborne sensing mainly for agricultural applications down to single leaf analysis in the context of precision and high-throughput plant phenotyping. All these applications have in common, that particular relevant compounds of the plant need to be determined by means of hyperspectral signatures as complement or substitute to extensive biochemical analyses.

Often the direct relationship between spectral information and biochemical target value or material category is not known in a closed mathematical form. In this case a machine learning approach is used to acquire an analysis model from reference data, a paradigm often referred to as 'soft-sensor'. Sensor data analysis becomes a pattern recognition task. Regarding pattern recognition and data mining in the acquired spectral data, computational intelligence based methods are still providing powerful tools to cope with this kind of high-dimensional and complex data.

In this paper we assess the ability of machine learning methods to robustly classify nutrition states and genotypic identity from input of three different hyperspectral cameras covering the VNIR/SWIR range.

2 Data acquisition

The data set originated from three genetically different tobacco varieties, namely *Nicotiana tabacum L., cv. SamsunNN (SNN), Nicotiana tabacum L., cv. undulata (NIC1015)* and *Nicotiana tabacum L., cv. undulata (NIC1019).* Plants were cultivated on quartz sand and maintained under controlled environmental conditions in a greenhouse. The plants were daily irrigated with a complete nutrient solution containing either 5 mM or 10 mM NH_4NO_3 (ammonium nitrate). Twelve weeks old plants were used in the experimental setup. Hyperspectral images were acquired from whole leaf blade (lamina). Leaves of different age were taken into account. Four leaves per plant were recorded. Leaves are numbered starting from the top downwards along the stem, therefore leaf age increases with the leaf number.

Images were acquired covering the complete VNIR/SWIR-band with three sensors simultaneously (Norsk Elektro Optikk A/S, VNIR 1600, SWIR 320i, SWIR 320m, 0.4-1.0, 0.9-1.7, 1.3-2.5 μm, respectively). The acquired images were read from 16 bit raw data using the vendors software. Blank images of the image background were also taken into account for inhomogeneous pixel sensitivities, which were found negligible. Reflectance calibration values were obtained from a standard optical PTFE (polytetrafluoroethylene) pad.

In a first k-means clustering [1], background pixels and pixels of non-leaf objects were removed. For display purposes and as input to the Support Vector Machine classifier in the classification stage, a Linear Discriminant Analysis (LDA) was performed. Figure 10.1a shows the data distribution in a one-dimensional LDA space per camera for the two-class problem of nutrition classification (5 mM and 10 mM NH_4NO_3). In Figure 10.2a, the mean spectrum (middle line) is depicted per camera. The seam around the mean spectra depicts the extend of the standard deviation per spectral band. Spectra were normalized to unit length. In both figures data originates from mutant NIC1019 and all leaf ages. Figure 10.1b shows the scatter plot in a two-dimensional LDA space per camera for the three-class problem of genotype classification while Figure 10.3a shows the mean spectra with standard deviation. Data originates from all leaf ages.

3 Theory

For machine learning, four different classification models are considered, a Radial Basis Function (rRBF) Network with Relevance Learning [2, 3], Generalized Relevance Learning Vector Quantization (GRLVQ) [4], Supervised Relevance Neural Gas (SRNG) [5] as well as a Support Vector Machine [6]. In general, rRBF, SRNG, and GRLVQ Networks are similar in terms that they process the input data in a layer of prototypical data points. While the rRBF generates activation due to the similarity with prototypes which is accumulated in a second layer for the network output, the GRLVQ and SRNG directly assign classes to prototypical data points. Prototypes usually represent central positions in a data cloud. In contrast, the Support Vector Machine stores support vectors, e.g. representative data points at the margin between data clouds. The used Support Vector Machine implementation of the v-SVM variant [7] from the freely available libSVM package[1] takes up a variable amount of support vectors.

In order to compute the distance of spectral data point $\mathbf{v}$ and a prototype $\mathbf{w}$ in the rRBF, SRNG and GRLVQ, we used the weighted Euclidean distance metric

$$d\left(\mathbf{v}, \mathbf{w}_r, \lambda\right) = \sum_i \lambda_i \left(v_i - w_{ir}\right)^2, \tag{10.1}$$

where λ_i is the relevance factor per spectral band which is adapted during the learning process to form the relevance profile. The rRBF, SRNG, and GRLVQ learning approach is essentially an energy minimization problem. In the standard learning scheme, stochastic gradient descent

---

[1] *www.csie.ntu.edu.tw/~cjlin/libsvm/*

with step-sizes manually set for different parameters are used. In order to avoid a manually chosen step-size, we used the non-linear conjugate gradient approach with automatic step size from the optimization toolbox 'minFunc'[2] available for Matlab. For this purpose we had to provide the objective/energy function along with the first derivatives according to the optimization parameters. The derivatives are accumulated for all data points (batch learning).

3.1 Radial basis function network with relevance

For the rRBF [2, 3] the objective function is the accumulated quadratic error of the network output y and target value t across network outputs and data samples $\mathbf{v}^j$.

$$E\left(\mathbf{V}, \mathbf{W}, \lambda\right) = \frac{1}{2} \sum_j \sum_k \left\{ y_k\left(\mathbf{v}^j\right) - \mathbf{t}_k^j \right\}^2,$$

with $y_k\left(\mathbf{v}\right) = \sum_r u_{rk} \phi\left(d\left(\mathbf{v}, \mathbf{w}_r, \lambda\right)\right)$ and $\phi\left(x\right) = \exp\left(-\frac{x}{2\sigma^2}\right)$. The partial derivatives are as follows

$$\frac{\partial E}{\partial w_{ir}} = \sum_j \sum_k \left\{ y_k\left(\mathbf{v}^j\right) - \mathbf{t}_k^j \right\}$$

$$u_{rk} \phi\left(d\left(\mathbf{v}^j, \mathbf{w}_r, \lambda\right)\right) \frac{\left(x_i^j - w_{ir}\right)}{\sigma_r^2}$$

$$\frac{\partial E}{\partial \sigma_r} = \sum_j \sum_k \left\{ y_k\left(\mathbf{v}^j\right) - \mathbf{t}_k^j \right\}$$

$$u_{rk} \phi\left(d\left(\mathbf{v}^j, \mathbf{w}_r, \lambda\right)\right) \frac{\sum_i \lambda_i\left(v_i - w_{ir}\right)^2}{\sigma_r}$$

$$\frac{\partial E}{\partial \lambda_i} = -\sum_j \sum_k \left\{ y_k\left(\mathbf{v}^j\right) - \mathbf{t}_k^j \right\}$$

$$\sum_r u_{rk} \phi\left(d\left(\mathbf{v}^j, \mathbf{w}_r, \lambda\right)\right) \frac{\left(v_i^j - w_{ir}\right)^2}{2\sigma_r^2}.$$

---

[2] http://www.di.ens.fr/~mschmidt/Software/minFunc.html

The output weights u_{rk} are yielded by direct update $\mathbf{U}^T = \Phi^\dagger \mathbf{T}$ where † denotes the pseudo inverse [8]. For the classification task a 1-out-of-N coding scheme for the target vector was used.

3.2 Generalized relevance learning vector quantization

For the GRLVQ the objective function is the accumulated difference in shortest distance of a data point to a prototype representing its class d_r^+ and a prototype representing any other class d_r^- [4]:

$$E\left(\mathbf{V}, \mathbf{W}, \lambda\right) = \sum_{v \in V} \frac{d_r^+ - d_r^-}{d_r^+ + d_r^-}.$$

The partial derivatives are as follows

$$\frac{\partial E}{\partial w_{ir}^+} = -\frac{2 \cdot d_r^-}{\left(d_r^+ + d_r^-\right)^2} 2\left(v_i - w_{ir}^+\right) \qquad \frac{\partial E}{\partial w_{ir}^-} = \frac{2 \cdot d_r^+}{\left(d_r^+ + d_r^-\right)^2} 2\left(v_i - w_{ir}^-\right)$$

$$\frac{\partial E}{\partial \lambda_i} = \frac{2 \cdot d_r^-}{\left(d_r^+ + d_r^-\right)^2}\left(v_i - w_{ir}^+\right)^2 - \frac{2 \cdot d_r^+}{\left(d_r^+ + d_r^-\right)^2}\left(v_i - w_{ir}^-\right)^2.$$

All partial derivatives not belonging to the winning prototype of same class w_r^+ and any other class w_r^- are set to zero.

3.3 Supervised neural gas

The SRNG [5] is a supervised version of the well known neural gas clustering algorithm [9]. Like in the GRLVQ a number of prototype vectors with pre-assigned class labels are distributed in the input space while minimizing the energy function

$$E\left(\mathbf{V}, \mathbf{W}, \lambda\right) = \sum_{\mathbf{v} \in \mathbf{V}} \sum_{\mathbf{w}_r \in \mathbf{W}_c} h_\gamma\left(r, \mathbf{v}, \mathbf{W}_c\right) \frac{d_r^+ - d_r^-}{d_r^+ + d_r^-},$$

where $h_\gamma\left(r, \mathbf{v}, \mathbf{W}_c\right)$ denotes the degree of neighborhood cooperation among all prototypes representing the respective spectral vector class.

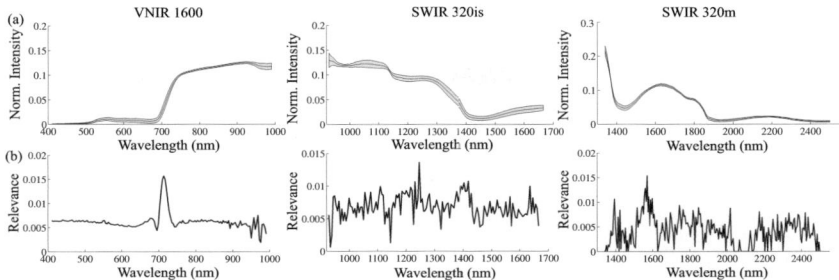

Figure 10.2: Nutrition state classification: (a) Mean spectral profile; (b) rRBF relevance profile for NIC1019; In VNIR 1600, a clear dominant frequency range around the intensity flank can be observed. This is known as "red edge" that corresponds to photosynthesis activity in plants as result of varying nitrogen supply.

The partial derivatives are as follows

$$\frac{\partial E}{\partial w_{ir}^+} = -\frac{2 \cdot d_r^-}{\left(d_r^+ + d_r^-\right)^2} h_\gamma\left(r, \mathbf{v}, \mathbf{W}_c\right) 2 \left(v_i - w_{ir}^+\right)$$

$$\frac{\partial E}{\partial w_{ir}^-} = \sum_{\mathbf{w}_r \in \mathbf{W}_c} \frac{2 \cdot d_r^+}{\left(d_r^+ + d_r^-\right)^2} h_\gamma\left(r, \mathbf{v}, \mathbf{W}_c\right) 2 \left(v_i - w_{ir}^-\right)$$

$$\frac{\partial E}{\partial \lambda_i} = \sum_{\mathbf{w}_r \in \mathbf{W}_c} h_\gamma\left(r, \mathbf{v}, \mathbf{W}_c\right) \left(\frac{2 \cdot d_r^-}{\left(d_r^+ + d_r^-\right)^2} \left(v_i - w_{ir}^+\right)^2 \right.$$

$$\left. - \frac{2 \cdot d_r^+}{\left(d_r^+ + d_r^-\right)^2} \left(v_i - w_{ir}^-\right)^2 \right).$$

4 Spectral band reduction

All three described machine learning modeling approaches optimize their respective energy function by adaptation of per-spectral band weighting. This weight vector is used to order the spectral bands according to their relevance. In order to check model performance on reduced spectral information, an rRBF network model was trained on the largest weighted bands as input and continuously added bands with

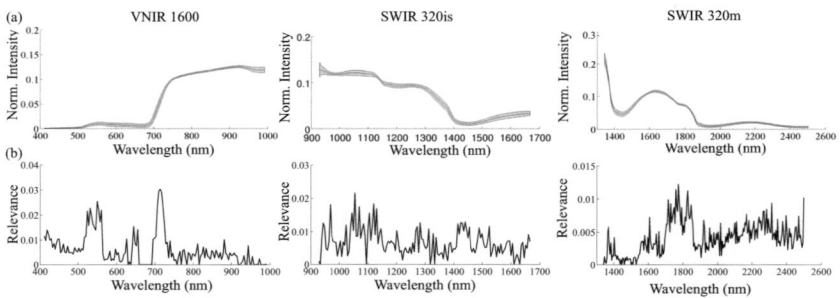

Figure 10.3: Relevance profiles for genotype classification: (a) Exemplary mean spectral profile; (b) rRBF relevance profile.

the highest input dimensionality of 70. The rRBF networks were trained with the same setup and parameters as above. The data is taken from the VNIR range for leaf 1. Test accuracy on unseen data for nutrition and genotype classification is evaluated for each n-dimensional input space. As control, a matching number of spectral bands are chosen at random (uniform distribution).

5 Results

For the prediction of nutrition states and genotypic identity, data sets were obtained from all three cameras for all leaves, for leaf one (youngest), and leaf three (second oldest) separately. Furthermore, for nutrition prediction, data was separated for each mutant condition to remove variation from genotype identity, which is a reasonable assumption since crop plant species should be known in advance in a precision farming environment. For the genotype classification, all nutrition conditions per genotype were included, since these could vary on the field. For each class 3, 000 randomly selected spectral samples were chosen. Data was partitioned into 50% training and 50% test data. A 5-fold cross validation with randomized assignment of data samples to test and training data under the given partition and randomized initialization in GRLVQ, SRNG, and rRBF was performed. Classifier accuracy was averaged and standard deviation was calculated.

Table 10.1 on the left shows test data accuracy for classification of nu-

	Nutrition			Genotype		
Class. Method	VNIR 1600	SWIR 320i	SWIR 320m	VNIR 1600	SWIR 320i	SWIR 320m
	Leaf 1-4					
SVM+LDA	79.2 (0.1)	70.8 (0.9)	80.3 (0.2)	79.2 (0.1)	70.8 (0.9)	80.3 (0.2)
SVM	59.0 (0.5)	53.6 (1.7)	55.2 (1.6)	59.0 (0.5)	53.6 (1.7)	55.2 (1.6)
SRNG	56.0 (5.1)	55.5 (3.8)	54.5 (2.0)	56.0 (5.1)	55.5 (3.8)	54.5 (2.0)
GRLVQ	58.4 (0.6)	55.4 (4.0)	53.4 (2.9)	58.4 (0.6)	55.4 (4.0)	53.4 (2.9)
rRBF	**83.7 (0.6)**	**75.2 (0.9)**	**81.5 (0.7)**	**83.7 (0.6)**	**75.2 (0.9)**	**81.5 (0.7)**
	Leaf 1 - youngest					
SVM+LDA	99.3 (0.1)	87.9 (0.7)	85.8 (0.3)	99.3 (0.1)	87.9 (0.7)	85.8 (0.3)
SVM	97.3 (0.1)	77.9 (0.3)	69.2 (1.5)	97.3 (0.1)	77.9 (0.3)	69.2 (1.5)
SRNG	92.6 (1.9)	74.3 (2.7)	57.6 (4.5)	92.6 (1.9)	74.3 (2.7)	57.6 (4.5)
GRLVQ	92.3 (0.3)	61.5 (8.9)	60.3 (0.7)	92.3 (0.3)	61.5 (8.9)	60.3 (0.7)
rRBF	**99.5 (0.1)**	**93.9 (0.6)**	**91.1 (0.8)**	**99.5 (0.1)**	**93.9 (0.6)**	**91.1 (0.8)**
	Leaf 3 - second oldest					
SVM+LDA	78.9 (0.4)	74.6 (0.5)	83.8 (0.5)	78.9 (0.4)	74.6 (0.5)	83.8 (0.5)
SVM	70.6 (0.3)	53.5 (0.4)	59.1 (0.9)	70.6 (0.3)	53.5 (0.4)	59.1 (0.9)
SRNG	70.6 (0.3)	60.3 (8.8)	52.9 (6.2)	70.6 (0.3)	60.3 (8.8)	52.9 (6.2)
GRLVQ	60.7 (5.4)	59.0 (1.3)	54.0 (1.8)	60.7 (5.4)	59.0 (1.3)	54.0 (1.8)
rRBF	**83.5 (0.4)**	**79.8 (1.4)**	**84.3 (0.5)**	**83.5 (0.4)**	**79.8 (1.4)**	**84.3 (0.5)**

Table 10.1: The table contains the classification test accuracy averaged over a five-fold cross validation and according standard deviation in brackets. Best performance per classification is highlighted.

trition from the NIC1019 mutant, other mutants showed comparable levels of performance. It is apparent that both GRLVQ and SRNG show poor performance in data sets containing all leaf ages while improving significantly if just the youngest leaf is considered, especially in the VNIR 1600 camera data. Furthermore, VNIR 1600 and SWIR 320m data performed better in classification than SWIR 320is. As to be expected, the SVM classifier gains much from data transformation by LDA and shows poor performance on plain spectra data for the data set with all leaves, gaining performance if the youngest leaf is considered only. Leaf age seems to be the most prominent confounding factor for prediction of the nutrition state. Finally we have to note that the RBF network performs robustly with levels of performance matching those of an SVM on LDA subspace. Classification performance is affected by the leaf age to a much smaller extend than seen in GRLVQ and SRNG staying around 80% accuracy in all cameras for all leaf ages.

Figure 10.2b shows relevance profiles obtained from the rRBF trained for nutrition classification for all three cameras and the NIC1019 mutant in the youngest leaf (which showed best classification performances). Some interesting properties can be learnt from these relevance profiles.

The relevance profile is altered in a way to minimize the mean square error between network output and target vector, e.g. to maximize network classification performance. In the VNIR 1600 data, a peak of relevance can be observed right at the position of the intensity flank between $0.7\mu m$ and $7.5\mu m$. In the SWIR 320m, increased relevance can be observed at the flank between $1.5\mu m$ and $1.6\mu m$ as well as the end of the intensity flank between $1.8\mu m$ and $1.9\mu m$. A similar behavior can be found for the other mutants.

Figure 10.4a compares the test accuracy of nutrition classification for the rRBF model trained on input spaces of different dimensionality for the three selection strategies (relevance, discriminance, and random selection). The data, taken from the VNIR range, contains mutant NIC1019 and leaf one. In general, accuracy saturated extremely fast for both strategies. From around 20 spectral bands onwards, all strategies converge. However, it is apparent that the selection based on the relevance vector yields test accuracy above 0.9 with even just one spectral band. This shows that the relevance weighting can identify bands that will contribute highly to the classification task at hand.

Table 10.1 on the right side shows test data accuracy for classification results of genotypes. Generally, the classification of genotypes proves to be a harder task then the classification of nutrition. Like in the nutrition classification both GRLVQ and SRNG show poor performance in data sets containing all leaf ages while in contrast to nutrition performance did not improve significantly if just the youngest leave was considered. There is also no clear difference of performance between VNIR 1600, SWIR 320m and SWIR 320is ranges across the board. The best results for genotypic classification were gained with an rRBF network in the VNIR range if just the youngest leaf is considered, yielding near 90% accuracy. From theory of plant nutrition it is known that young leaves are most active in terms of photosynthesis while older leaves show weaker photosynthesis related signals up to beginning senescence. From the application point of view this fact offers excellent perspectives for smart farming set-ups because typically only the youngest leaves are visible from above.

Figure 10.3b shows relevance profiles obtained from the rRBF network trained for genotype classification for all three cameras in the youngest leaf (which showed best classification performances). Like for the nutrition classification, some interesting properties can be derived from these relevance profiles. In the VNIR 1600 data, a peak of relevance can be observed right at the position of the intensity flank

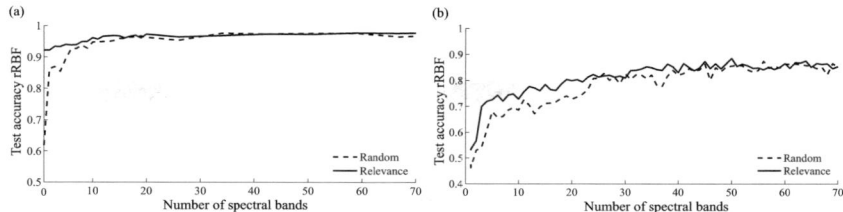

Figure 10.4: Model accuracy on reduced spectral bands: Spectral bands are chosen due to rRBF relevance profile or at random; rRBF Models are trained on reduced data set and test accuracy is depicted for (a) nutrition state prediction and (b) genotype classification.

between $0.7\mu m$ and $7.5\mu m$ but additionally, the range between $0.5\mu m$ and $0.6\mu m$ gains high relevance factors. In the SWIR 320m, increased relevance can be observed at the flank between $1.7\mu m$ and $1.9\mu m$.

Figure 10.4b compares the test accuracy of genotype classification for the rRBF model trained on input spaces of different dimensionality for the three selection strategies (relevance, discriminance, and random selection). The data, taken from the VNIR range, contained all nutrition conditions and leaf one. In general, accuracy saturated slower than for the nutrition classification showing that more spectral information is needed for this classification task. The relevance selection strategy yields a slight advantage in the classification performance. In general, this graph shows that the number of dimensions can be reduced massively and still retaining the classification accuracy.

6 Summary

Leaf age showed a strong impact on reducing classification performance for nutrition states by GRLVQ, SRNG, and SVM (plain spectra) down to near guessing level. Both SVM on LDA subspace and rRBF showed a robust nutrition prediction under leaf age variation. Such performance is needed for the utilization of machine learning methods in precision farming where other than under laboratory conditions recorded data cannot be controlled for individual leaf age for example. The genotype classification task proved to be much harder compared to nutrition classification. Here an rRBF trained on young leaf data in the VNIR range showed best results while performance dropped significantly when all leaf ages are considered in the same model.

From the application point of view the obtained results clearly demonstrate the usefulness and suitability of this framework for precision phenotyping and smart farming. While detecting unknown genotypes is typically not in the focus of this kind of applications, recognition and quantitative modeling of the abundance of several metabolites, caused by various abiotic and biotic stress factors, is much more relevant. For example, quantitative changes in the plant's metabolism based on different supply of nutrients is the key to a wide range of smart farming applications. This also paves the way for modeling further metabolic effects that are relevant in plant breeding and pathogen response.

References

1. J. B. MacQueen, "Some methods for classification and analysis of multivariate observations," in *Proc. of the fifth Berkeley Symposium on Mathematical Statistics and Probability*, L. M. L. Cam and J. Neyman, Eds., vol. 1.   University of California Press, 1967, pp. 281–297.

2. J. Moody and C. J. Darken, "Fast learning in networks of locally tuned processing units," *Neural Computation*, vol. 1, pp. 281–294, 1989.

3. A. Backhaus, F. Bollenbeck, and U. Seiffert, "Robust classification of the nutrition state in crop plants by hyperspectral imaging and artificial neural networks," in *In Proc. 3rd Workshop on Hyperspectral Image and Signal Processing: Evolution in Remote Sensing*, Lissabon, Portugal, 2011.

4. B. Hammer and T. Villmann, "Generalized relevance learning vector quantization," *Neural Networks*, vol. 15, pp. 1059–1068, 2002.

5. B. Hammer, M. Strickert, and T. Villmann, "Supervised Neural Gas with general similarity measure," *Neural Processing Letters*, vol. 21, pp. 21–44, 2005.

6. V. Vapnik and A. Chervonenkis, *Theory of Pattern Recognition*.   Nauka, 1974.

7. B. Schölkopf, A. Smola, R. Williamson, and P. Bartlett, "New support vector algorithms," *Neural computation*, vol. 12, no. 5, pp. 1207–1245, 2000.

8. C. M. Bishop, *Neural Networks for Pattern Recognition*.   Oxford University Press., 1995.

9. T. M. Martinetz and K. J. Schulten, "A Neural-Gas network learns topologies," in *Artificial Neural Networks*, T. Kohonen, K. Mäkisara, O. Simula, and J. Kangas, Eds.   North-Holland, Amsterdam, 1991, pp. 397–402.

Improving optical fruit sorting by non-destructive determination of quality parameters affecting wine quality

M. Lafontaine[1] and M. Freund[2]

[1] Geisenheim University, Institute for General and Organic Viticulture
Von Lade Str. 1, 65366 Geisenheim (Germany)
[2] Geisenheim University, Institute for Oenology,
Von Lade Str. 1, 65366 Geisenheim (Germany)

Abstract The scope of this project is finding suitable parameters correlated with grape and wine composition to be implemented as a quality criteria to sort harvested grapes. Grape quality is not only defined by sugar concentration but by a complex equilibrium of parameters depending on the type of wine to be produced. Moreover, measuring berry composition is not always linked to the amount that will finally be extracted into wine. Sorting the berry according to their density and berry size showed that measuring berry size could be another good tool to segregate groups. It was possible to relate berry color with sugar accumulation and anthocyanin accumulation until berry coloration process (veraison). However, after veraison, berry color was not a suitable parameter anymore to describe differences in maturity. It was also possible to correlate berry color with aroma precursors in Riesling white grapes, showing that VIS measurements in white grapes could indeed be a possible way to sort the berries according to quality. A multiparametric optical sensor, Multiplex® (Force A, France) showed that change in simple fluorescence ratio in green excitation was correlated to sugar concentration in white berries. Two ratios showed promising results: Firstly, the NBI_G indicating amino acid in berries and juice then secondly the ANTH_G correlating red color pigments (anthocyanin) concentration. This will have potential to determine quality parameters and in combination with user-friendly interfaces will improve grape sorting devices.

1 Introduction

In recent years, grape sorting has gained in importance and there is a growing interest in optical food evaluation technologies for grape and wine analysis [1]. This development can be observed particularly for the production of hand-picked, high-quality wines and the further processing of mechanically harvested grapes. Grape sorting provides an opportunity to actively increase the quality of the harvested grapes by sorting out green parts of plants, as well as unripe, damaged or partly rotten berries, insects such as ladybugs or earwigs and other foreign substances such as material of the trellising-system (e.g. wood, nails) (Fig. 11.1). Especially in the field of red wine production, such a selection is important because the grapes are processed with skin contact during several weeks to extract the desired substances such as anthocyanins and tannins. However, when unsorted, undesirable flavor components can be extracted. In the past, grape sorting was mainly done manually; either by selective hand-picking in the vineyard or by means of manual sorting devices such as vibrating or belt sorting tables. The growing use of mechanical harvesting leads to an increasing relevance of sorting grapes. Therefore growing interest in automatisation of the process can be observed [2].

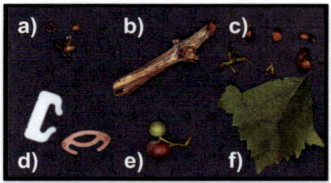

Figure 11.1: Materials Other than Grapes (MOG) to be sorted out for the harvest: insects (a), wood (b), stem pieces (c), material of the trellising-system, nails (d), unripe, smallest berries (e) and leaf pieces (f).

Nowadays, automatic sorting lines are already available, selecting the harvested grapes using mechanical or optical methods. The automatic sorting lines are positioned downstream of a destemming machine where the berries first fall onto a conveyer belt or vibration tables. During convey, juice that has accumulated as well as part of the small pieces of stems, petioles, and smallest berries are separated by means of a perforated plate imbedded in the table. By means of mechanical sorting systems, larger pieces of stems and entire rachises are separated at the end of the conveyor via different systems. The remaining berries and berry parts fall from the conveyer belt and go through an adjustable air nozzle or fall onto a perforated stainless steel roller to separate damaged berries and parts of stems. After spreading out, the berries get to a perforated sorting belt that accelerates the berries to about 2-3 m/s. At this speed, the fruit is passed alongside an optical system made up of camera, laser and/or LED technology allowing systematic selection according to colour, structure and/or form. The elements that the optical evaluation system recognizes as foreign materials or generally as negative are blown into a separate collecting system. The automatic evaluation of the harvested grapes provided by the existing systems therefore involves only a determination of foreign bodies (stem, leaves), affected berries and unripe berries [3], [4]. However, the remaining healthy berries differ largely in quality or ripeness, leading to different wine styles. The aim of this project is to determine suitable parameters correlated with grape and wine composition to be implemented as a quality criteria.

2 Quality parameters to be taken into account for wine production

Compared to many other agricultural products, grape production still holds one of the highest cash returns . Around 70% of this production is aimed for winemaking. Wine contains many different components, the majority originating from the vineyard and others produced during the winemaking process. Therefore most of the compounds responsible for wine quality depend on the quality of the grapes. Grape either produced in leaves (sugars and acids) or in berries (acids and phenolics). Grape berries contain three major types of tissue: skin, flesh, and seeds and the maturation process follows a two sigmoid curve [5]. Many of the solutes are accumulated in the grape berry during the first period of development yet their concentration is significantly reduced towards harvest due to the increase in berry volume. A grape berry is mostly composed of *water* and overall the berry approximately doubles in size and weight between veraison and harvest. Although the first growth period contributes to the final quality of the berry, the most important events occurs during the second growth period with an increase in *sugar (glucose and fructose)*, organic acids, mostly *tartaric and malic acids* that are responsible for the acidity of the wine and therefore critical to its quality. Malic acid is metabolised and used as an energy source during the ripening phase, resulting in a significant decrease of its levels relative to tartaric acid. *Nitrogen*, present in mineral or organic forms in the grapes is accumulated during ripening and metabolized by the yeast during the fermentation process. However, sugar accumulation is not well related to flavor and aroma compounds therefore phenolic and aromatic ripeness may be reached at a different time. *Phenolics* contribute to the color, color stability, structure and mouthfeel of a red wine. Tannins also decline considerably on a per-berry basis after the onset of ripening, veraison, whilst the anthocyanins accumulation begins in berry skin of red grapes. The complexity of wine *aromas* is issued from primary aromas synthesized in grapes and secondary aromas released during winemaking process. Aromatic compounds produced during the first growth period also decline on a per berry basis during fruit ripening. From a winemaking point of view, optimal grape maturity is essential for wine quality, but is difficult to assess because it is controlled by many factors, involving grapevine variety and environmental parameters such as soil, temperature, exposure to sun, and hormonal regulation.

3 Sorting berries according to berry size

Among many secondary components, phenolic components are important for red wine color (anthocyanins) and mouthfeel (tannins), therefore for the quality of a red wine. However heterogeneity of grape composition at one given date is well known and changes observed through the ripening process would be more related to berry ripeness than harvest date [6]. Phenolic compounds can be found in berry skin and seeds, however structure and accumulation differ. Therefore differences in berry size or maturity may affect their contribution to wine composition. Pinot noir berries from a vineyard at Geisenheim (Germany) were first segregated into size groups at harvest and then each group in different density subgroups as described previously [7]. As

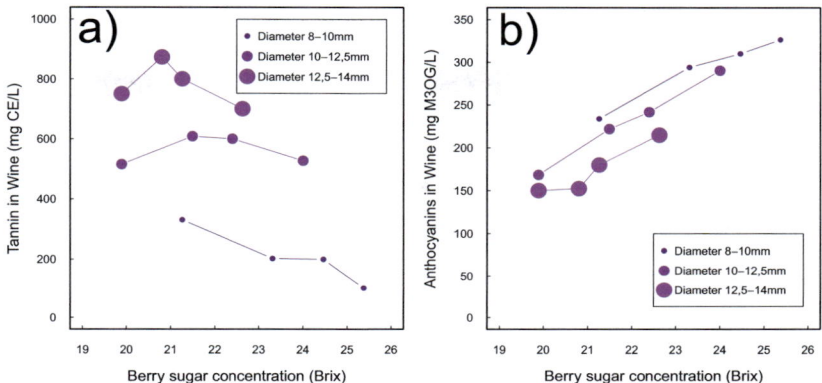

Figure 11.2: Phenolics in micro scale wines produced from berries sorted according to their density depending on 3 diameter classes. **a)** Tannin concentration in wines as mg catechin equivalent (CE) per L wine, **b)** Anthocyanin concentration in wines as malvidin 3-O Glucoside equivalent (M30G) per L wine.

grape secondary components can differ in extractability into wine, measuring berries cannot always predict the type of wine that will finally be made at the end of the process. Thus, a nanoscale winemaking technique was developed for red wine fermenting of 100 berries to be able to mimic higher scale fermentation and obtain wines from different discriminated groups. When sorting berries according to their total soluble solids (density), wine tannin concentration decreased with increasing maturity (Fig. 11.2). Flotation method has already been suggested for grape sorting method [8] and is already implemented in some systems on the market. When maturity was even, wines produced from smaller sized berries showed higher anthocyanin extraction compared to wines from bigger sized berries (Fig. 11.2b) probably a result of the greater skin to juice ratio in the fermentation process as hypothesized before [9]. On the other hand, wines produced from smaller sized berries showed lower tannin concentration compared to wines from bigger sized berries (Fig. 11.2a) [10]. Therefore segregating berries according to their size diameter would be a good tool to sort berries according to the type of wine aimed to be produced.

4 Sorting berries according to reflection in visible part of the spectrum

4.1 Red grapes

When a red grape undergoes maturation, the color is changing from green to dark blue due to anthocyanin accumulation in berry skin (Fig. 11.3). One parameter to sort the berries would be to measure the change in color in the visible part of the spectrum. Colorimetry is an approach to evaluate grape ripeness from diffuse light reflectance which is then converted into values that represent human visual perception according to the Commission Internationale de l'Eclairage (CIE) tristimulus values (CIELab). A color index for red grapes (CIRG) was developed [11] and was already used to correlate against anthocyanins concentration (coefficient of determination 0.92) [12, 13]. Pinot noir grapes were first sorted according to their density at different time during the maturation period to obtain homogen groups in terms of sugar concentration. Single berry reflection was measured with a spectrometer in visible (VIS) part of the spectrum (Minolta 3500d, Konica Minolta, Germany). The parameters lightness (L*), red/green (a*), and yellow/blue (b*) were calculated using the D65 illuminant and a 10 degree standard observer. The berry color b* in CIELAB system (blue to yellow) was correlated with sugar accumulation and anthocyanin accumulation until berry coloration process began. However, after berry coloration, blue color (negative b*) in VIS was not anymore suitable to describe differences in maturity. Such poor estimates were also found giving maximum a 0.50 for the coefficient of determination in the correlation with anthocyanins in whole grape berries [14].

4.2 White grapes

When a white grape undergoes maturation, the color is changing from green to yellow due to loss of berry skin chlorophyll and therefore carotenoids and phenolics become responsible for the color. Carotenoids are important for grape quality as they are aroma precursors so as C13-norisoprenoids and terpenes. Grape exposition to sunlight is a critical factor for berry coloration as berry skin secondary components act as a barrier defense against UV light. Again the problem of

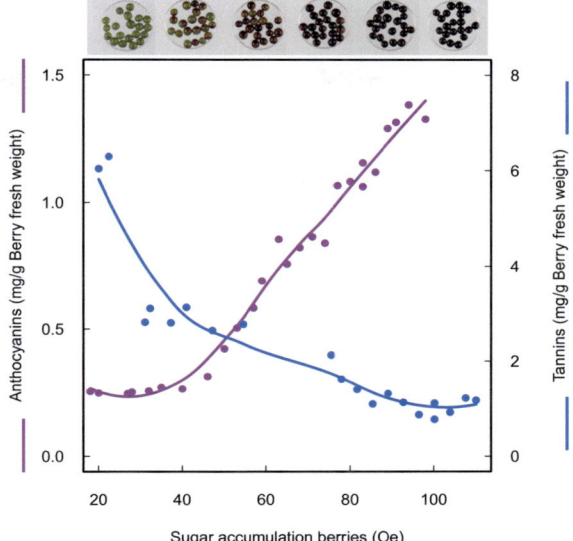

Figure 11.3: Change in berry color for Pinot noir grapes from green to blue accompanied with an increase of anthocyanins and a decrease of tannins in grapes as mg per g homogenate.

the wide range in berry color was contourned when first sorting Riesling grapes according to their red/green color (a*) [15]. It was possible to correlate the berry a* color parameter with glycosidic aroma precursors (so called Glycosyl Glucose -GG) in grapes (Fig. 11.4), showing that VIS measurements in white grapes could indeed be a possible way to sort white berries according to quality.

5 Sorting berries according other parameter than visible part

Another way for non destructive measurement would be to use berry properties in emitting specific light emission – fluorescence – under UV excitation for flavonols or visible light for anthocyanins. The tech-

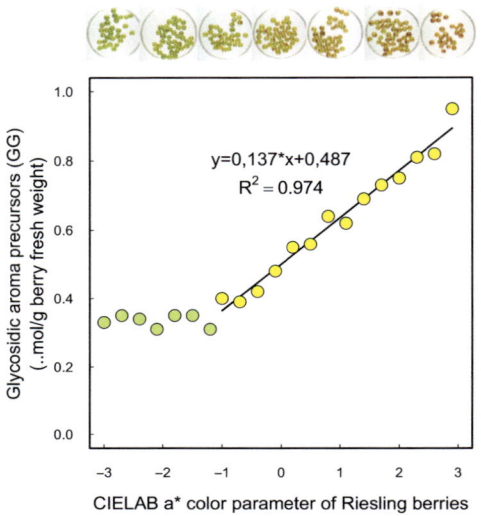

Figure 11.4: Color of Riesling berries sorted according to a* parameter measured in CIELab system as linear correlated to glycosidic aroma precursor measured as Glycosyl Glucose (GG as µmol /g berry fresh weight) in grape homogenate.

nique, based on intrinsic fruit fluorescence, called chlorophyll fluorescence screening method, has been successfully used to determine anthocyanin in berry skin [16]. An optical sensor, Multiplex® (Force A, Orsay, France), relies on such principles. The device measures the yellow fluorescence(YF-590nm), red fluorescence (RF-685nm) and far-red fluorescence (FRF-735nm) , excited by ultraviolet (_UV-375nm), blue (_B-470nm), green (_G-516nm) or red (_R-635nm) light. This fluorescence sensor would be insensitive to ambient light [17].

5.1 Red grapes

To validate the method, Pinot noir grapes were first sorted according to their density at different time during the maturation period to obtain homogen groups in terms of sugar maturity. Then population of 20 berries were measured with the Multiplex® (Force A, Orsay, France). An index called ANTH_RG, was defined as the ratio between Far-Red Fluorescence (FRF) under red excitation (FRF_R) and Far-Red Fluorescence (FRF) under green excitation (FRF_G): ANTH_RG = log(FRF_R/FRF_G). The index ANTH_RG was correlated to anthocyanin concentration proving that blue colored berries could indeed be separated in different groups when using other part of the spectrum than visible light. Similar results were found when sampling Pinot noir berries during maturation period (coefficient of determination 0.96) [16]. The Multiplex® SFR index is linked to the changes in skin chlorophyll content. This index is defined as the ratio between Far-Red Fluorescence (FRF) emitted under red excitation (FRF_R) and Red Fluorescence (RF) emitted under red excitation (RF_R): SFR_R = FRF_R/RF_R [17]. It was possible to correlate this index SFR_R with tannin concentration in berry skin, however not really for tannin concentration in berry seeds.

5.2 White grapes

Change in simple fluorescence ratio in green excitation (SFR_G) is related to berry chlorophyll content and was correlated to sugar concentration in white berries of Riesling collected at Geisenheim (Germany). Similar results were obtained for Chardonnay grapes showing the strong correlation of sugar accumulation and chlorophyll decrease [17]. However, an absolute calibration for the use as non-destructive prediction remains to be done for different varieties and seasons. Another index, NBI_G is defined as the ratio between Far Red Fluorescence emitted after UV excitation (FRF_UV) to red fluorescence emitted in red excitation (RF_R): NBI_G = FRF_UV/RF_R. The NBI_G index was correlated to amino acid concentration of the grape juice (measured as N-OPA), important substrate to assure complete fermentation of the juice.

5.3 NIR spectroscopy

Near Infrared spectroscopy (NIR) was found to be linked with berry composition and indeed, NIR spectroscopy was shown to be a good tool for acidity prediction in grapes [18]. Grape ripeness (Brix) could be predicted with NIR spectroscopy for red and white grape with however better results for red grapes. [19]. Together with sugar content (Brix) and pH, it was shown that anthocyanin content from red grapes could be predicted with spectroscopy measurements in the visible-NIR range [20]. Measurements were undertaken in 2012 to confirm the validity of assessing NIR spectroscopy to determine quality parameters in grapes of this project.

6 Summary

In the past, grape sorting was mainly done manually. With the use of mechanical harvesters, a selection is crucial for sorting out undesirable substances, i.e. material other than grapes (MOG). Automatic sorting lines are already available for negative selection of such components. However, despite the negative selection it is of major interest to sort the fruit towards quality and hence improve the final wine. The aim of this project is to find optical non-destructive parameter to assess quality of the grapes affecting wine quality. We found that measuring berry size could be a good tool to segregate groups. Moreover, berry color gives interesting hints about grape quality for white berries showing that VIS measurements could indeed be a possible way to sort the berries according to quality. The implementation of an optical sensor, Multiplex® (Force A, France) showed promising results. Further, measurements aside the visible range of the spectrum, in UV or NIR part, are tested to validate the use of such parameters for quality segregation. This work represents the basis of an on-going project implementing these techniques on a sorting machine with a user-friendly interface to improve existing systems for sorting grapes in different quality levels.

Aknowledgements

Thanks is due to the laboratory team of the viticulture section of the Geisenheim Research Center, notably Sabrina Samer and Angelika Baer for the analyses as well as the skillful contribution of Dennis Lehmen (HSRM, University of Applied Sciences).

References

1. D. Cozzolino, W. U. Cynkar, N. Shah, R. G. Dambergs, and P. A. Smith, "A brief introduction to multivariate methods in grape and wine analysis," *International Journal of Wine Research*, vol. 1, pp. 123–130, 2009.

2. M. Christmann and M. Freund, *Advances in grape processing equipment.* Woodhead Publishing Limited, 80 High Street, Sawston, Cambridge, CB22 3HJ, UK, 210, ch. 15, pp. 547–588.

3. J. Feltes, "Sortierung am laufenden Band: Beere und Stiel," *Der Deutsche Weinbau*, no. 11, pp. 12–15, 2012.

4. R. Falconer, B. Liebich, and A. Hart, "Automated Color Sorting of Hand-Harvested Chardonnay," *American Journal of Enology and Viticulture*, vol. 57, no. 4, pp. 491–496, 2006.

5. C. Conde, P. Silva, N. Fontes, A. C. P. Dias, R. M. Tavares, M. Sousa, A. Agasse, S. Delrot, and H. Gerós, "Biochemical Changes throughout Grape Berry Development and Fruit and Wine Quality," *Food*, 2007 Global Science Books.

6. L. Rolle, S. Río Segade, F. Torchio, S. Giacosa, E. Cagnasso, F. Marengo, and V. Gerbi, "Influence of Grape Density and Harvest Date on Changes in Phenolic Composition, Phenol Extractability Indices, and Instrumental Texture Properties during Ripening," *Journal of Agricultural and Food Chemistry*, vol. 59, no. 16, pp. 8796–8805, 2011.

7. V. L. Singleton, C. S. Ough, and K. E. Nelson, "Density Separations of Wine Grape Berries and Ripeness Distribution," *American Journal of Enology and Viticulture*, vol. 17, no. 2, pp. 95–105, 1966.

8. L. Rolle, F. Torchio, S. Giacosa, S. R. Segade, E. Cagnasso, and V. Gerbi, "Assessment of Physicochemical Differences in Nebbiolo Grape Berries from Different Production Areas and Sorted by Flotation," *American Journal of Enology and Viticulture*, vol. 63, no. 2, pp. 195–204, June 2012.

9. V. L. Singleton, "Effects on Red Wine Quality of Removing Juice before Fermentation to Simulate Variation in Berry Size," *American Journal of Enology and Viticulture*, vol. 23, no. 3, pp. 106–113, 1972.

10. M. Lafontaine, M. Stoll, and H. R. Schultz, "Berry size and maturity affecting phenolic extraction in Pinot Noir wines," in *Proceedings GIESCO Conference*, 2013.

11. J. Carreno, A. Martinez, L. Almela, and J. Fernandez-Lopez, "Proposal of an index for the objective evaluation of the colour of red table grapes," *Food Research International*, vol. 28, no. 4, pp. 373–377, 1995.

12. J. A. Fernandez-Lopez, L. Almela, J. A. Munoz, V. Hidalgo, and J. Carreno, "Dependence between colour and individual anthocyanin content in ripening grapes," *Food Research International*, vol. 31, no. 9, pp. 667–672, 1998.

13. G. Agati, S. Meyer, P. Matteini, and Z. G. Cerovic, "Assessment of Anthocyanins in Grape (*Vitis vinifera* L.) Berries Using a Noninvasive Chlorophyll Fluorescence Method," *Journal of Agricultural and Food Chemistry*, vol. 55, no. 4, pp. 1053–1061, 2007.

14. D. Cozzolino, M. Elser, R. Dambergs, W. Cynkar, D. Boehm, I. Francis, and M. Gishen, "Prediction of colour and pH in grapes using a diode array spectrophotometer (400-1100nm)," *Journal of Near Infrared Spectroscopy*, vol. 12, pp. 105–111, 2004.

15. D. Lehmen, "Untersuchungen zur Korrelation von Farbparametern intakter Rieslingbeeren mit Inhaltsstoffen als Beitrag zur Lesereifebestimmung," Master's thesis, HSRM, University of Applied Sciences, 2009.

16. Z. G. Cerovic, N. Moise, G. Agati, G. Latouche, N. Ben Ghozlen, and S. Meyer, "New portable optical sensors for the assessment of winegrape phenolic maturity based on berry fluorescence," *Journal of Food Composition and Analysis*, vol. 21, no. 8, pp. 650–654, 2008.

17. N. Ben Ghozlen, Z. G. Cerovic, C. Germain, S. Toutain, and G. Latouche, "Non-Destructive Optical Monitoring of Grape Maturation by Proximal Sensing," *Sensors*, vol. 10, no. 11, pp. 10 040–10 068, 2010.

18. F. Chauchard, "Application of LS-SVM to non-linear phenomena in NIR spectroscopy: development of a robust and portable sensor for acidity prediction in grapes," *Chemometrics and Intelligent Laboratory Systems*, vol. 71, no. 2, pp. 141–150, 2004.

19. J. Herrera, A. Guesalaga, and E. Agosin, "Shortwave–near infrared spectroscopy for non-destructive determination of maturity of wine grapes," *Measurement Science and Technology*, vol. 14, no. 5, p. 689, 2003.

20. M. Larrain, A. Guesalaga, and E. Agosin, "A Multipurpose Portable Instrument for Determining Ripeness in Wine Grapes Using NIR Spectroscopy," *IEEE Transactions on Instrumentation and Measurement*, vol. 57, no. 2, pp. 294–302, 2008.

Active infrared thermography as a tool for quality control in the food industry

Jochen Aderhold[1], Peter Meinlschmidt[1] and Volker Märgner[2]

[1] Fraunhofer Institute for Wood Research (WKI),
Bienroder Weg 54E, D-38108 Braunschweig
[2] Technical University of Braunschweig,
Schleinitzstraše. 22, D-38106 Braunschweig

Abstract Active infrared thermography is a technique which can visualize differences in the thermal properties of the objects under inspection. It is an interesting alternative to existing methods in various fields of quality control in foodstuff. Possible applications include the detection of foreign bodies in almonds and potatoes and the detection of bruises in apples. This chapter explains the principles of active thermography, gives typical examples and discusses the options and limits of the technique as wells as some aspects of infrared image processing.

1 Introduction

Consumers of food expect high quality and low prices at the same time. Consequently, automated techniques for quality control in the food industry are essential and still gain in importance. While well-established methods based on image processing in the visible part of the electromagnetic spectrum exist, little use is made today of the differences in thermal properties such as thermal capacity and thermal conductivity of foodstuff. These differences can be made visible by means of active infrared thermography. In such a way, thermography can help to solve some problems e.g. in the detection of foreign bodies in food. Potatoes coming from the producer, for example, can contain a lot of foreign bodies such as wood, bones, objects from plastic and even golf balls. Many of these can be separated by means of heavy media separation: Potatoes sink in normal water, any object with lower density than potatoes will swim and can be removed. In salt water, on the other hand, the potatoes will swim, and objects with a higher density can be separated. However, wooden objects, bones, and also the golf balls cannot be removed in this way. Furthermore, they also look very much like potatoes, so that conventional image processing is difficult or impossible. As will be shown below, these objects can be detected using active infrared thermography.

2 Principles of infrared imaging

The basis of infrared thermography is the fact that every object having a temperature above absolute zero emits electromagnetic radiation which is called thermal or Planck radiation. At a given wavelength the radiated power density (for a so-called black body) depends on the temperature only so that the temperature can be calculated by measuring the radiated power density. The dependence of the power density on temperature and wavelength is given by the famous Planck equation:

$$M_\lambda^0 = \frac{C_1 \lambda^{-5}}{\exp(\frac{C_2}{\lambda}) - 1}$$

In this equation, M_λ^0 is the power density per wavelength interval emitted by an ideal ("black") radiator (unit: W/m^3), whereas λ stands for the wavelength and T for the absolute temperature. The constants C_1 und C_2 contain only natural constants such as h (Planck's constant), c (speed of light) und k_B (Boltzmann's constant):

$$C_1 = 2\pi hc^2$$

$$C_2 = \frac{hc}{k_B}$$

For room temperature, the emissivity curve peaks around $10\mu m$ (see Fig. 12.1). A large number of cameras exist on the market which are sensible to infrared radiation in this wavelength range. Basically, there are two groups of cameras. In the first type, the so-called uncooled or bolometer cameras, the infrared radiation is focussed on an array of small silicon plates. The resulting increase in temperature is detected by means of the increasing electrical resistance. In the second

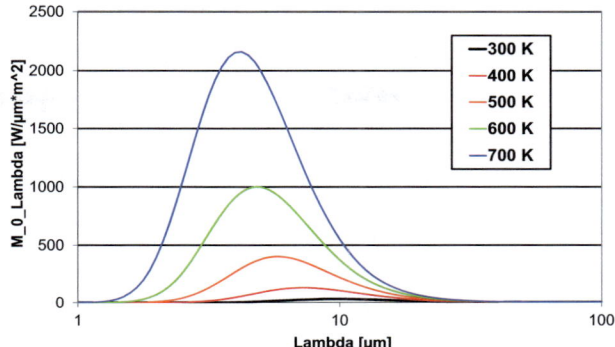

Figure 12.1: Power density radiated by a black radiator between $300\,\mathrm{K}$ and $700\,\mathrm{K}$.

group of cameras, mostly called cooled cameras, the infrared photons create electron-hole pairs in semiconductors such as HgCdTe or InSb. These detectors have to be cooled to temperatures around 90K in order to avoid excessive thermal noise. Typical pixel numbers are 640 x 512 for both camera types. The temperature sensitivity is given by the so-called noise equivalent temperature difference which is in the range of 50mK for uncooled and 15mK for cooled cameras. It is often said that infrared cameras image the surface temperature of objects. This is not exactly true since Planck's formula as written above is valid only for the ideal black radiator. Any real object radiates at a given temperature less power than the black radiator This is mathematically described by a multiplicative constant called ϵ which is between 0 and 1 by definition:

$$M_\lambda^\epsilon = \epsilon(\lambda)M_\lambda^0$$

While polished metals can have very low emissivity values (Al: 0.03), most organic materials have emissivities close to one.

3 Active infrared thermography

The idea of thermography for quality control in foodstuff is to generate temperature differences between "good" and "bad" regions which can

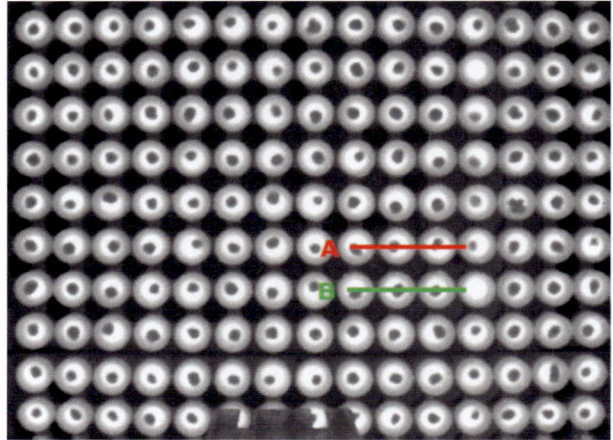

Figure 12.2: Thermal image of caramel cups (light grey) filled with hot chocolate (white) and nuts (dark). A: half nut. B: mising nut.

subsequently be detected by infrared imaging. The flow of heat in solid matter is described by Fourier's law:

$$\nabla Q = \nabla(\nabla \kappa T)) = \rho C_{sp} \frac{\partial T}{\partial t} - q$$

where Q is the heat flow, κ the thermal conductivity, ρ the mass density, C_{sp} the specific heat capacity, and q the internally generated heat. In order to have $\nabla T \neq 0$, one needs either internally generated heat ($q \neq 0$) or a change of temperature in time ($\partial T / \partial t \neq 0$), or both. Only the second case is of practical importance in quality control of foodstuff since there are normally no internal heat sources. A change of temperature in time can simply be achieved by letting cool down some foodstuff which was heated in a preceding production step (passive heat flow thermography). A typical example for passive heat flow thermography is presented in Fig. 12.2, showing the top view of an array of caramel cups (light grey) filled with ot chocolate (white) and hazelnuts (dark). Missing nuts (B) and half nuts (A) can be clearly detected.

A second and more important way to achieve a change of temperature in time is to apply a transient heat pulse to the foodstuff. An

Figure 12.3: Photographic (left) and infrared (right) image of almonds with stones as foreign bodies.

easy way to this is to let the foodstuff pass an infrared heater on a conveyor belt. This corresponds to a single rectangular heat pulse. Since infrared cameras are very sensitive, a temperature increase of a few degree Kelvin is sufficient. In order to better understand the underlying physics, let us first consider the homogeneous thermal excitation of an infinite half plane by a sinusoidally (with frequency ω) modulated heat source. In this case we get a sinusoidal, but exponentially damped thermal wave [1]. Its amplitude is described by

$$T(z,t) = \frac{Q}{2\sqrt{\rho C_{sp}\kappa\omega}} \exp\left(\frac{z}{\mu}\right)$$

where

$$\mu = \sqrt{\frac{2\kappa}{\rho C_{sp}\omega}}$$

is the damping factor, also called penetration depth, Q the external heat flow, and z the distance from the surface. It can be seen that a thermal contrast can arise when there is a difference in $\rho C_{sp}\kappa$. The contrast and the penetration depth increase with decreasing ω. Following Fourier, rectangular pulses can decomposed in a series of sinusoidal waves. The lowest efficiently excited frequency is inversely proportional to the pulse length. Consequently, the penetration depth under rectangular excitation can be tailored to a desired value by adjusting the

Figure 12.4: Infrared images of potatoes with different foreign bodies including golf ball and pumice stone (left) as well as peices of wood and bone (right).

pulse length. A typical result of this technique can be seen in Fig. 12.3 which shows almonds with stones as foreign bodies. In the infrared image (right) these appear darker because of their higher thermal capacity.

4 Application: Detection of foreign bodies in potatoes

Figure 12.4 shows infrared images of potatoes and foreign bodies taken with active thermography. Interestingly, the grey values of the potatoes are all the same, independent of their size. The reason is that the penetration depth was chosen in such a way that it is much smaller than the smallest dimension of the potatoes. Thus, the heat front is confined a region close to the surface, and size effects do not appear. The foreign bodies can be clearly identified by their differing grey values. A piece of bone (right part of the right image) appears brighter since it has a rather low thermal capacity. The thermal capacities of a golf ball and a pumice stone (left image) are higher than those of the potatoes, consequently they appear darker. The same is true for a wet piece of wood (left part of the left image). The presented images are already the result of some image preprocessing routines. First of all, the pixels of infrared detectors have very different response curves so that a so-called non-uniformity correction has to be carried out. To this end, two reference images of a homogeneous area are taken at different temperatures. By assuming linear response curves, correction factors for most pixels can

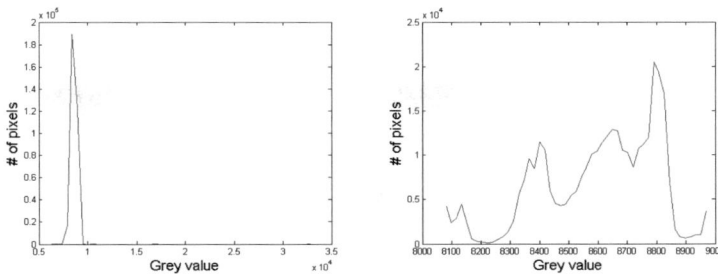

Figure 12.5: Histogram of the left image in 12.4 before (left) and after (right) outlier removal.

be calculated. However, some pixels cannot be corrected in this way since they do not give any signal at all (dead pixels) or have very non-linear or unstable response curves. These pixels have to be removed because they could lead to wrong results in further processing steps. A possible way to do this is to identify them manually, register them in a look-up table and replace their values by those of a good neighbour pixel. In case the bad pixels do not form too big cluster, a median filter is an alternative solution. Even after bad pixel correction, the histogram of a typical infrared image like the left image in Fig. 12.4 looks like the left histogram in Fig. 12.5: It is dominated by outliers whereas the actual signal is confined to a small grey value range. A good method to remove the outliers is to clip the histogram at the lowest and highest 1 percent of the grey values (right histogram in Fig. 12.5). For a segmentation of the foreign bodies one can in principle use the histogram and set a grey value threshold. However, the potatoes and also the foreign bodies can have various temperatures, depending on the storage conditions. Consequently, a fixed grey value threshold will not work, and an adaptive calculation of the threshold is necessary. There are several ways to do this. Fortunately, foreign bodies are rare. Thus, one can simply take images of the potato stream and calculate the histograms. This will normally have two peaks: those of the potatoes, and those of the conveyor belt. It helps when the grey value of the conveyor belt is close to that of the potatoes or at least between the grey values of the "dark" and the "bright" foreign bodies. When a third peak appears in

Figure 12.6: Apple with bruise.

the histogram, some action has to be taken. Alternatively, one could take two images, one before the thermal excitation and one afterwards. The grey value difference between both images depends only on the heating power and the speed of the belt. However, this requires two of the rather expensive infrared cameras.

5 Application: Detection of bruises in apples

Another promising application of this principle is the recognition of bruises in apples. When the apple tissue is damaged by the application of a certain force, subsequent chemical processes lead within several hours to brown spots on the apple surface which many customers do not accept. These spots can easily be detected by conventional image processing. Fresh bruises, however, are not visible. But the damaged tissue has a different thermal conductivity than sound tissue (see Fig. 12.6), so that even fresh bruises can be detected by thermography. This is demonstrated in Fig. 12.7. Three apples were subjected to forces of 20N, 40N, and 60N, respectively, on an area with 1cm diameter. The left part of the picture shows the apples before thermal excitation, whereas the right image was taken after thermal excitation. The bruises can clearly be detected, and different pressures apparently cause different patterns in the infrared image.

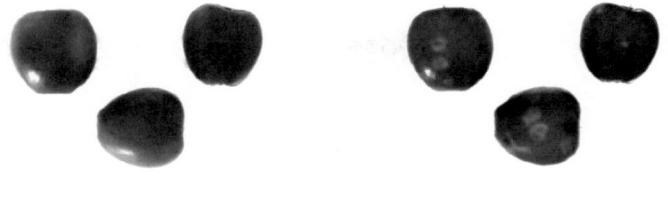

Figure 12.7: Infrared images of apples with bruises caused by defined pressure before (left) and after thermal excitation.

6 Summary

It was shown that active infrared thermography is a versatile tool for quality control in foodstuff since it can visualize differences in thermal capacity and/or thermal conductivity and thus opens the way to utilize physical properties not used before. Thermal excitation can be achieved by simply installing an infrared heater over a conveyor belt. Significant changes to the production line are not necessary. Furthermore, no safety concerns as in x-ray technologies exist. Typical applications include the detection of foreign bodies in almonds and potatoes and of bruises in apples. Whereas many algorithms of conventional image processing can be adapted for the use in thermography, infrared images have some peculiarities which have to betaken into account.

References

1. D. P. Almond and P.-M. Patel, *Photothermal Science and Techniques*.   London, UK: Chapman and Hall, 1996.

Inline HSI food inspection and concentration measurements of pharmaceuticals – a report from an industrial environment

M. Kerschhaggl[1], W. Märzinger[2], E. Leitner[3], N. Haar[3], M. Zangl[4], M. Jeindl[4] and P. Kerschhaggl[1,4]

[1] EVK DI Kerschhaggl GmbH, R&D
Josef Krainer Str. 35, A 8074 Raaba
[2] i-RED Infrarot Systeme GmbH
Hafenstrasse 47-51, A 4020 Linz
[3] Institut für Analytische Chemie und Lebensmittelchemie, TU-Graz
Stremayrgasse 9/II, A 8010 Graz
[4] Insort GmbH
Europastrasse 26, A 8330 Feldbach

Abstract Current food diagnostic measurement techniques tend to suffer from unreliable chemometric quantification and poor spatial resolution. Chemical components in food such as sugar, fat,water and dry substance are today inferred from destructive, lab based, techniques that measure chemical composition albeit with limited statistical accuracy and insufficient precision for food quality monitoring. Technologies such as NIR hyperspectral imaging (HSI) and FTNIR offer the potential for accurate, fast and efficient evaluation of chemical components accurately over the whole food production cycle. In this regard, the disentanglement of spectral endmembers from a mixed detector response due to background and multiple chemical constituents is both crucial and scientifically challenging for a reliable signal detection in terms of illumination technique, data pre-processing and multivariate analysis. In this talk various inline applications employing NIR hyperspectral imaging using the HELIOS camera system will be presented, including examples and results from a prototype project in pharmaceuticals and a joint study in which HSI quantitative analysis of chemical concentration gradients found in potatoes and wheat grains are discussed.

1 Introduction

Near infrared spectroscopy (NIRS) has proven to be one of the most powerful techniques for (quantitative) analysis and classification of materials as well as continuous controlling the quality of e.g. food and feed. NIRS uses normally a spectral range from 780-2500 nm, where mainly overtones and combinations of vibrational modes from C-H, O-H and N-H chemical bonds are located, carrying most of the information of the chemical composition of organic materials, food, feed and beverages [1]. The advantage of NIRS is the fact that no sample preparation is necessary and there are several ways to collect spectra in a non-destructive way like transmittance, interactance, transflectance, diffuse transmittance, and diffuse reflectance. In addition the advantage of NIRS in comparison to mid infrared spectroscopy is the higher energy due to shorter wavelengths penetrating the products to get information from under the surface like the ripeness of fruits [2, 3]. Attention must be paid for the calibration models which can be a very time consuming and costly procedure. Changes of the composition of the target product like new harvest or new varieties must be taken into account and the training set should be updated and checked on a regular base [4]. Beside water several other components like fat, carbohydrates and proteins can be quantified using NIRS to optimize quality parameters from raw materials to the finished product. Moreover, beside the determination of the chemical composition of the (food) material even other parameters like authenticity [5] or sensory properties [6] are inferable. Problems can arise from interferences from uneven surfaces during online monitoring or when the chemical information is not evenly distributed in the sample.

In the following we describe two different applications of NIRS from the pharmaceutical as well as the food industry employing near infared hyperspectral imaging (NIR HSI) and/or Fourier transform near infrared (FTNIR) spectroscopy cameras.

1.1 The camera systems

The EVK HELIOS camera is a hyperspectral imaging system operating in push broom mode yielding spatially resolved NIR spectra from a moving sample [7]. It features an 320(spectral) × 256(spatial) InGaAs

(a) HELIOS CORE camera.

(b) Setup including HELIOS hyperspectral camera, halogen light source and driving unit.

Figure 13.1:

sensor array and covers a spectral range of 0.9-1.7 μm. A powerful FPGA unit is part of the camera and allows for integrated real time data processing and analysis (Fig. 13.1 (a)). With a sampling rate of up to 330 Hz (full frame) the camera is suitable for fast inline applications with bulk flows of several m/s of input material.

The i-RED FTNIR spectrometer operates from 900-2600 nm and acquires up to 100 spectra per second with DSP based high speed data processing [8]. Light reflected from the sample surface is directed to a spectrograph with 0.15 nm bandpass at 2600 nm via one channel fibre optics. The data are streamed to a PC where further (real time) analysis of the spectra is possible.

2 HSI concentration monitoring

In the following we describe the inference of concentration gradients of thin layers of dry chemicals from HSI data. Figure 13.2 (a) shows a patch covered with a thin layer made from baking a white pharmaceutical powder. The problem in related pharmaceutical quality moni-

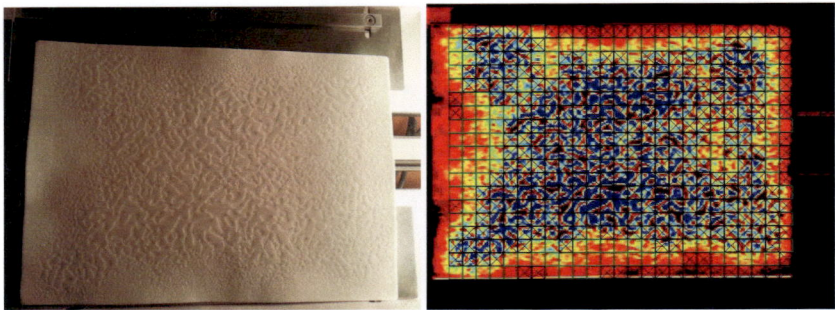

(a) Patch covered with baked white powder showing concentration gradients.

(b) Hyperspectral concentration gradient (colour coded) of dry chemicals.

Figure 13.2:

toring is the reliable measurement of concentration gradients due to ill deposition of the dry chemical prior to the baking process. The data analysis discussed here is based on measurements using the $1.7 \, \mu m$ HE-LIOS CORE camera as desrcibed in sec. 1.1 and multivariate analysis techniques as e.g. described in [9].

2.1 The model

The underlying quantitative model is the *partial least squares regression* (PLS) a standard technique where the spectral data is optimized with respect to the target data to be inferred (see e.g. [9] and [10]). The set of equations

$$X = tp^T + E \tag{13.1}$$
$$Y = uq^T + F \tag{13.2}$$

represents the decomposition of the spectral and chemical concentration data, X and Y, respectively, into loadings and scores according to standard *principal component analysis* (PCA). The t, u and p, q denote the *scores* and *loadings* vectors of X and Y, respectively, and E and F are the residual variance matrices. The PLS regression adapts the chemical concentrations with respect to the spectral data during the optimization

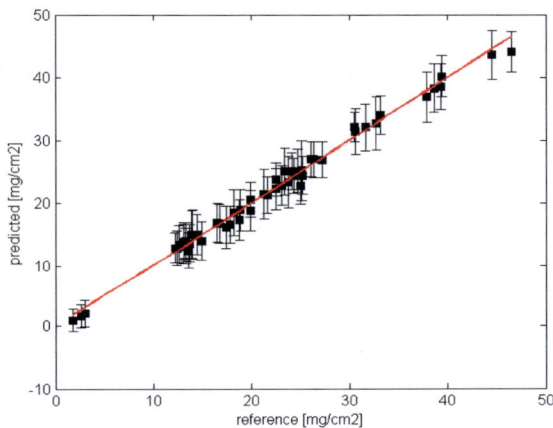

Figure 13.3: PLS regression of 53 NIR spectra of dry chemicals using two PLS components. Shown are nominal vs. measured concentrations in units of mg/cm^2.

process via the relations [9]

$$Y = X^T B + B_0 \tag{13.3}$$
$$B = W(p^T W)^{-1} q^T \tag{13.4}$$
$$B_0 = Y^T - X^T B \tag{13.5}$$
$$W = X^T u / \sqrt{(X^T u)(X^T u)^T} \tag{13.6}$$

Such, information from the target data influences the PCA of the spectral data and vice versa. Figure 13.3 shows the outcome of a two component PLS regression of 53 NIR spectra of dry chemicals recorded with the HELIOS camera. The fit shows the measured against the nominal concentration values in units of mg/cm^2. The correlation between predicted and nominal concentrations is $R^2 = 0.99$. The inferred (normalized) PLS coefficients B along with the teach spectra are shown in Fig. 13.4.

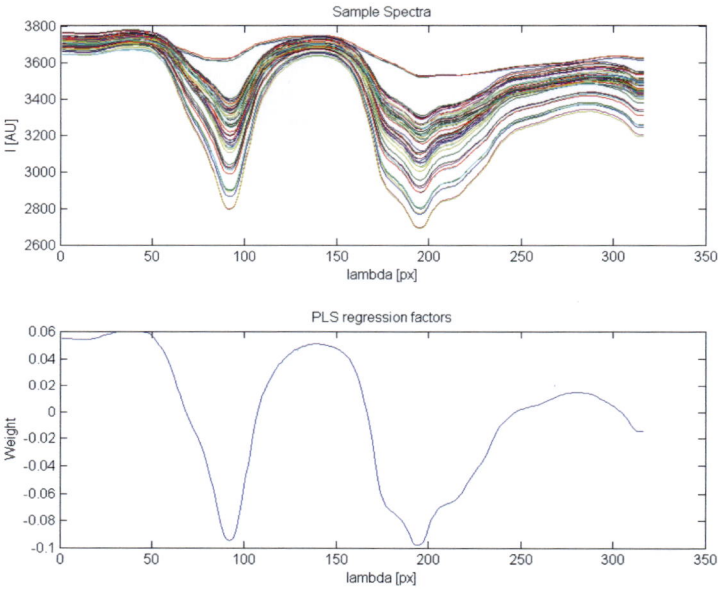

Figure 13.4: NIR teach spectra for the PLS regression model (upper panel). PLS coefficients B for a two component regression (lower panel).

2.2 Measurement

The sample sheets coated with different concentrations of a dry chemical (Fig. 13.2) were scanned with the HELIOS camera in *push broom* mode using a driving unit (see Fig. 13.1). Using the model described in sec. 2.1 it is thus possible to assign a concentration value to every scanned sample pixel containing a full spectrum. An instructive example of the spatially resolved colour coded concentration gradient is shown in Fig. 13.2. The already to the naked eye visible inhomogeneous deposition of the investigated chemical substance can be reproduced with high accuracy quantitatively in the NIR regime (see Fig. 13.2) and help identifying quality issues in the production process following statistical bench marks.

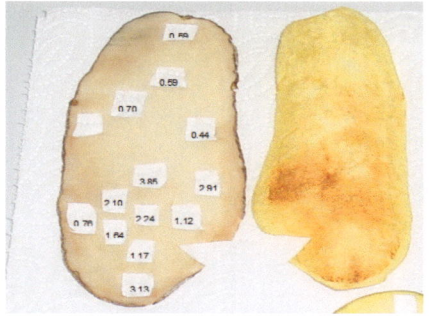 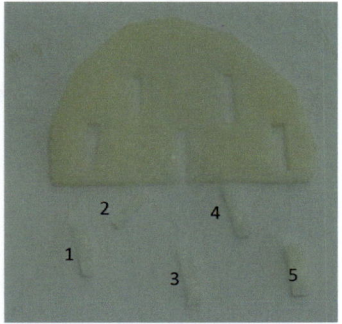

(a) Chemical reference analysis of dry substance combined with brown reactions.   (b) Chemical reference analysis of sugar content.

Figure 13.5:

3 Quantitative analysis of potatoes and wheat grains

Objective of this study was the feasibility of measuring chemical constituents concentrations in foods using NIR technology with the ultimate goal of constructing an inline food analyser in the near future. In particular, we focussed on the investigation of concentration gradients found in potatoes and wheat grains. For potatoes a crucial parameter for subsequent food processing is the distribution of water vs. dry substance and sugar, since gradients of e.g. sugar can have unwanted effects during the frying stage present e.g. in the French fries production. Concerning wheat grains, the parameters of interest are the baking properties of flour usually inferred from an amylograph which displays the viscosity of dough as a function of (linearly increased) temperature. In order to be able to correlate hyperspectral information with the wanted target parameters, such as sugar content in potatoes and gluten found in flour, chemical reference analysis is needed.

3.1 Potatoes

Slices of different potato varieties were investigated using FTNIR, HSI and chemical reference analysis. The latter provided both the spatial information of sugar content as well as unwanted correlated browning

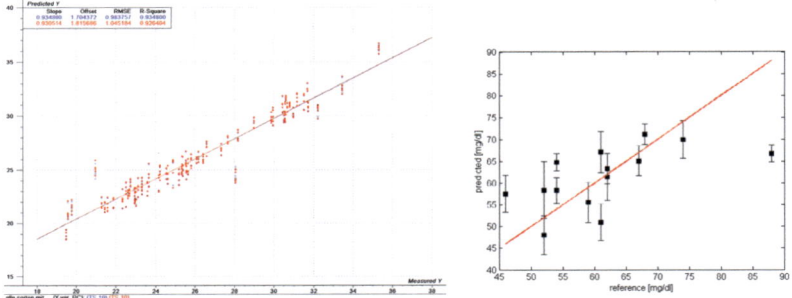

(a) FTNIR calibration dataset of 4 different potato varieties for dry substance determination. (blue) calibration data, (red) validation data.

(b) PLS calibration dataset (using two PLS components) of spatially resolved HELIOS spectra for the sugar content of potatoes.

Figure 13.6:

due to Maillard's reaction [11] during frying as shown in Fig. 13.5. The amount of glucose at different locations across the potato slide was extracted using a highly sensitive blood sugar test (tab. 13.1). Such the reference analysis yields glucose concentrations as target data Y being input for a PLS regression of NIR spectra X along the lines of sec. 2.1.

Table 13.1: Chemical reference analysis of glucose content in mg/dl across potato slices. Sample locations are depicted in Fig. 13.5 (b).

Slice #	1	2	3
Sample #		[mg/dl]	
1	61	62	-
2	62	67	54
3	52	61	59
4	54	52	46
5	74	88	68

The regression of a calibration data set for dry substance inferred from 4 different potato varieties is depicted in Fig. 13.6 (a) for FTNIR spectral data measured with a *Thermo Nicolet Antaris* analyzer. The spectral data show a very high correlation with the inferred reference analysis independent of the potato variety. Since an inline food analyser should

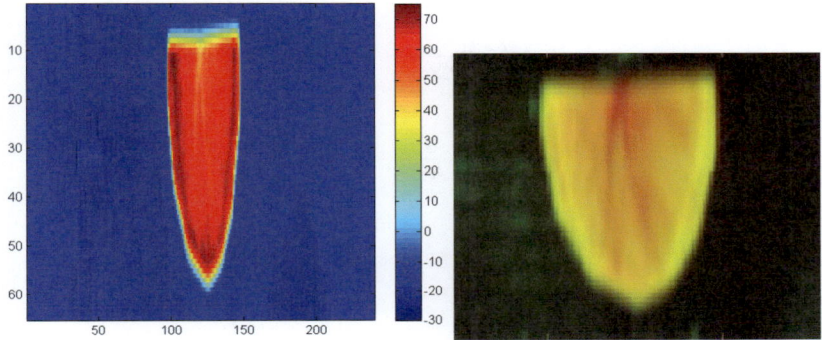

(a) sugar distribution in a potato as inferred from a quantitative hyperspectral PLS model. colour bar in units of mg/dl

(b) spatial distribution of two PCA components of the same hyperspectral image. PC1 (red) presumably traces water abundances in the fruit.

Figure 13.7:

ultimately deliver spatially resolved dry substance and sugar gradients the analysis was also performed using the HELIOS hyperspectral imager.

Figure 13.6 (b) shows the calibration curve inferred from PLS regression using spatially resolved NIR spectra for the sugar content. There is only a moderate correlation of $R^2 = 0.42$ between the reference analysis and the spectral prediction. While the FTNIR usually features better spectral statistics based on averaging over the whole spatial sample domain, the hyperspectral approach suffers from reduced spectral statistics but gains spatial information of sugar gradients in the potato. Such it was already possible to detect so called *sugar ends* [12] in whole potatoes as shown in [13]. But rather than merely classifying different constituents such as sugar, peel or dry substance it is interesting to get more quantitative information as well in order to gain quality and process analysis data for the production. Figure 13.7 (a) shows the quantified sugar gradient for one of the analysed potato slices. It appears that glucose increases towards the rim of the potato while the inner parts are dominated by fine channel like structures presumably tracing water (Fig. 13.7 (b)).

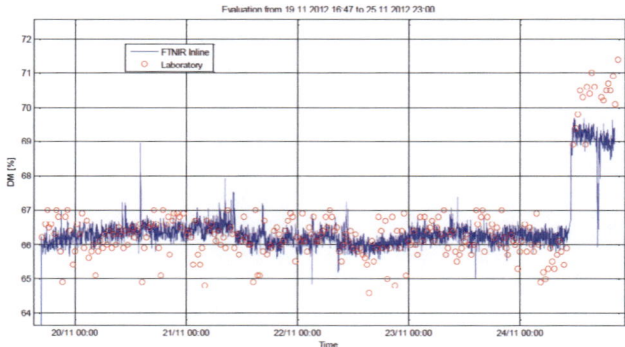

Figure 13.8: Dry substance content of French fries vs. time in a production process. (red) lab references (blue) inline FTNIR measurements.

An inline measurement of the dry substance content of French fries integrated in the production process was performed employing the i-RED FTNIR process spectrometer system and compared with lab references inferred from the material stream at the same time. The measured values from the FTNIR data based on PLS regression show an overall good agreement with the lab references over time following the same global trend while featuring reduced scatter (Fig. 13.8).

3.2 Wheat grains

Along the same lines, i.e. correlating chemical reference data with FT-NIR spectral data, the baking properties of whole wheat grains as well as flour was modelled. The relevant baking parameters are the start/end of agglutination and its maximum in terms of dough viscosity as shown in the amylogram Fig. 13.9 (a). The according data was correlated with the agglutination maximum similarly as for the potato dry substance content (Fig. 13.9 (b)). A correlation coefficient of roughly $R^2 \sim 0.7$ for predictions inferred from whole wheat grain spectra vs. viscosity maxima as measured with the amylograph represents aigain a promising result with respect to an inline food analysing application.

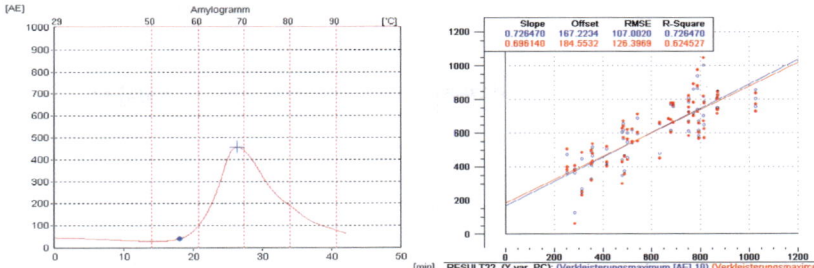

(a) Amylogram of wheat showing dough viscosity vs. temperature and time, respectively.
The blue spot denotes the beginning of agglutination and the cross its maximum.   Taken
from [14].

(b) Correlation of whole wheat grain
FTNIR spectral data vs. agglutination
maxima taken from amylograph data.

Figure 13.9:

4 Conclusion

Quantitative analysis of material parameters such as chemical concentrations, constituent gradients and food components using inline NIR
technologies is possible and ready for industrial application. Hyperspectral imaging and FTNIR cameras provide sufficient spectral (and in
case of HSI spatial) resolutions at fair data processing speeds to tackle
industry relevant process analysis problems at typical bulk flow veloci-
ties of several m/s. Albeit comprising limited statistical accuracy compared to chemical lab methods with respect to the individual sample
test the great benefit of quantitative inline analysis comes with the enor-
mous increase of the sample size, ultimately monitoring the entire input
stream on-line. The prototype studies for a dry chemical concentration
as well as inline food analyser presented in this article show that quantitative results inferred from NIR spectra are compatible with lab references within their statistical accuracy. Further work has to be done to
increase the methods accuracies mainly with respect to quality (S/N)
and selection criteria of relevant NIR spectra for the model building involved.

Acknowledgments

The project *Forschung-Technologie-Innovation (FTI) – Inline Food Analyser* is supported by the Austrian research council FFG under the project number 834298.

References

1. H. Huang, H. Yu, H. Xu, and Y. Ying, "Near infrared spectroscopy for on/inline monitoring of quality in foods and beverages: A review," *Journal of Food Engineering*, vol. 87, pp. 303–313, 2008.

2. S. Kawano, H. Watanabe, and M. Iwamoto, "Determination of sugar content in intact peaches by near infrared spectroscopy with fiber optics in interactance mode." *Journal of the Japanese Society for Horticultural Science*, vol. 61, pp. 445–451, 1992.

3. S. Kawano, T. Fujiwara, and M. Iwamoto, "Nondestructive determination of sugar content in satsuma mandarin using near infrared (nir) transmittance." *Journal of the Japanese Society for Horticultural Science*, vol. 62, pp. 465–470, 1993.

4. Y. Ni, M. Mei, and S. Kokot, "Analysis of complex, processed substances with the use of nir spectroscopy and chemometrics: Classification and prediction of properties - the potato crisps example," *Chemometrics and Intelligent Laboratory Systems*, vol. 105, pp. 147–156, 2011.

5. N. Ballin, "Authentication of meat and meat products," *Meat Science*, vol. 86, pp. 577–587, 2010.

6. R. Karoui, L. Pillonel, E. Schaller, J.-O. Bosset, and J. D. Baerdemaeker, "Prediction of sensory attributes of european emmental cheese using nearinfrared spectroscopy: A feasibility study," *Food Chemistry*, vol. 101, no. 3, pp. 1121–1129, 2007.

7. www.evk.co.at/downloads/download.php?ID=539.

8. www.i-red.at/index.php?id=268.

9. W. Kessler, *Multivariate Datenanalyse.*   Weinheim: John Wiley & Sons, 2007.

10. S. Wold, M. Sjöström, and L. Eriksson, "Pls-regression: a basic tool of chemometrics," *Chemometrics and Intelligent Laboratory Systems*, vol. 58, no. 2, pp. 109–130, 2001.

11. L. C. Maillard, "Action of amino acids on sugars. formation of melanoidins in a methodical way." *Comptes rendus de l'Académie des sciences*, vol. 154, p. 66, 1912.

12. J. R. Sowokinos, C. C. Shock, T. D. Stieber, and E. P. Eldredge, "Compositional and enzymatic changes associated with the sugar-end defect in russet burbank potatoes," *American Journal of Potato Research*, vol. 77, no. 1, pp. 47–56, 2000.

13. M. Groinig, M. Burgstaller, and M. Pail, "Industrial application of a new camera system based on hyperspectral imaging for inline quality control of potatoes." *ÖAGM/AAPR Workshop, Graz*, 2011.

14. Farina, "Muster r960 fa.teschl," internal FTI project protocol, Nov 2012.

Detection of non-metallic impurities and defects through radar measurements

Dirk Nüßler, Christian Krebs and Ralf Brauns

Fraunhofer Institute for High Frequency Physics and Radar Techniques FHR
Fraunhoferstraße 20, D-53343 Wachtberg

Abstract The detection of non-metallic impurities and defects during the production of food is a critical task for every inspection system. Through recall campaigns caused by the contamination of food during the production process can corrupt the good reputation of companies for a long time. To minimize the risk a huge number of sensor technologies is implemented. The spectrum of sensors starts from the optical region over sensors in the infrared region to x-ray systems. The main disadvantage of most of the systems is the inability to detect non-metallic contaminations inside a product. The paper describes the possibilities of modern radar systems to fulfill these tasks.

1 Introduction

For the surveillance of production process a huge number of different sensors and systems are today available. The spectrum of the sensors starts with a less or more simple measurement of the weight of the product followed by metal detectors. Camera systems in the optical or infrared region offers a wide spectrum of additional information and finally x-ray systems allow a view inside the product. A critical task for all of these sensors are non-metallic impurities inside a product. X-ray systems allows the detection of metallic and non-metallic impurities inside a product as long as the contrast between the product and the impurity is high enough. For those applications radar sensors working in the millimetre wave range offers an alternative to present systems. High frequency sensors have the advantage that many dielectric materials in the microwave and millimetre wave region are transparent. Based on the used frequency range, high frequency sensors could not realize the same spatial resolution, like sensors which work in a higher frequency range with a shorter wavelength. The frequencies of interest are in the millimetre wave region starting at 30 GHz and ending around 100 GHz. Systems in the frequency range above 100 GHz are technical possible but economically unviable. For this frequency range three different types of radar systems are possible, continuous wave (CW), frequency modulated wave (FMCW) and stepped frequency radar systems. For the calculation of the material parameters we need the physical dimensions of the device under test (DUT) and the phase information. In Particular the phase information is an important information for the detection of impurities which have an equal attenuation coefficient like the ambient material. The ability to measure the phase allows high frequency sensors to detect inclusions which are even invisible for a regular x-ray system. Like other sensors high frequency systems have a weak spot. Electrically conductive coatings and materials with a high water concentration are not transparent for electromagnetic waves.

2 Measurement set-up

For the measurement set-up to main configuration are common. The simplest measurement configuration is a transmission configuration. Comparable to x-ray systems transmitter and receiver are on opposite sides with the DUT moved between. This configuration can be used for CW and FMCW systems. The second configuration is a reflection geometry with transmitter and receiver on the same side. This configuration is only for systems with a range resolution usable like FMCW systems. Both configurations have advantages and disadvantages, but from a more economical view CW systems can be realized much cheaper than systems with a range resolution. For every measurement system the antenna configuration is an important device. There are several possibilities to realize a compact configuration with a high resolution. Based on the system approach and the signal processing small antennas like open waveguides or patch antennas with small lenses are used or rectangular antennas in combination with a focusing lens. The pixel resolution depends on the selected wavelength, comparable to the optical region the resolution is approximately between 0.5 and 1 wavelength. Through the chosen wavelength of maximum 100 GHz with a wavelength of 3 mm, the resolution is limited in millimetre wave region. For many industrial applications this resolution is insufficient. To realize a resolution better than 1 mm, we need a more sophisticated concept. One alternative is the use of near field probes for the measurements. With near field probes theoretical resolution better than 1% of the chosen wavelength can be realized. The biggest drawback of a measurement system with near field probes is the short measurement distance between the probe and the DUT. Depending on the measurement principal, resolution decreases when the distance between probe and DUT increases. For the performed measurements dielectric tips were used. For this configuration a compromise between distance and resolution was searched. Measurements have shown a good compromise between resolution and distance for a measurement distance of 10 mm. The results in this paper were all measured with a near field probe. Near field probes offer a good resolution in combination with a compact design for a low price and can easily be integrated in a high frequency system.

3 Measurement results

In a first step we compare the results of a amplitude measurement with a phase measurement. Amplitude measurements in the millimetre wave region follows the same restrictions like x-ray measurements. The contrast in the amplitude measurements is created through the different attenuation coefficient of the materials. Through the lower frequency range and the longer wavelength scattering effects appear which allows the detection of inclusions which have the same or an equal attenuation coefficient like the ambient material. There are many interesting research fields and over the last decade different applications were investigated and analysed. To find technology and economical successful applications for millimeter wave imaging systems, is the biggest challenge today. We need applications with a moderate number of systems, over hundred and not more than a few thousands, for a moderate price, over ten thousand but less than hundred thousand EURO, in a mass compatible technology like FMCW or better CW systems. Food industry is a perfect environment for radar sensors. The speed of production lines is moderate, typically not faster than 4 m/s and the products are normallytypically well separated. Figure 14.1 shows a cookie which was prepared for tests with a small piece of glass. Both glass and chocolate have a comparable attenuation coefficient in the measured frequency range. Through the scattering effects at the boundary between glass and chocolate the impurity can be easily detected. Unfortunately this effect is

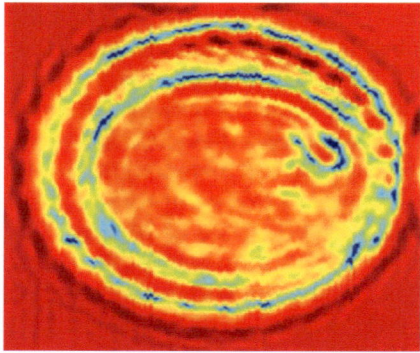

Figure 14.1: Picture of the amplitude measurement of a chocolate cookie prepared with a piece of glass.

only useable in a homogenous material. For cookies with nuts or other soughted ingredient, it is nearly impossible to separate desired from undesired components, when the attenuation coefficient and the physical dimensions are similar. We look again on our prepared chocolate filled cookie (Fig. 14.2). The phase measurements uses the dielectric properties of the material. Through the different material constant of glass and chocolate the runtime of the signal allows to discriminate between the two materials. In a CW system the different material parameters can be measured through the phase differences. The possible applications are not limited to the detection of inclusions and impurities inside of food. The measurements allows the detection of undesired defects in the production process. Through the ability to view through packaged products, defects like the missing pieces of chocolate in Fig. 14.3 can be easy visualized. Through the variation of the frequency range in combination with the phase measurement, the composition and concentration of ingredients can be controlled or the water content which could be an indicator for the freshness of a product. Especially in the production of food the humidity ratio or the concentration of ingredients should

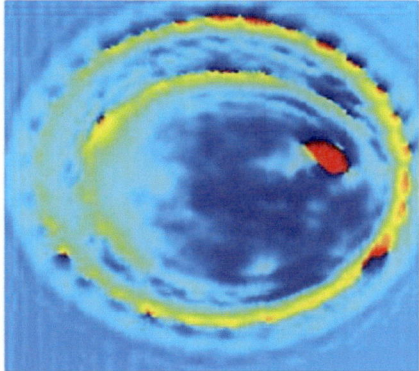

Figure 14.2: Picture of the phase measurement of a chocolate cookie prepared with a piece of glass.

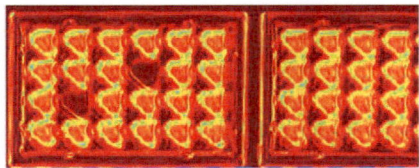

Figure 14.3: Picture of two packages of chocolate. On the left side two pieces are missing.

be constant. Through the comparison of the measured samples with a golden sample production processes can be monitored. As mentioned above radar measurements are sensitive to changes in the water concentration, many processes of maturing changes the water content inside the fruit which offers the opportunity to observe the degree of ripeness.

4 Conclusion

The ability of radar sensors to create high resolution images for quality control processes has been demonstrated. Through the combination of amplitude and phase measurements, high frequency sensors offer a wide spectrum of applications for the control of production processes especially in the area of food. The sensors can be used in a transmission or reflection geometry and in contrast to other sensors like x-rays high frequency sensors combine the ability to transmit a product with non-ionizing radiation.

Image analysis of natural products

Daniel Garten[1], Katharina Anding[2], Steffen Lerm[2], Gerhard Linß[2]
and Peter Brückner[2]

[1] GFE – Society for Production Engeneering and Development Schmalkalden
Naeherstiller Strasse 10, D-98574 Schmalkalden
[2] Ilmenau University of Technology, Department for Quality Assurance and
Industrial Image Processing,
Gustav-Kirchhoff-Platz 2, D-98693 Ilmenau

Abstract Natural products are exposed to various environmental influences resulting in a high phenotypical variability. This makes it very difficult to develop automatic recognition algorithms in contrast to the recognition of manufactured products. Recent developments in the field of computer science, especially the development of powerful classification algorithms like the support vector machine make it possible to face also such complicated tasks. In this paper we present an approach to classify the impurities of a wheat sample to analyse the quality.

1 Introduction

The analysis of a wheat sample for determinating the grain quality is called "Besatz analysis." The standard for this procedure is the manual sorting and weighting of the impurities of the sample by laboratory assistants or leading millers. This is an expensive, time-consuming and error-prone procedure. Our task was to automate this procedure by image processing in combination with intelligent machine learning algorithms. For the studies nearly 20,000 sample objects were pre-classified by human experts.. The image below shows the high variability on some sample classes. Flawless wheat kernels have a very high phenotypical variability like natural objects in general. Based on optical characteristics the boundaries between the various object classes in feature space are fluid. This leads to a very complex recognition problem.

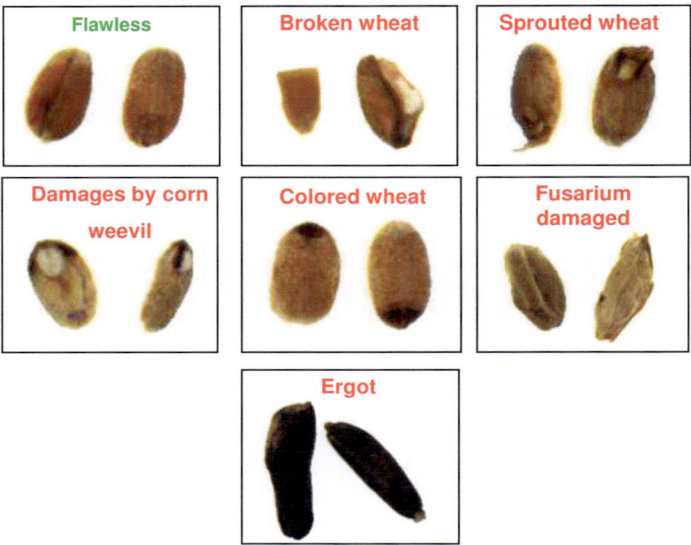

Figure 15.1: Sample objects for the different Besatz classes.

2 Hardware

For this complex optical recognition problem we need a stable image acquisition setup in terms of good single kernel separation and a stable and homogeneous object field illumination. For imaging every single object of a grain sample of nearly 500 g we used a setup consisting of a color line scan camera from the canadian manufacturer JAI with 2048 pixels running at nearly 2000 Hz line frequency and a Zeiss macro lens with a focal length of 50 mm. The object stream needs to be singularized before it passes the image acquisition unit because overlapping objects and occlusions result in recognition errors. Object singularization in the dimension perpendicular to the moving direction of the object stream was achieved by using partition walls. The separation in the dimension parallel to the moving direction was attained by two conveyer belts running at different speed. With this setup a sample with 500 g (nearly 10,000 single objects) can be analysed within 6 minutes. We achieved singularization rates of nearly 99 %. The whole setup is illustrated in the schematic diagram below.

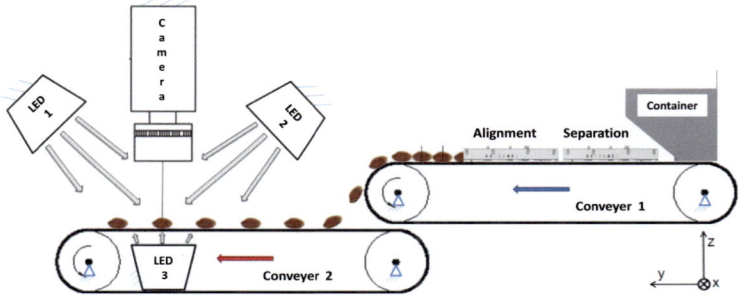

Figure 15.2: Setup for single kernel separation and image acquisition.

For object illumination a combination of transmitted (LED 3) and reflected light (LED 1 and 2) was used. The material of the conveyer belt is semi-transparent and thus a light source located thereunder provided a diffused background illumination. This generates a basis of the simplified object segmentation. A simple thresholding operation in combination with run length encoding makes a realtime line-wise segmentation possible. Right after the last row of the object image is transferred to the evaluation program the image can be classified by the classification module, implemented with a support vector machine [1]. The complete analysis is put into practice in terms of the European Commission Regulation (EC) No 856/2005 [2].

3 Image features

For an image recognition task in general, we have a high amount of possible image features. Detecting relevant features out of these is a very crucial step. In this experiment a bag-of-features with nearly 240 standard operators from the image processing library Halcon [3] as well as self-developed features based on texture information and gray value morphology [4] where used. For detecting relevant features the whole dataset with nearly 20,000 object images was separated randomly into 3 datasets – dataset 1 with 22 % of all available objects for feature scoring, dataset 2 with 45 % for training and dataset 3 with 33 % for the final test. Then the information gain [5] was calculated within dataset 1 which results in a relevance score for every single feature. Thus it is not clear at which threshold a feature can be considered to be irrelevant. This threshold can only be defined in combination with a classifier within a semi-wrapper approach. So we ordered our features in ascending order by the information gain score [5] and iteratively removed the 10 lowest ranked features from the feature vector, trained a classifier on dataset 1 and tested its performance on dataset 2. This results in the curve shown below. From this, the relevance threshold and consequently the final feature set could be estimated.

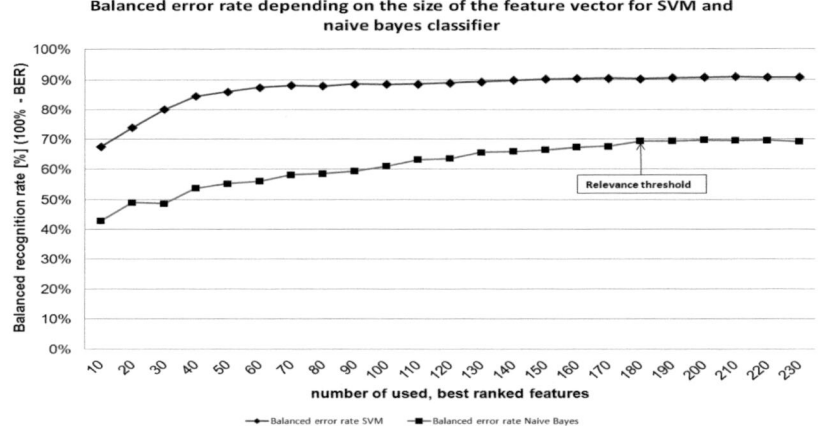

Figure 15.3: Total recognition rate on test set depending on feature set size.

The total recognition rate of about 91 % on the final test set shows that there is a significant improvement due to the introduction of problem-adapted image features. The reduction of the feature set to the most relevant features resulted into a significant speedup. In the new feature set problem-adapted features based on texture operators and morphological operations were introduced. This leads to the significant improvement. The results in the form of recognition rates accomplished with the feature set contraining of standard image operators in contrary to the optimized feature set are shown in Fig. 15.4.

class	recognition rate - feature set with all standard operators	recognition rate optimized feature set	difference
Sprouted wheat	79.10 %	82.00 %	+2.90 %
Broken wheat	82.80 %	86.80 %	+4.00 %
Durum wheat	91.60 %	94.40 %	+2.80 %
Wheat damaged by pests	80.60 %	85.00 %	+4.40 %
Oats	96.50 %	96.20 %	-0.30 %
Canola	99.00 %	98.10 %	-0.90 %
Rye	91.60 %	93.20 %	+1.60 %
Shrivelled wheat	84.00 %	87.60 %	+3.60 %
Sunflower seeds	98.10 %	97.80 %	-0.30 %
Husks	89.10 %	90.00 %	+0.90 %
Stones	95.40 %	96.20 %	+0.80 %
Weed seeds	94.00 %	94.70 %	+0.70 %
Other contaminations	77.50 %	80.80 %	+3.30 %
Flawless wheat	82.10 %	86.90 %	+4.80 %
total recognition rate	88.92 %	90.95 %	+2.03 %

Figure 15.4: Improvement of the recognition rate by feature optimization.

4 Classifier optimization

The SVM classifier is considered the most powerful classifier today. Tests indicated that the SVM will be the best classifier for our task also. So we used a SVM classifier with the radial basis function kernel (rbf):

$$k(x, x') = e^{-Gamma|x-x'|^2} \qquad (15.1)$$

The kernel parameter Gamma and the regularization parameter Nu for the training of the SVM need to be chosen before the training process very carefully. To find an optimal parameter set a grid search method in combination with 3-fold crossvalidation on the training dataset with all available data was conducted. For the grid search optimization, the position of the grid points in the interval $[0, Max_{Nu,Gamma}]$ are calculated according to the following formula, with Nu as a threshold for the termination of the optimization process and Gamma as the kernel parameter:

$$Pos_{Nu,Gamma} = \frac{Max_{Nu,Gamma}}{2^{i-n+1}} \quad with \quad 0 \le i \le 9 \quad n = 10 \qquad (15.2)$$

The formula leaves an exponential characteristic for the distribution of the nodes. The interval width grows with increasing values for Nu and Gamma. As expected, the optimal values of both parameters are small. To handle the imbalanced dataset the predictive power is measured in terms of the balanced recognition rate (BRR). This measure is defined as the average of the recognition rates of each classes. For many recognition problems with natural material the influence of Gamma is much higher than of Nu. Nu controls the training set error as well as the number of training vectors which become support vectors and thus affects the decision border to become more complex. With growing Gamma the influence of each of these support vectors on the decision border grows. To cover the high intra-class-variance in the dataset many relevant training vectors are needed with each relatively less but equal distributed influence among them on the decision border. This results in a low value for Gamma and a mid-sized for Nu (see figure below). As we see from the figure for this recognition problem we can also choose a simpler optimization strategy because of the low influence by Nu. We can take a fixed low value for Nu and increase the value for Gamma till the recognition rate starts to decrease.

5 Complexity visualization with Principle Component Analysis (PCA)

The given recognition task and the results so far indicate a very high complexity. One way to understand the complexity of the recognition problem is to establish a suitable visualization of the distribution of the different object clusters in the feature space. The feature space has got 200 or more dimensions and can not be visualised in an easy way. To reduce the dimensions of the feature space a principle component analysis (PCA) [6] could be used. The PCA allows the visualisation of the given high dimensional data in a lower dimensional space with loss of information. The goal of the PCA is the approximation of the n features by a smaller number m of meaningful linear combinations (principal components). On the given dataset a visualisation of the object clusters in feature space was realised with Matlab® for the subclasses of wheat. The result of the PCA confirmed the high complexity and further indicated the need to use a powerful classifier which is able to handle com-

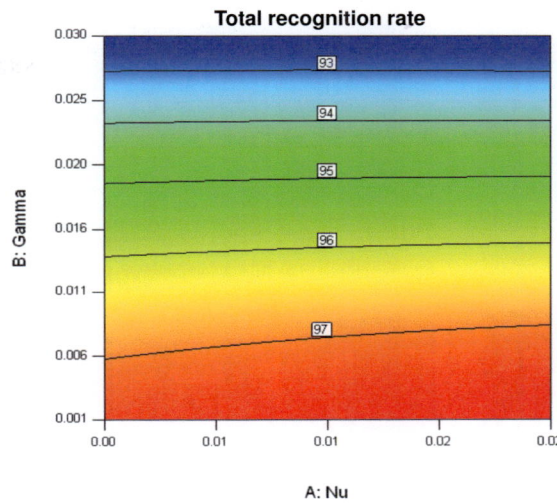

Figure 15.5: Total recognition rate in dependency of Nu and Gamma.

plex borders between the classes in feature space. The PCA can be seen as a quick and simple way to get a first impression on the complexity of the recognition problem, especially in line with a feasibility study.

It can be clearly seen that the subclasses of wheat in Fig. 15.6 show far more overlap in feature space after PCA due to a higher intra-class-variability in combination with less inter-class-variability. The clusters of the different grain types (Fig. 15.7) can be visualy separated also in the 3-dimensional space after PCA. For Further results about complexity visualisation you can refer to [7].

The task to separate foreign grain and also weed seeds from flawless grain can be implemented with more simple color-based image features like done within optical sorting machines. But in practice this also comes along with a higher false-positve rate for objects not belonging to the class of flawless wheat. For the purposes of sorting this is tolerable; for the purposes of analysis, the rate of false-positives is considered to high to be reliable.

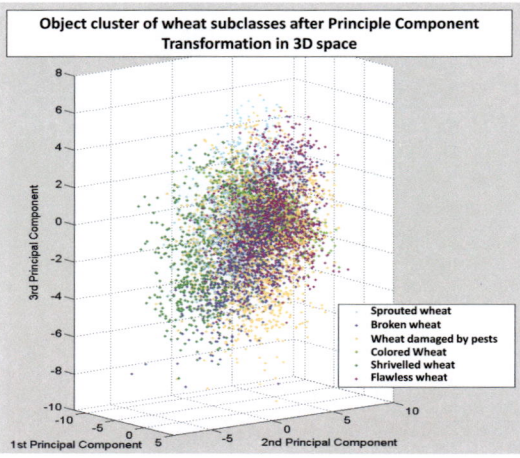

Figure 15.6: Cluster of the wheat subclasses after PCA in 3-dimensional space.

6 Results

After this optimisation the dataset has been expanded with toxic ergot and fusarium-damaged wheat and further samples for every class. With optimized features and optimized SVM parameters (regularization parameter Nu and parameter Gamma of the radial basis function kernel) we created a classifier for practical testing. It could be demonstrated that the whole system consisting of automatic sample separation, single kernel imaging and classification is able to achieve a high accuracy of recognition. Therefore, sample material with known composition from different crop years, also from later years than the material used for training has been analysed in a comprehensive test. It turned out that recognition rates of 90 % could be reached.

The whole system was also tested within a field test in two grain mills. The results confirmed the findings from the presented laboratory test and validated the applicability of the system.

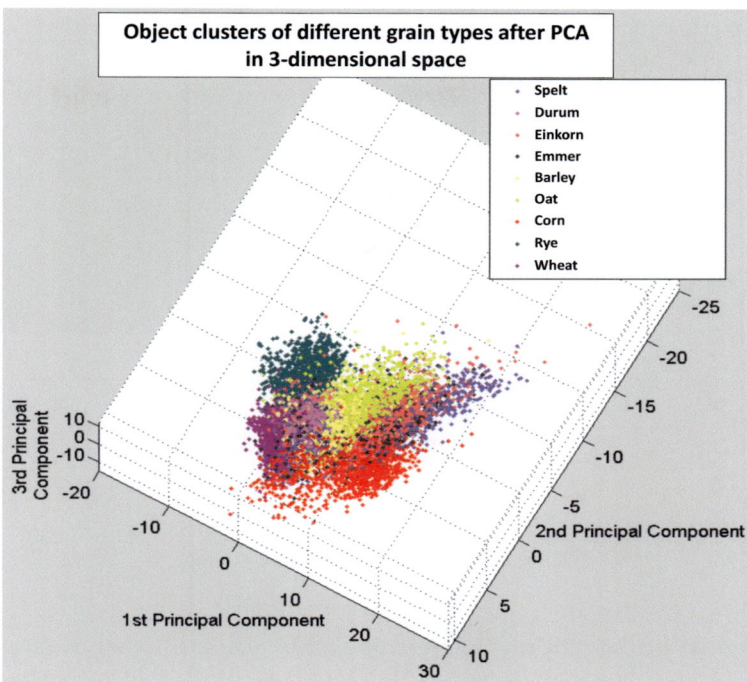

Figure 15.7: Cluster of the different grain types after PCA in 3-dimensional space.

7 Summary

The automatic recognition of natural material like grain is always a challenging task. Recent advantages in the development of new classification algorithms like support vector machines, random forest classifiers and neural networks now make it possible to solve many of these problems. With our setup for objects separation and image acquisition it is possible to acquire the images of 10,000 objects of a wheat sample in less than 10 minutes. With problem-adapted feature extraction and a highly optimized classifier it is possible to reach an accuracy of nearly 90 % under practice conditions. This seems to be a very good result. We as-

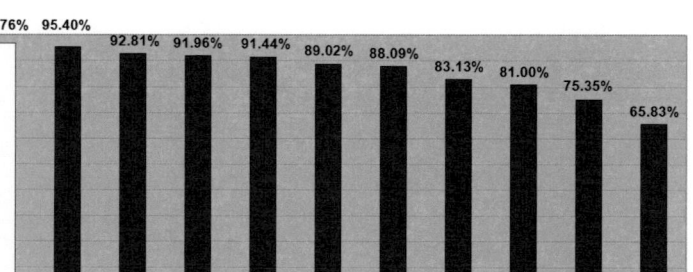

Figure 15.8: Recognition rates per class.

sume that further improvements come up by using a higher resolution, e. g. a colour line scan camera with 4096 pixels. With a decreasing price hyperspectral cameras can also be considered in the future for this problem. Especially ultra-violet light can deliver information for the recognition of broken wheat and other whear subclasses. Also the detection of fusarium seems to be improvable by using spectral information. Recent research, for example [8] strongly indicates this. Discussions with future users of the system indicated that the time for an analysis is sufficient but the precision could be improved. Accordingly the main focus in future research will be the increase of the recognition rate.

Acknowledgements

A project, funded by the Federal Ministry for Economic Affairs and Technology under the promotional reference 16INO496, forms the basis of this paper. The responsibility for the content of this paper lies with the author.

References

1. N. Cristianini and J. Shawe-Taylor, *An Introduction to Support Vector Machines and other kernel-based learning methods.* Cambridge: Cambridge University Press, 2000.

2. N.U., "Commission regulation (ec) no 856/2005," *Official Journal of the European Union*, vol. 143, no. 3, 2005.

3. ——, *Halcon 8.0.3 Reference Manual.* Munich: MVTec Software GmbH, 2009.

4. D. Garten, *Einfluss von Bildaufnahme und Bildmerkmalen auf die Erkennungsguete bei der automatischen Besatzanalyse von Brotweizen (Influence of image acquisition and image features on the recognition rate for the automatical Besatz analysis of wheat).* Ilmenau: ISLE Verlag Ilmenau, 2011.

5. T. M. Mitchell, *Machine Learning.* Pittsburgh: The Mc-Graw-Hill Companies, Inc, 1997.

6. I. T. Jolliffe, *Principal Component Analysis, Series: Springer Series in Statistics.* New York: Springer, 2002.

7. K. Anding, *Automatisierte Qualitätssicherung von Getreide mit überwachten Lernverfahren in der Bildverarbeitung (Automated quality assurance with supervised machinge learning in image processing).* Ilmenau: ISLE Verlag Ilmenau, 2010.

8. G. Polder, "Detection of fusarium in single wheat kernels using spectral," *Seed Science and Technology*, vol. 33, pp. 655–668, 2004.

Evaluation of spectral unmixing using nonnegative matrix factorization on stationary hyperspectral sensor data of specifically prepared rock and mineral mixtures

Wolfgang Gross[1], Sven Borchardt[2] and Wolfgang Middelmann[1]

[1] Fraunhofer Institute of Optronics, System Technologies and Image Exploitation, Departement Scene Analysis, Gutleuthausstraße 1, D-76275 Ettlingen

[2] University of Potsdam, Institute of Earth and Environmental Science, Am Mühlenberg 3, D-14476 Potsdam

Abstract Hyperspectral sensors are used to identify materials via spectroscopic analysis. Often, the measured spectra consist of mixed materials and depending on the problem, the mixture ratio and the pure material spectra are wanted. In this paper, linear spectral unmixing is performed using the Nonnegative Matrix Factorization to analyze its correlation to ground truth data. The results are compared to Nonnegative Least Squares unmixing using manually selected endmembers from the image. Additionally, the effect of different endmember extraction algorithms and abundance initialization methods for NMF are investigated. To test the validity of the method, several checkerboard patterns of different ground minerals/rocks with predefined mixtures were prepared. It was shown that good initialization is beneficial in terms of approximation error and correlation to ground truth.

1 Introduction

Hyperspectral sensors are used to identify materials via spectroscopic analysis. They are widely used in areas such as satellite/airborne imaging, mining and recycling. The value of hyperspectral data can be increased by having a fair knowledge about the physical composition of the recorded data. Considering that certain materials only occur in small quantities on a sub-pixel level, typical classification approaches can be insufficient depending on the scope of work. Instead, spectral unmixing can be used to determine the individual material spectra, so called endmember and their abundances in a measured sample. As the amount of materials in an image is generally much less than the number of spectral bands, data reduction is achieved simultaneously [1].

Usually, the endmembers must be provided by the user and the abundances are computed by a Nonnegative Least Squares (NNLS) approach to approximate the original data set. However, this is only applicable when they are known in advance or can be selected manually from the data. When the data sets become larger, manual selection is increasingly difficult and automatic endmember extraction algorithms should be used. Small deviations from the actual endmember spectra, e.g. noise in the data set or variation in illumination, can lead to errors. The Nonnegative Matrix Factorization (NMF) can be used to alternately optimize endmembers and abundances to increase approximation accuracy [2].

When the focus lies on the physical interpretation of a hyperspectral data set, generally two constraints have to be introduced to the process [3]. The most important is the nonnegativity constraint for endmembers and abundances as the measured reflectance is per definition nonnegative and mutual cancellation of endmembers is impossible. The second constraint states that the abundances of one sample must sum to one. In that case, each abundance directly stands for the ratio of its associated endmember.

2 Linear spectral unmixing and initialization

The underlying optimization problem of linear spectral unmixing can be written as

$$\min_{W,H} \|V - WH\|_F,$$
$$\text{subject to } W, H \geq 0 \text{ per element,} \tag{16.1}$$

where V is the data matrix with m bands and n samples, W is the $m \times k$ endmember matrix and H the $k \times n$ abundance matrix. $\|\cdot\|_F$ denotes the Frobenius norm. All entries of the matrices are real and nonnegative numbers. When the endmember matrix W is already known, it can be considered as constant and optimization is done only for H. Thus, the optimization problem becomes convex and a global minimum can be computed via NNLS.

In practice, data dimensionality will always be m due to sensor noise. However, the number of materials and thus the inherent dimension of a data set is usually much smaller than m and a set of k vectors, with $k \ll m$ can approximate the data very well [1]. In this paper, we act on the assumption that k is known, as determination of the actual number of endmembers for a data set is a problem by itself. Further information on the selection of k can be found in [4].

The NMF is basically computed using the method of alternating steepest descent. As the underlying optimization problem is nonlinear due to the nonnegativity constraint, multiple (sub)optimal solutions exist and a good initialization improves the outcome [5].

The alternating multiplicative update proposed by [6] is basically a steepest descent algorithm with efficient step size calculation, to comply with the nonnegativity constraint. W and H are alternately updated. The NMF can be used when the endmembers are not known *a priori* or cannot be determined with sufficient accuracy. However, linear spectral unmixing is an ill-posed inverse problem. Because of model inaccuracies, sensor noise, external measurement conditions and variability in material spectra, it is impossible to analytically determine the solution. Depending on the initialization the steepest descent algorithm can get stuck in a local minimum due to initialization.

The endmembers can be regarded as extreme directions of the minimal convex cone containing the data cloud in m-dimensional space. All spectra within the cone can be reconstructed without residuals, using abundances as coefficients for the linear combination of endmembers. NMF iteration alternately adjusts the endmembers and their abundances to better fit the data cloud and thus reduce the approximation error.

Using the notation from (16.1), NMF can be performed as follows:

$$
\begin{aligned}
H^{(t+1)} &= H^{(t)} * \frac{((W^{(t)})^T V)}{(W^{(t)})^T W^{(t)} H^{(t)} + \epsilon} \\
W^{(t+1)} &= W^{(t)} * \frac{(V(H^{(t+1)})^T)}{W^{(t)} H^{(t+1)} (H^{(t+1)})^T + \epsilon}
\end{aligned}
\qquad (16.2)
$$

Here, (t) is the iteration index and $*$ and $\div$ denotes multiplication/division per element. ϵ is a small, strictly positive value to prevent division by zero. The proof of monotony can be found in [6], further discussion on convergence in [3].

One of the most useful properties of NMF is that it usually produces a sparse representation of the data set. This means that most of the information is concentrated in a few abundances [6]. As the mixed spectra usually consist of only two or three different materials, this is a great benefit when compared to an unconstrained least squares approach where all endmembers are used per sample.

2.1 Initialization of W

Several approaches exist to extract endmember spectra directly from the data and use them to initialize the endmember matrix for linear spectral unmixing. This section contains a short explanation of the most frequently used algorithms. Further information and examples for implementation can be found in [2,5,7,8].

Random initialization: The random methods are among the fastest and easiest to code. W is initialized as a dense matrix with random numbers between 0 and 1. According to [9], these initializations have the potential to outperform every other method in terms of approximation error.

Spherical k-Means Clustering: The cluster centers are used as initialization for W. In this paper, the spectral angle is used as a metric for clustering. This is a reasonable choice, as spectra of identical mixtures should be treated identical, regardless of illumination. The algorithm, which is very similar to conventional k-Means Clustering, can be found in [2].

Pixel Purity Index (PPI): The data is projected onto random unit vectors and the most extreme samples are collected. This is repeated several times and the resulting samples are thinned out till only a set amount of spectra remains. The PPI algorithm used for endmember extraction can be found in [7].

Sequential Orthogonal Subspace Projection (SOSP): The SOSP is an analytical approach to determine the most significant vertices of the data set in m-dimensional space. Thus, an approximation to the convex hull of the data set is computed. The algorithm can be found in [8] and performs exceptionally well on simulated data satisfying the linear mixture model. In contrast to the other methods discussed here, no random procedures are used making the result reproducible.

2.2 Initialization of H

Only two notable initialization methods exist for the abundance matrix H. The first being random initialization similar to W from Subsect. 2.1. This usually provides good results, but specifically when a sparse solution is needed another method must be chosen.

After initialization of W with an endmember extraction algorithm, the abundances in H are estimated by their fractional part, that is not accounted for by any other endmember. Each row $H_{i:}$ of H is calculated separately by

$$H_{i:} = w_i^T P_{\text{OSP}}^{-i}, \text{ where}$$
$$P_{\text{OSP}}^{-i} = (I - W_{-i}(W_{-i}^T W_{-i})^{-1}W_{-i}^T)V \tag{16.3}$$

I is the unit matrix of suitable dimension and W_{-i} is the endmember matrix W without the i-th endmember w_i. A discussion of this method can be found in [10].

3 Experiments and discussion

Evaluation of linear spectral unmixing was performed using a 4×4 checkerboard pattern of ground minerals/rocks with known abundances per square. Experiments with three to nine classes were performed. To evaluate the effect of different endmember extraction methods at least one square was provided containing the pure material. Also, the experiments were limited to having three different materials per square at most.

For every pattern, regions of interest (ROI) were manually selected to outline the homogeneous parts of each sample. This was done to restrict the endmember extraction algorithms to spectra that comply with the linear mixture model. However, NMF was performed on the whole data set. Restricting NMF to the homogeneous regions was considered to be impractical when working with data that is not specifically prepared. The setup for three classes is shown in Fig. 16.1. The ground

Figure 16.1: Ground truth masks (left) and corresponding abundance images (right) for basalt (top), trachyte (middle) and rhyolite (bottom); endmembers by SOSP, random initial abundances.

truth masks depict homogeneous regions of each square, light blue corresponding to a fraction of 25%, green 50%, orange 75% and red 100% of the corresponding material.

The data was recorded in a laboratory using an AISA sensor with 238 spectral bands in the wavelength range from $1 - 2.5\mu m$ and artificial illumination.

On the left side of Fig. 16.1 the ground truth images for basalt, trachyte and rhyolite are depicted from top to bottom. On their right are the corresponding abundance images. In this case, assignment was done manually as the similarities are clear. The abundances from Fig. 16.1 were calculated by initializing W with SOSP and H randomly.

To evaluate the results, the mean approximation error per sample as well as the mean correlation between the abundance images and the corresponding ground truth images were calculated. This was done for all initialization methods in section 2.1 including the random and OSP initialization for H. All methods that use random procedures were computed 10 times and the best result was saved. Only the combination of SOSP initialization for W and OSP for H can be computed analytically, always producing the same outcome. The NMF algorithm was terminated after 2000 iterations of (16.2). Without parallel processing the computation time of NNLS and NMF was comparable. The results of NMF and NNLS solutions are shown in tables 16.1 and 16.2 respectively. Depicted are the mean results over all available test sets.

Selecting the endmember candidates manually from visual judgment usually results in a good unmixing. However, manual selection is susceptible to errors especially on extensive data sets. The random initialization for both W and H gives good results in terms of correlation. However, the approximation error, especially in the case of NNLS, is worse when compared to other methods. Also, initialization methods with random procedures were evaluated 10 times due to the dependency of NMF and NNLS on a good initialization. When random procedures are involved and no ground truth is available, selecting the best among multiple solutions remains to be investigated. In the case of NNLS, random initialization of W has a very high approximation error per sample as it is treated as a fixed endmember matrix and the results depend on its similarity to the actual endmembers.

Spherical k-Means Clustering, PPI and SOSP have similar performance. When manual initialization is not possible SOSP in combination with OSP initialization of H is preferable due to analytic computation. It was shown that SOSP always finds the correct endmembers, when the linear mixture model holds [8]. On simulated data sets a correlation of 0.9986 could be achieved while simultaneously the approximation error was the lowest among the tested methods. However, outliers and regions with nonlinear mixtures must be ignored during initialization.

Table 16.1: NMF results: Approximation error and mean correlation between abundances and corresponding ground truth images.

NMF:	H_{OSP}		H_{random}	
	approx. error	mean corr.	approx. error	mean corr.
Random	0.1850	0.8891	0.1387	0.9111
Manual initialization	0.1330	0.9012	0.1958	0.8665
k-Means Clustering	0.1247	0.8790	0.1954	0.8517
Pixel Purity Index	0.1550	0.8418	0.2417	0.9543
Sequential OSP	0.1147	0.9273	0.1942	0.9386

Table 16.2: NNLS results: Approximation error and mean correlation between abundances and corresponding ground truth images.

NNLS:	H_{OSP}		H_{random}	
	approx. error	mean corr.	approx. error	mean corr.
Random	3.6586	0.9015	3.7402	0.8900
Manual initialization	0.1541	0.9380	0.1580	0.9452
k-Means Clustering	0.1563	0.8978	0.1562	0.8955
Pixel Purity Index	0.6656	0.6475	0.6656	0.6475
Sequential OSP	0.2036	0.8239	0.2036	0.8239

4 Conclusion

Comparison of linear spectral unmixing algorithms has shown that NNLS generally gives good results provided the initial endmember matrix closely resembles the actual endmember spectra in the scene. The iterative approach of NMF is able to compensate for worse initialization by alternately updating abundances and endmembers. While the accuracy of the result, measured here by correlating the abundance images with their corresponding ground truth information, is comparable, good results are computed more consistently with NMF and the approximation error is lower. In a measurement where no ground truth data is available to quantify the result, NMF is generally more forgiving of bad initialization and the chance to get a result close to the actual physical composition in the first attempt is higher.

Considering the different initialization methods, random initialization for W and H has the potential to outperform every other method with the downside that multiple computations may be necessary. The SOSP initialization for W most consistently gave good results as the computation does not rely on random procedures. Additionally, when H is initialized with random values the NMF is able to iterate towards a result that allows easy assignment between ground truth and abundance images. It has to be noted that for this to work properly on a real data set, areas where nonlinear effects occur should be ignored while initializing W. Otherwise, endmembers might be chosen from these areas. NNLS and NMF would then be preset to prioritize the approximation of these areas over the actual linear mixtures. This can result in a lower approximation error, when a lot of nonlinear mixtures are in the scene, but in terms of comparability to the physical composition of the scene the result is worse.

Initialization of H by (16.3) already limits optimization problem (16.1) to certain solutions resulting in slightly lower correlations in our tests. This limitation can be advantageous, where nonlinear mixtures should be ignored. Also, when computation time is especially important, tests have shown that it can already be used as a crude unmixing or reduce the number of iterations needed for NMF.

The arranged test sets are valuable for further analysis as barely any hyperspectral data is available with ground truth about the mixture ratios per sample. More checkerboards were prepared where some materials were only included in mixtures. The arranged data sets can also be used to analyze nonlinear mixtures as well. Nonlinear unmixing usually needs a lot of *a priori* information about the data set, but the ground truth information is already available. This can help to improve the understanding of unmixing and the degree of model complexity that is needed for accurate results.

In future work the performance of NMF will be analyzed when no pure spectra are available for endmember extraction. Additionally, the effects of over- or underestimating the real amount of endmembers have to be explored.

References

1. C. Chang and Q. Du, "Estimation of number of spectrally distinct signal sources in hyperspectral imagery," *IEEE Transactions on Geoscience and Remote Sensing*, vol. 42, no. 3, pp. 608–619, 2004.

2. S. Wild, J. Curry, and A. Dougherty, "Motivating non-negative matrix factorizations," *SIAM*, vol. 8, 2003.

3. M. Berry, M. Browne, A. Langville, V. Pauca, and R. Plemmons, "Algorithms and applications for approximate nonnegative matrix factorization," in *Computational Statistics & Data Analysis*, vol. 52, 2007, pp. 155–173.

4. J. Bioucas-Dias and J. Nascimento, "Hyperspectral subspace identification," *IEEE Transactions on Geoscience and Remote Sensing*, vol. 46, no. 8, pp. 2435–2445, 2008.

5. A. Langville, C. Meyer, and R. Albright, "Initializations for the nonnegative matrix factorization," *Proceedings of the Twelfth ACM SIGKDD International Conference on Knowledge Discovery and Data Mining*, 2006.

6. D. Lee and H. Seung, "Algorithms for non-negative matrix factorization," *Adv. Neural Info. Proc. Syst.*, vol. 13, pp. 556–562, 2001.

7. F. Chaudhry, C. Wu, W. Liu, C. Chang, and A. Plaza, "Pixel purity index-based endmember extraction for hyperspectral data exploitation," *Image Processing*, vol. 661, no. 2, 2006.

8. W. Gross and W. Middelmann, "Sparseness-inducing initialization for non-negative matrix factorization in hyperspectral data," *Proc. DGPF*, vol. 32, 2012.

9. S. Wild, J. Curry, and A. Dougherty, "Improving non-negative matrix factorizations through structured initialization," *Pattern Recognition*, vol. 37, no. 11, pp. 2217–2232, 2004.

10. C. Kwan, B. Ayhan, G. Chen, J. Wang, B. Ji, and C. Chang, "A novel approach for spectral unmixing, classification, and concentration estimation of chemical and biological agents," *IEEE Transactions on Geoscience and Remote Sensing*, vol. 44, no. 2, pp. 409–419, 2006.

Spectral and spatial unmixing for material recognition in sorting plants

Matthias Michelsburg and Fernando Puente León

Institute of Industrial Information Technology (IIIT),
Karlsruhe Institute of Technology (KIT),
Hertzstr. 16, 76187 Karlsruhe, Germany

Abstract In optical inspection systems like automated bulk sorters, hyperspectral images in the near infrared range are used more and more for identification and classification of materials. However, the possible applications are limited due to the coarse spatial resolution and low frame rate. By adding an additional multispectral image with higher spatial resolution, the missing spatial information can be acquired. In this paper, a method is proposed to fuse the hyperspectral and multispectral images by jointly unmixing the image signals. Therefore, the linear mixing model, which is well-known from remote sensing applications, is extended to describe the spatial mixing of signals originated from different locations. Different spectral unmixing algorithms can be used to solve the problem. The benefit of the additional sensor and the unmixing process is presented and evaluated, as well as the quality of unmixing results obtained with different algorithms. With the proposed extended mixing model, an improved result can be achieved as shown with different examples.

1 Introduction

Recognition and classification of a variety of objects consisting of different materials is a challenging task in automated optical inspection systems as bulk sorters. Such sorting plants are widely used in the fields of mining, food production, and recycling to distinguish between objects according to the material they are made out of, i.e., their chemical composition. Many optical detectors used to discriminate materials work in the near-infrared spectral range (NIR), as the reflected light in this range gives information on the molecular bindings. This is due to the combination vibrations and its overtones which yield to material-specific spectral signatures. If a precise distinction between different materials is needed, hyperspectral cameras, which usually acquire more than 100 channels simultaneously, are of great importance. These cameras provide a narrowly sampled spectrum for each pixel and thereby allow to recognize different materials at different places.

While the fine spectral resolution provided by the high number of spectral channels is the main advantage of hyperspectral imaging systems, the coarse spatial resolution and low frame rate are its drawbacks. Thereby, light reflected by different objects or several parts of a single object is mixed, which reduces the capabilities of an inspection system. Hence, many industrial constraints concerning speed and resolution cannot be met.

By adding a multispectral (less than 10 channels) or monochrome camera, which meets the requirements for resolution and frame rate, the desired spatial information can be obtained. Therefore, the additional image is fused with the hyperspectral image and a classification in the required spatial resolution is possible. There are several approaches for fusing the different images. When fusing a panchromatic image with a hyperspectral image, the procedure is called pansharpening [1]. A widely used method of this kind is the replacement of a single principal component with the panchromatic image after having transformed the hyperspectral image by principal component analysis. Other methods are based on adding high-frequency components of the monochrome image to the hyperspectral image.

In this paper, a new method for fusing images of different spectral and spatial resolution is proposed. Therefore, the image signals are regarded as mixtures of different material signatures and combined in a common model.

The problem of mixing and its inversion are known as spectral unmixing from the field of remote sensing [2]. Here, mixing coefficients which represent the contribution of each material to the overall signal are assigned to each pixel. In conventional spectral unmixing, the mixing of signals takes place only within each pixel. This approach will be extended by spatial unmixing. This allows images with different spatial resolutions to be merged. The purpose of the proposed method is not the fusion of the different images into one resulting image, but the determination of the mixing coefficients. These coefficients can be used as feature vectors for a subsequent classification process.

This paper is structured as follows. In the following section, the problem is stated in more detail and the procedure of spectral unmixing is introduced. Then, an approach for extending spectral unmixing to several images of different cameras is proposed. The properties of the proposed methods are discussed on the basis of different example signals in the subsequent section.

2 Spectral unmixing

Spectral unmixing is based on the assumption that the reflected spectrum of a pixel is composed of a mixture of different signals originated from different endmembers. These endmembers are usually pure materials. By spectral unmixing of hyperspectral images, the ratios of the endmembers are determined. This can be done in a supervised or unsupervised way. For supervised unmixing, the spectral signatures of the endmembers must be known in advance. Whereas, the spectral signatures are extracted from the hyperspectral image when using unsupervised techniques. There are also methods which do not need endmember spectra at all. Different measures like the pixel purity index or the volume of the simplex spanned by the endmember spectra can be used to determine the endmember signatures. A comparison of different endmember extraction methods can be found in [3]. Instead of extracting endmembers from the image, they also can be taken from several databases. The number of endmembers must be known a priori or can be specified with several methods such as the concept of virtual dimensionality [4].

Spectral unmixing is often used in remote sensing to investigate the earth surface and its geological composition, its development, and vegetation. The areas viewed by a single pixel of a hyperspectral imaging system can be several meters due to the long distance between the image sensor based in an airplane or satellite and the observed object. Hence, different objects and materials are usually found in the field of view of one pixel. Similar effects can be observed when using hyperspectral images in inspection systems like automated bulk sorters. While the distance between sensor and object is small, signal components are also mixed due to the high speed of the objects and the low frame rate of the camera. By spectral unmixing, the mixture is attempted to be inverted and, as a result, the relative contribution of each material is determined.

There are different mixing models which are based on different constraints. The linear mixing model is the simplest and most widely used model. Here, additively mixed signal compounds are assumed. The linear mixing model is presented in the next section. Other mixing models, as the bilinear mixing model, allow for more complex mixtures caused by scattering and other nonlinear effects taking place in the material [5].

2.1 Linear mixing model

In the following, all signals are regarded as discrete variables for mathematical descriptions. Thereby, they can be written in matrix notation.

The linear mixing model assumes a signal $\mathbf{y}$ to conform

$$\mathbf{y} = \mathbf{X} \cdot \mathbf{a} + \mathbf{n}, \tag{17.1}$$

where $\mathbf{X}$ is a $N \times M$ matrix whose columns $\mathbf{x}_i$ represent the spectra of the M endmembers. N stands for the number of channels of the sensor, $\mathbf{n}$ is a noise term which combines model errors and sensor noise. Vector $\mathbf{a}$ consists of the mixing coefficients. There are two restrictions for these coefficients. The coefficients need to be non-negative

$$a_i \geq 0 \qquad \text{for} \qquad i = 1, \ldots, M, \tag{17.2}$$

and all coefficients of one pixel need to sum up to one:

$$\sum_{i=1}^{M} a_i = 1. \tag{17.3}$$

The different endmembers contribute only positively to the overall signal, which is ensured by the first constraint. The second restriction accounts for the signal is being fully described by the endmembers. The assumptions yield

$$a_i \leq 1 \qquad \text{for} \qquad i = 1, \ldots, M. \tag{17.4}$$

All possible combinations of mixing coefficients are found within an M dimensional simplex with edges of length one.

2.2 Unmixing algorithms

The inversions of the mixing problem, i.e., the estimation of the mixing coefficients $\hat{\mathbf{a}}$, can be done by different approaches. Methods that minimize the reconstruction error

$$e(\hat{\mathbf{a}}) = \|\mathbf{y} - \mathbf{X}\hat{\mathbf{a}}\|^2 \tag{17.5}$$

are widely used. The least-squares method, which can be extended to fulfill the requirements of (17.2) and (17.3), belongs to this kind of algorithms. The nonnegativity constraint of the mixing coefficients is ensured by the nonnegativity constrained least-squares algorithm (NNLS) [6], the normalization is ensured by the sum-to-one constrained least-squares algorithm (SCLS) [7]. Both methods can be combined into the fully constrained least-squares method (FCLS), which meets both requirements.

Beside the least-squares approaches, there are methods based on stochastic models. Here, the unmixing problem is resolved by a maximum-likelihood estimator or by hierarchical Bayesian models [8]. The nonnegative matrix factorization (NMF) determines the endmember spectra and the mixing coefficients simultaneously and, hence, does not need any endmember spectra at all [9].

3 Extended signal model

The linear mixture model is extended to represent also spatial mixtures. Therefore, the linear mixture model is defined for the whole image instead of only for a single pixel. The linear mixture model in (17.1) is assumed to be valid for each pixel of the image. Hence, all signals $\mathbf{y}$ and the corresponding mixing coefficients $\mathbf{a}$ can be combined into matrices. This yields

$$\mathbf{Y} = \mathbf{X}\mathbf{A}, \tag{17.6}$$

where the columns of $\mathbf{Y}$ and $\mathbf{A}$ represent the signals and mixing coefficients of the single pixels. Here and in the following, the noise term is not mentioned for simplicity.

The individual images are acquired with different spectral and spatial resolutions and are combined in one common model. The effects caused by the different resolutions are called spectral and spatial mixing, respectively.

Spectral mixing   The spectral resolution describes the spectral sensitivity of the single sensor channels. This resolution is referred to as a spectral base resolution. For convenience, the spectral channels of the hyperspectral image sensor are used as the base resolution. Matrix $\mathbf{X}$ consists of the spectral signatures of the endmembers at base resolution. The specific spectral sensitivity of each channel of a camera is modeled as a linear combination of the channels in $\mathbf{X}$. This yields an adapted matrix of endmember signatures for each sensor

$$\mathbf{X}_i = \mathbf{C}_i \cdot \mathbf{X}. \tag{17.7}$$

Here, matrix $\mathbf{C}_i$ consists of the relative spectral sensitivities of camera i.

Spatial mixing   The spatial resolution of a sensor is affected by the region, out of which a signal of a pixel is composed. The signal of a pixel is written as linear combination of signals of a high spatial base resolution. For the linear mixing model, this can be regarded as a linear combination of the mixing coefficients $\mathbf{A}$. For the coefficients at lower resolution, this results in

$$\mathbf{A}_i = \mathbf{A} \cdot \mathbf{B}_i. \tag{17.8}$$

Matrix $\mathbf{B}_i$ describes the mixing of signals originating from different locations and can be derived from the point-spread function of the sensor.

3.1 Combination of spatial and spectral mixing

For each sensor with the spectral and spatial mixing effects described above, one has

$$\mathbf{Y}_i = \mathbf{X}_i\mathbf{A}_i = \mathbf{C}_i\mathbf{X} \cdot \mathbf{A}\mathbf{B}_i, \tag{17.9}$$

rearranging by using the Kronecker product yields

$$\mathrm{vec}\{\mathbf{Y}_i\} = \left(\mathbf{B}_i^{\mathsf{T}} \otimes \mathbf{C}_i\mathbf{X}\right) \cdot \mathrm{vec}\{\mathbf{A}\}. \tag{17.10}$$

Here, the operator $\text{vec}\{\mathbf{Z}\}$ denotes the column representation of matrix $\mathbf{Z}$ by stacking the columns of $\mathbf{Z}$ into a single column vector, and $\otimes$ stands for the Kronecker product.

In this representation, the signals of multiple sensors can be combined by stacking the vectors and matrices column-wise:

$$\underbrace{\begin{bmatrix} \text{vec}\{\mathbf{Y}_1\} \\ \text{vec}\{\mathbf{Y}_2\} \\ \vdots \\ \text{vec}\{\mathbf{Y}_k\} \end{bmatrix}}_{\bar{\mathbf{y}}} = \underbrace{\begin{bmatrix} \mathbf{B}_1^T \otimes \mathbf{C}_1 \mathbf{X} \\ \mathbf{B}_2^T \otimes \mathbf{C}_2 \mathbf{X} \\ \vdots \\ \mathbf{B}_k^T \otimes \mathbf{C}_k \mathbf{X} \end{bmatrix}}_{\bar{\mathbf{X}}} \cdot \underbrace{\text{vec}\{\mathbf{A}\}}_{\bar{\mathbf{a}}} . \tag{17.11}$$

This yields a common linear model

$$\bar{\mathbf{y}} = \bar{\mathbf{X}}\,\bar{\mathbf{a}} \tag{17.12}$$

that needs to be solved. As this problem is similar to the linear mixing model, the approaches for spectral unmixing described above can be used to solve it.

4 Studies

The proposed method for fusing different images is illustrated and evaluated with an example. Therefor, images of different spectral and spatial resolution need to be created.

4.1 Example data

Five different materials with spectra shown in Fig. 17.1 are evaluated. The spectra were extracted from a single hyperspectral image of minerals. For further evaluation, a simulated image is created, which consists of 100×100 pixels at the highest spatial resolution. The spatial distribution of the five mixing coefficients is shown in Fig. 17.2 and were chosen based on the examples in [3]. The brighter a pixel the higher the contribution of the endmember to the overall signal of the pixel. Every material is represented by a pure pixel. The other pixels are mixtures of multiple materials. The mixing coefficients fulfill the constraints in (17.2) and (17.3).

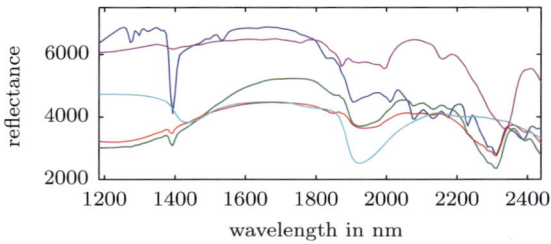

Figure 17.1: Spectra of endmembers.

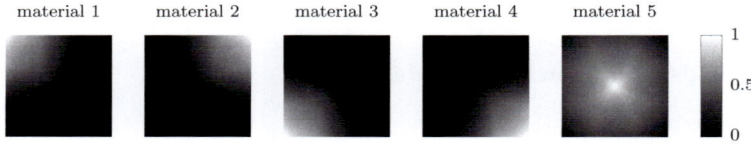

Figure 17.2: Spatial distribution of mixing coefficients for the different materials.

Different signals can be simulated with the spectra shown in Fig. 17.1 and the mixing coefficients shown in Fig. 17.2. Gaussian noise is added to the signal to account for sensor noise. The signal-to-noise ratio (SNR) is the ratio of half the mean signal value to the standard deviation of the noise (compare [3]). Unless otherwise stated, the SNR is 50 : 1.

4.2 Evaluation

Different measures can be used to evaluate the results of spectral unmixing algorithms. As simulated data is used, measures can be determined on the error of the mixing coefficients and on the reconstructed image signal. Therefor, the root-mean-square error of the estimated mixing coefficients can be used. The ERGAS index is another widely used error measure for the fusion of images of different spatial and spectral resolutions [10]:

$$\text{ERGAS} = 100 \cdot \frac{h}{l} \cdot \sqrt{\frac{1}{K} \sum_{k=1}^{K} \frac{\text{RMSE}(Y_k))^2}{\overline{Y}_k^2}} \,. \tag{17.13}$$

Here, h is the spatial resolution of the high-resolution image and l the resolution of the low-resolution image. $RMSE(Y_k)$ stands for the RMSE of the k-th channel of the reconstructed image, $\overline{Y}_k$ denotes the mean value of a channel. Unlike the RMSE of the mixing coefficients, the ER-GAS index is related to the reconstitute image and not to the mixing coefficients themselves. The lower the values of the ERGAS index the better the fusion of the two images.

4.3 Impact of the resolution

A scenario with one hyperspectral and one multispectral camera is evaluated. The spectral resolution of the hyperspectral camera is the same as the one of the base resolution, i.e., 200 channels. The spatial resolution is smaller than the base resolution. A single pixel of the hyperspectral image is composed of 6×6 pixels of the base resolution. The number of channels of the multispectral camera and its spatial resolution are modified. To minimize the spatial correlation of the mixing coefficients, the image pixels are randomized spatially. Figure 17.3 shows the RMSE of the mixing coefficients for different resolutions of the multispectral sensor with a varying number of spectral channels.

One can see that the effect of the additional image is higher the higher

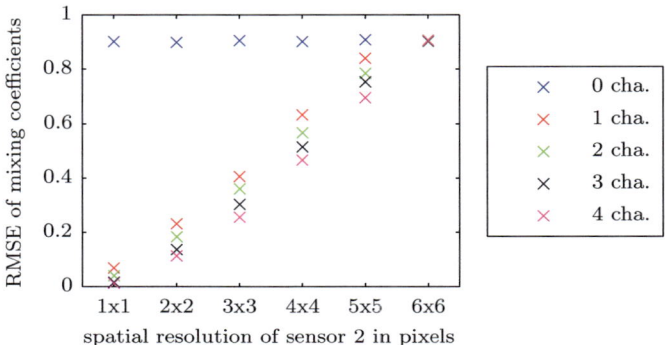

Figure 17.3: RMSE as a function of the spatial resolution of the multispectral sensor and its number of spectral channels in combination with a hyperspectral sensor with a spatial resolution of 6×6 pixels.

the spatial resolution. For all spatial resolutions, the RMSE is lower than when using only the hyperspectral sensor. The RMSE decreases with an increasing number of channels of the multispectral sensor.

4.4 Impact of the algorithms

To evaluate the different algorithms, a different scenario is used. Here, a hyperspectral image with 200 channels is combined with a multi-spectral image with 3 channels. The spatial resolution of the hyper-spectral image is 3×3 pixels and 1×1 for the multispectral image, respectively. Four different algorithms are compared. Firstly, the un-constrained least-squares algorithm (UCLS), NNLS and FCLS, all de-scribed above. The fourth algorithm is a successive algorithm (sFCLS), which at first solves the hyperspectral image with low resolution and subsequently solves the high resolution image constrained by the first result. The results in terms of the RMSE and ERGAS index are listed in Tab. 17.1.

	UCLS	NNLS	FCLS	sFCLS
ERGAS	1.13	1.12	0.81	0.81
RMSE	0.16	0.16	0.11	0.11

Table 17.1: ERGAS index and RMSE for unmixing results with different al-gorithms. The results were obtained with the combination of a hyperspectral image with resolution 3×3 and a multispectral image with 3 channels and a resolution of 1×1.

UCLS and NNLS yield similar results. The same holds for FCLS and sFCLS. The unmixing result of the FCLS algorithms is better than the one of the unconstrained algorithm. There is no big difference of the combined and the successive variant of the FCLS algorithm. However, the advantage of the combined method is the possibility to apply it to more than two images.

5 Summary

An extended mixing model based on the linear mixing model and spec-tral unmixing was proposed. It can be used to jointly unmix image signals of different spatial and spectral resolutions. Thereby, an improvement of the unmixing result can be achieved in applications where there is sufficient spectral information, but too low spatial information. The proposed method is fully based on the mixing model which has been established in remote sensing applications for object classification. Hence, many remote sensing methods can also be used for analysis of the material composition in visual inspection.

The proposed sensor model can be easily extended to multiple sensors. An extension by image registration and other spatial transformations is also possible. Different sensor noise models can be considered when solving the unmixing problem. The possibility of applying the methods to non-linear mixing models and the benefit for the final classification will be further investigated.

References

1. I. Amro, J. Mateos, M. Vega, R. Molina, and A. K. Katsaggelos, "A survey of classical methods and new trends in pansharpening of multispectral images," *EURASIP Journal on Advances in Signal Processing*, vol. 1, no. 79, pp. 1–22, 2011.

2. N. Keshava, "A survey of spectral unmixing algorithms," *Lincoln Laboratory Journal*, vol. 14, no. 1, pp. 55–78, 2003.

3. A. Plaza, P. Martínez, R. Pérez, and J. Plaza, "A quantitative and comparative analysis of endmember extraction algorithms from hyperspectral data," *IEEE Transactions on Geoscience and Remote Sensing*, vol. 42, no. 3, pp. 650–663, Mar. 2004.

4. C.-I. Chang and Q. Du, "Estimation of number of spectrally distinct signal sources in hyperspectral imagery," *IEEE Transactions on Geoscience and Remote Sensing*, vol. 42, no. 3, pp. 608–619, Mar. 2004.

5. A. Halimi, Y. Altmann, N. Dobigeon, and J.-Y. Tourneret, "Nonlinear unmixing of hyperspectral images using a generalized bilinear model," *IEEE Transactions on Geoscience and Remote Sensing*, vol. 49, no. 11, pp. 4153–4162, Nov. 2011.

6. R. Bro and S. De Jong, "A fast non-negativity-constrained least squares algorithm," *Journal of Chemometrics*, vol. 11, no. 5, pp. 393–401, Sep. 1997.

7. E. Ashton and A. Schaum, "Algorithms for the detection of sub-pixel targets in multispectral imagery," *Photogrammetric Engineering & Remote Sensing*, vol. 64, no. 7, pp. 723–731, 1998.

8. N. Dobigeon, J.-Y. Tourneret, and C.-I. Chang, "Semi-supervised linear spectral unmixing using a hierarchical Bayesian model for hyperspectral imagery," *IEEE Transactions on Signal Processing*, vol. 56, no. 7, pp. 2684–2695, 2008.

9. V. P. Pauca, J. Piper, and R. J. Plemmons, "Nonnegative matrix factorization for spectral data analysis," *Linear Algebra and its Applications*, vol. 416, no. 1, pp. 29–47, Jul. 2006.

10. L. Wald, "Quality of high resolution synthesised images: Is there a simple criterion?" in *Proceedings of the third conference "Fusion of Earth data: merging point measurements, raster maps and remotely sensed images"*, T. Ranchin and L. Wald, Eds., 2000, pp. 99–103.

Understanding multi-spectral images of wood particles with matrix factorization

Mark Asbach[1], Dirk Mauruschat[2] and Burkhard Plinke[2]

[1] Fraunhofer IAIS,
Schloss Birlinghoven, 53754 Sankt Augustin
[2] Fraunhofer WKI,
Bienroder Weg 54 E, 38108 Braunschweig

Abstract Multispectral image data can be used to quantify the concentrations of chemical substances in material compounds by differential spectroscopy. In this paper, we describe Simplex Volume Maximization (SiVM), a matrix factorization method derived from Archetypal Analysis (AA), that is well suited to separate spectra. Exemplarily, we apply the technique to multispectral images of wood strands partially covered with adhesives and wood-polymer composites and show how to determine the concentration of the adhesives and how to distinguish the polymer types.

In the multispectral domain, our objective is to separate the spectral characteristics of the adhesives and polymers from those spectral components caused by variation in the natural wood, including differences in moisture.

Our experiments show that wood particles with different concentrations of adhesives or different polymer components can be distinguished after applying SiVM-based factorization to NIR spectral imaging. We therefore conclude that this technique has great potential for quality control applications that rely on multispectral imaging.

1 Introduction

Wood is an important raw material for the enterprises producing particle boards and other wood-based material like e.g. wood polymer composites (WPC). Because wood is an eco-friendly renewable material many efforts in research and development take place to reduce production costs [1] and to increase possibilities for recycling [2].

Spectral imaging in the near-infrared range (NIR) is one of many measurement techniques with great potential for classification and sorting processes [3]. However, the requirements are much higher than e.g. in recycling of plastic packages, because better resolution is needed and because the signals acquired by NIR cameras are superposed by optical scattering due to rough surfaces and statistical/temperature noise in the detector. The "classical" method to classify spectra using chemometric methods like linear filtering and principal component analysis (PCA) works but has its limitations [4]. Especially for wood particles improved methods would help to optimize wood products and to increase the recycling rate.

In addition to improved classification performance, a second motivation to use alternative methods results from the fact, that classical subspace transformation methods like PCA result in numerical representations of the data that have no physical meaning and are hard to interpret. In contrast, non-negative matrix factorization (NMF) has been shown to provide meaningful results, if the data are inherently non-negative [5]. But because the underlying problem is NP hard [6], optimal solutions are costly to obtain for real-world problems. Instead, recent extensions to NMF introduce additional constraints on the basis vectors to reduce the search space. Several of these extensions have been demonstrated successfully on hyperspectral image data for remote-sensing applications [7,8].

In order to obtain a meaningful decomposition of the multispectral NIR imagery with low algorithmical complexity, we apply Archetypal Analysis (AA) [9] or rather its approximative implementation Simplex Volume Maximization (SiVM) [10]. SiVM requires efforts of only $O(kn)$ to derive basis functions and was shown to provide highly accurate reconstructions [11].

2 Wood particles

Two tasks are presented here as examples where the evaluation of multispectral image data could be improved by new approaches for factorization and classification:

2.1 Adhesive coverage of wood strands

Oriented strand boards (OSB) are made from big wood particles (e.g. 120mm $\times$ 25mm $\times$ 0.8mm) in automatic production lines. Emulgated adhesive (or resin) is sprayed onto the surface of the strands while they pass a rotating drum, then the strands are oriented and formed to a mat on a conveyor, pass a continuous hot press and leave it as particle boards. The board quality depends on many manufacturing conditions. An important one is the adhesive distribution on the strands before the mat enters the press.

But the adhesive is "visible" only in the NIR range by using spectral cameras and detection methods which are suitable also for the surface of an OSB mat. Figure 18.3 shows a scene with strands made from aspen wood and partially covered with urea-formaldehyde (UF) resin. The adhesive concentrations, based on the dry mass of wood, were 0% (definitely too low), 6% (good concentration) and 12% (too high because resin is an important cost factor). These concentrations are estimated from the amount of glue added to the rotary drum, but cannot be deduced from the visible light image.

2.2 Detection of different polymer types in WPC granulate

Wood polymer composites (WPC) consist of approx. 50 to 70 mass percent wood fibers and a polymer component, e.g. polyethylene (PE), polypropylene (PP), polyvinyl chloride (PVC), or a bio-based polymer like poly-L-lactic acid (PLLA). They are produced in a compounding/extrusion process as profiles and can substitute solid wood in applications as terrace deckings, windows, and door frames or car interior parts. Recycling of WPC has proven to be possible. However, methods for material management and especially for grading and sorting are not yet available, and therefore most of the material is only reused as fuel [12].

Developments for WPC sorting are ongoing but require a sorting or grading method for WPC granulate to make sure that the material stream is free of impurities and contains only one polymer component. The second example in Fig. 18.4 shows WPC granulate with four types of polymer components (from top to bottom: PLLA, PVC, PP, PE) which can not be distinguished in the visible light range.

3 Multispectral image decomposition

We interpret multispectral imaging as a discrete form of reflectance spectroscopy: a sample reflects light to a sensor that measures a discrete reflectance spectrum per pixel. A multispectral image with F spectral bands is then represented as a matrix $X = [x_1, x_2, \ldots, x_N]$ of N pixels $x_n \in \mathbb{R}^F$.

The run of the spectrum is characteristic of the chemical substance under investigation. For a mixture of different substances, the measured spectrum is a weighted sum of the individual spectra. If a pixel x_n shows a mixture of K chemical components with reflectance spectra $s_k \in \mathbb{R}^F$ and mixture weights w_{nk}, the pixel can be expressed as a linear combination

$$x_n = w_{n1}s_1 + w_{n2}s_2 + \cdots + w_{nK}s_K = SW_n, \tag{18.1}$$

with

$$w_{nk} \geqslant 0, \sum_K w_{nk} = 1.$$

This is schematically depicted in Fig. 18.1: A pure substance A shall have a flat spectral reflectivity of 0.8, thus reflecting 80 % of spectrally white light, while a second, pure substance B shall have a spectral reflectivity of 1.0 over all but a given spectral band, where it has a reflectivity of 0. When measuring the spectral reflectivity of a compound material consisting of 60% of substance A plus 40% of substance B, we expect a combined spectral reflectivity that is the linear combination of the pure spectra, weighted with the respective lots of the substances. For our assumed compound substance, we would therefore expect a spectral reflectivity of $0.88 = 0.6 \cdot 0.8 + 0.4 \cdot 1.0$ over most of the spectrum and

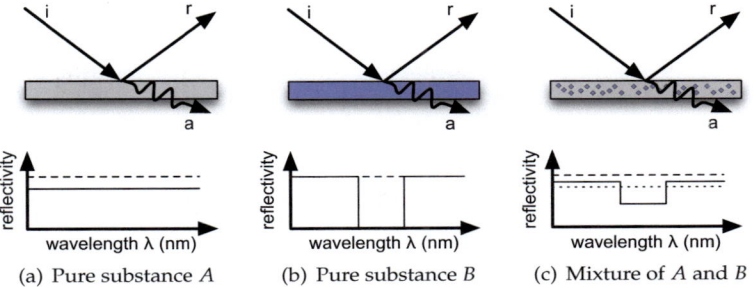

(a) Pure substance A (b) Pure substance B (c) Mixture of A and B

Figure 18.1: We consider three different, thick materials with diffuse surface scattering, where incident light i is split into a fraction a that is absorbed and a second part r that is reflected. The spectral reflectivity of a material mixture with 60% of substance A and 40% of substance B is considered to be the weighted sum of the spectral reflectivities of the pure substances.

$0.48 = 0.6 \cdot 0.8 + 0.4 \cdot 0$ over the band where substance B is fully absorbent.

4 Archetypal analysis

The spectra s_k of simple chemical substances are known, but natural materials like wood exhibit mixtures of a high number of components that can be learned from sample data only. Analogous to Equation 18.1, we approximate a multispectral image X with N pixels from K spectral components $s_k \in \mathbb{R}^F$ and K weights $w_k \in \mathbb{R}^F$ as

$$X \approx S \cdot W, \tag{18.2}$$

with

$$S = [s_1, s_2, \ldots, s_K], W = [w_1, w_2, \ldots, w_K]^T$$

with the approximation error $E = \min ||X - SW||^2$. While non-negative matrix factorization (NMF) provides a solution to Equation 18.2 satisfying the physical requirements for the spectra s_k, convex-NMF [13] and

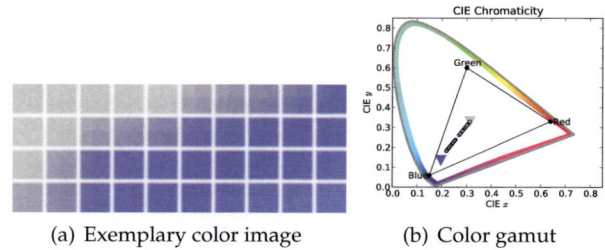

(a) Exemplary color image   (b) Color gamut

Figure 18.2: Color mixing example: All pixel colors in (a) can be composed as linear combination of two archetypal colors light blue and light gray (triangular color entries in (b)). They form the convex hull (here: a line) enclosing all other pixel colors.

convex-hull-NMF [14] further guarantee meaningful weights w_k satisfying the requirements for w_{nk} from Equation 18.1.

The resulting spectra s_k typically coincide with actual data points x_n, which makes convex-hull-NMF representations readily interpretable: If an individual image location n' exist, at which only a single substance k is present, the discrete spectrum of this substance $s_k = x_{n'}$ resides on the convex hull of all data points x_n.

For illustrational purposes, we can interpret RGB colors as a colorspace with three spectral bands. Figure 18.2 depicts an image containing various colors mixed from light blue and light gray. As can be seen from the gamut diagram, these colors represent data points in a subspace of the full RGB spectrum. The "pure" colors light blue and light gray reside on the convex hull. Given an image like the one depicted in Fig. 18.2(a), our goal is to find the "pure" colors and to unmix the colors of all pixel spectra. Archetypal Analysis (AA) is a method that selects suitable data points as basis functions for the above mentioned convexity-constrained matrix factorization techniques. We use its speeded up derivate—Simplex Volume Maximization (SiVM)—to quickly identify archetypal datapoints in our multispectral image data. Then, all other pixels of the image can be approximated by linear combinations of the archetypes. By definition, all resulting coefficients are of the range $[0, 1]$ and we can interpret them as relative amount of "pure" ingredients (archetypes) used to "mix" a certain pixel's spectrum.

5 Results

We apply the Archetypal Analysis to two material characterization problems from the woodworking industry.

5.1 Adhesive coverage of wood strands

In our first experiment, we seek to analyze the glue coverage of wood strands. Data were acquired with an InGaAs line scan camera that records 316 spectral bands in the near infrared (NIR) range between 1032 nm and 1656 nm. The image depicted in Fig. 18.3 shows about twenty strands of aspen wood. Four strands are covered with $\approx$ 6%, four other strands are covered with $\approx$ 12% of adhesive.

With Simplex Volume Maximization, 15 archetypes were extracted from the pixel spectra. We expect to need several different archetypes to model the spectra of the wooden texture, the spectrum of the adhesives, moisture, image background, and the spectrum of the graphite used to mark the strands. Using a slightly higher number of archetypes allows to model shadows, specular highlights, and noise as well. Figure 18.3(c) and Fig. 18.3(d) show archetype s_{13} and the corresponding mixture weights w_{13}, that seem to model the absorption spectrum of wood covered with $\approx$ 12% adhesives.

The 15-dimensional SiVM space can be used to classify image pixels based on the adhesives coverage. Exemplarily, we have marked small regions with known (compare section 2) glue coverage as training data for a simple nearest-neighbor classifier (light green is used for 12% and dark green for 6%). In addition, areas showing strands not covered with adhesives were marked with light blue and visible background marked in light grey. The trained classifier was then used to predict the glue coverage of all other image pixels. Classification result and training data (marked by boxes) are depicted in Fig. 18.3(b).

5.2 Detection of different polymer types in WPC granulate

In a second experiment, we use the same method to disambiguate pellets made from wood fibres and different sorts of polymers. WPC pellets with four different polymer components (PLLA, PVC, PP, and PE

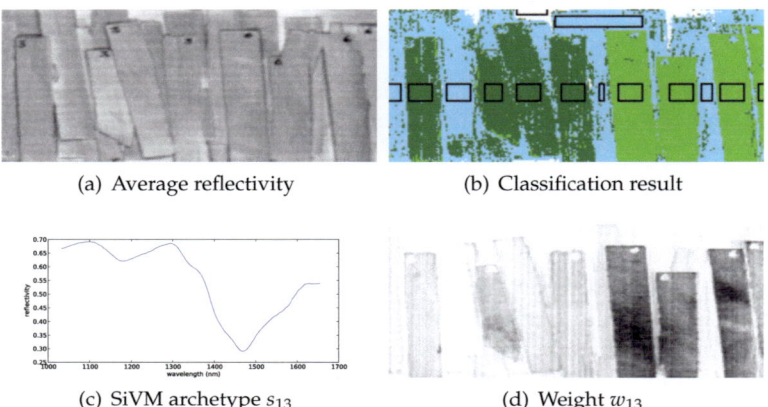

(a) Average reflectivity   (b) Classification result

(c) SiVM archetype s_{13} (d) Weight w_{13}

Figure 18.3: Wood strands, partially covered with adhesives. The adhesive is transparent in visible light as well as in the averaged NIR reflectivity (a). After decomposition with SiVM into 15 basis functions and training a nearest-neighbor classifier (training regions marked with black boxes), it can be predicted for the whole image (b). An exemplary basis function (c) with corresponding weight (d) seems to model adhesive concentration quite well.

respectively) have been placed in a wooden box together with paper labels. The wooden box has walls that cast shadows on part of the scenery and the whole setup is far from an ideal laboratory environment but nevertheless closer to industrial conditions. We chose it to illustrate the resilience of our method against adverse data acquisition conditions. The image data was captured with an Extended-InGaAs line scan camera with a spectral resolution of 248 bands in the range of 1161 nm to 2262 nm, of which the 20 lowest and 25 highest wavelengths were discarded because of extremely low signal-to-noise ratio.

Again, SiVM with 15 archetypes was used in combination with a nearest-neighbor classifier to learn the characteristics of the different plastics from some image pixels and predict it for the remainder of the image. Figure 18.4 depicts the wood-plastic-compound (WPC) dataset, including classification result and an exemplary archetype. Archetype 13—depicted in Fig. 18.4(d)—shows contributions in the area of PLLA pellets.

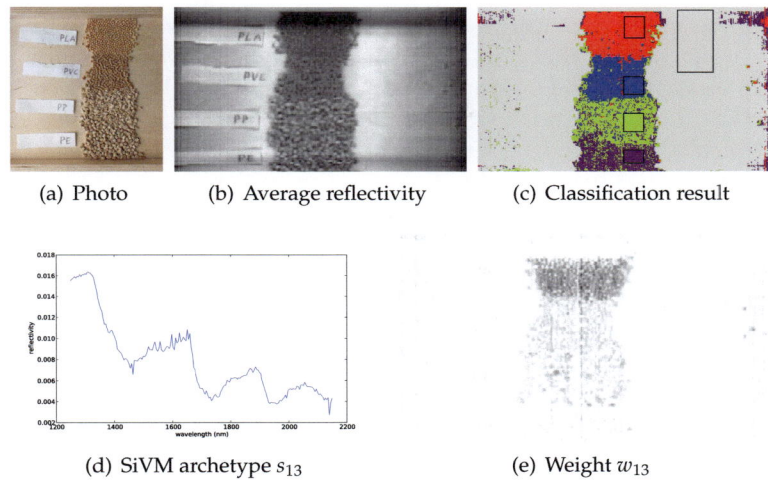

(a) Photo   (b) Average reflectivity   (c) Classification result

(d) SiVM archetype s_{13} (e) Weight w_{13}

Figure 18.4: Composite pellets made from PLLA, PVC, PP, and PE, in a wooden box. From a conventional color photo (a) or the averaged NIR reflectivity (b), polymer components can not be estimated. The decomposition of the multispectral NIR image with SiVM into 15 basis functions, however, allows classification even with a simple nearest-neighbor classifier. Training data (black boxes) and result are shown in (c). An exemplary basis function is depicted together with its corresponding weights in (d) and (e).

The nearest-neighbor classification result was obtained by selecting per class one rectangular image region as training samples. The wooden box was learned from a slightly larger region. Overall, this— really simple—attempt already results in acceptable classification performance. Errors are only visible in shadowed areas. As the pellets themselves generate small shadows, classification errors looking like speckle noise are observed especially in the area of PP and PE pellets.

6 Summary

In this paper, we have demonstrated the application of Archetypal Analysis (AA) / Simplex Volume Maximization (SiVM), a matrix factorization method, to multi-spectral image analysis for wooden materials. It was shown that adhesive concentrations on wood strands and polymer types in WPC granulates can be distinguished with simple classification algorithms using the image decompositions derived from SiVM/AA.

The proposed method allows for a better understanding of the multispectral image decomposition than standard methods from chemometry. And while the latter are usually sensitive to outliers, surface and acquisition conditions rather than to the chemical composition of the material, the proposed approach appears to deliver predictable results, invariant to small changes in the initialization.

An objective for future research will be to quantitatively evaluate the algorithms—shown here as a prove-of-concept—on a larger set of image data and to optimize the computational performance.

References

1. J. Aderhold and B. Plinke, "Innovative methods for quality control in the wood-based panel industry," in *Wood-based Panels: An Introduction for Specialists*, H. Thoemen, M. Irle, and M. Sernek, Eds.   London: Brunel Univ. Press, 2010, pp. 225–249.

2. P. Meinlschmidt and B. Plinke, "Optical infrared detection of contaminations in recovered wood," in *Sensor Based Sorting*, Aachen, 2012.

3. S. Wendel and B. Plinke, in *7. Kolloquium Prozessanalytik*, Linz.

4. B. Plinke and D. Ben Yacov, "Detection of adhesives on wood surfaces: Spatially resolved monitoring of adhesive application," in *Adhesion Adhesives & Sealants*, vol. 4, 2010, pp. 25–29.

5. D. Lee and S. Seung, "Learning the Parts of Objects by Non-Negative Matrix Factorization," *Nature*, vol. 401, no. 6755, pp. 788–791, 1999.

6. S. Vavasis, "On the Complexity of Nonnegative Matrix Factorization," *SIAM J. on Optimization*, vol. 20, no. 3, pp. 1364–1377, 2009.

7. L. Miao and H. Qi, "Endmember Extraction From Highly Mixed Data Using Minimum Volume Constrained Nonnegative Matrix Factorization," *IEEE Trans. on Geoscience and Remote Sensing*, vol. 45, no. 3, pp. 765–777, 2007.

8. J. Nascimento and J. B. Dias, "Vertex Component Analysis: A Fast Algorithm to Unmix Hyperspectral Data," *IEEE Trans. on Geoscience and Remote Sensing*, vol. 43, no. 4, pp. 898–910, 2005.

9. A. Cutler and L. Breiman, "Archetypal Analysis," *Technometrics*, vol. 36, no. 4, pp. 338–347, 1994.

10. C. Bauckhage and C. Thurau, "Making Archetypal Analysis Practical," in *Pattern Recognition*, ser. LNCS, J. Denzler and G. Notni, Eds., vol. 5748. Springer, 2009, pp. 272–281.

11. C. Thurau, K. Kersting, and C. Bauckhage, "Yes We Can – Simplex Volume Maximization for Descriptive Web-Scale Matrix Factorization," in *Proc. ACM CIKM*, 2010.

12. C. Gahle, "Wpc: Recyclingfrage noch nicht abschließend geklärt," *Holz-Zentralblatt*, pp. 253–254, 2009.

13. C. Ding, T. Li, and M. Jordan, "Convex and Semi-Nonnegative Matrix Factorizations," *IEEE Trans. on Pattern Analalysis and Machine Intelligence*, vol. 32, no. 1, pp. 45–55, 2010.

14. C. Thurau, K. Kersting, and C. Bauckhage, "Convex Non-Negative Matrix Factorization in the Wild," in *Proc. IEEE ICDM*, 2009.

A framework for storage, visualization and analysis of multispectral data

Stephan Irgenfried[1] and Christian Negara[2]

[1] Karlsruhe Institute of Technology KIT,
Institute of Process Control and Robotics IPR,
Engler-Bunte-Ring 8, D-76131 Karlsruhe
[2] Fraunhofer Institute of Optronics, System Technologies and Image
Exploitation, Fraunhoferstr. 1, D-76131 Karlsruhe

Abstract In this paper we describe our database centered workflow for acquisition, enrichment, long-term storage and web-based analysis of multi- and hyperspectral image data and measurement metadata. We propose a standardized way of storing large amounts of measurement data using a hybrid approach consisting of a relational database and direct file access through a common data access layer. Data import and export is performed by either using proprietary file formats like ENVI or by using an universal XML-based data format. To allow preview and analysis of image data, a web-based application has been developed which supersedes the need for client-side installation of tools like MATLAB to perform spectral or spatial analysis of the data while still allowing third-party applications to retrieve data from the database to perform in-depth analysis like automated filter design. Successful implementation of the workflow is demonstrated by the example of rapid application development for mineral sorting.

1 Introduction

While classification of materials based on their spectral reflectance properties has been an area of research in remote sensing applications for a long time, it is attracting more and more attention in the area of industrial applications, e.g. sorting materials as part of the recycling process, quality assurance in food production or enrichment of primary resources. Common to those applications is the need to measure the reflectance spectrum of the materials to be detected using appropriate equipment and to analyze the acquired data to define classification features and optical filters. To be able to build productive and robust applications, the whole process from sample selection and spectral measurement as well as data storage and analysis up to filter and application design has to be taken into account and is preferably standardized. In this work we propose a workflow for this process, describe our implementation and present results. We especially focus on a solution for the long term raw measurement data storage, which tackles the problem of the loss of measurement information over time as described by Michener and Brunt [1]. The rest of the article is organzied as follows: in Chapter 2 related work is discussed. Chapter 3 describes our approach and the implementation details. In chapter 4 we finish with a summary and an outlook on future work.

2 Related work

Acquiring, storing and analyzing hyperspectral information has a long history in remote sensing applications. A couple of databases have been set up to make hyperspectral material information publically available, e.g the ASTER spectral library [2], USGS digital spectral library [3], hyperspectral.info [4], SPECCHIO [5], Vegetation Spectral Library [6]. Also background work on the design and implementation of hyperspectral databases, metadata and measurement process was published by some authors, e.g. Ruby [7] or Pfitzner [8, 9], who introduced 12 rules to be taken into account when measuring and storing hyperspectral data. There are some very good analysis and visualization tools for multispectral data available like the Environment for Visualizing Images (ENVI) [10] and Gerbil [11]. Also the use of MATLAB [12] is very common. While all these programs are desktop applications and mostly used by experts in the image processing or statistical domain, our software is designed to provide some basic visualization tools, e.g the mean spectral reflectance and its standard deviation, to anybody via a user-friendly web application replacing the need for installation of dedicated analysis software on the user computer.

3 Our work

Within our work we focus on design and implementation of a consistent workflow for hyperspectral data to improve long term availabilty of measurement data and to support analysis and application development. Fig. 19.1 gives a basic overview of our framework which will be described in more detail in the following chapters.

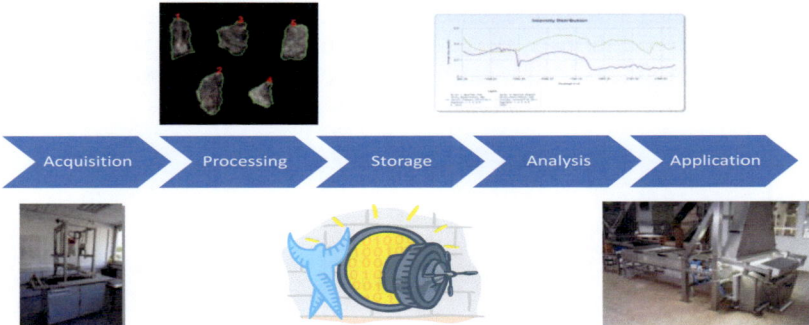

Figure 19.1: A consistent workflow from data acquisition to application development.

3.1 Data acquisition

The data acquisition is performed in the lab at the Fraunhofer IOSB with different types of sensors: There are high speed and high resolution RGB cameras, single-channel UV/NIR cameras and low speed and low resolution hyperspectral cameras ranging from 240-400nm, 366-720nm and 1000-2500nm. The data processing chain consists of the following semi-automatic steps to prepare measured data to be imported to the database:

White balance, outlier detection and normalization

To get comparable results, the spectra have to be normalized. This is obvious when using different measurement stations, but also has to be done for measurements using only one spectrometer, because the illumination might change. The spectra are normalized to the interval $[0, 1]$ because the sensors have different dynamic ranges. The white balance is computed in two steps. For every hyperspectral image I, an image I_w of a shading bar is also acquired. I is a function that maps x, y, λ to an intensity value, whereas x, y define the pixel position and λ the wavelength. Because in our lab we only use line sensors for multispectral data acquisition, the x-value defines the position on the line, the y-value defines a time-line which results from moving the probe on a linear table through the viewing plane of the camera. After subtracting the dark current, the following formula is used to compute the white balanced image I' from the original image I:

$$I'(x, y, \lambda) = \frac{I(x, y, \lambda)}{\bar{I}_w(x, \lambda)} \cdot \frac{t_w}{t} \tag{19.1}$$

$$\bar{I}_w(x, \lambda) := \frac{\sum\limits_{y} I_w(x, y, \lambda)}{\sum\limits_{y} 1}$$

t, t_w are the respective exposure times. The normalization function $\bar{I}_w(x, \lambda)$, which is computed from the image of the shading bar, is invariant of y because the illumination effects don't change during the movement of the linear table. In the literature some further normalizations like the spectral gradient [11] or the division by the cumulative intensity [13] are applied to remove the effects of the illumination or object geometry. Some of these normalizations are not always applicable, because they assume a hyperspectral image as input data, but we often only use up to four discrete wavelength bands in our sorting machines. Another drawback is the loss of the cumulative intensity information, which can be an important feature for classification, especially when only a few bands are measured.

The image I' is normalized according to the shading bar. Therefore the spectrum has to be divided by the reflectance spectrum $R(x, \lambda)$ of the shading bar:

$$I''(x, y, \lambda) = \frac{I'(x, y, \lambda)}{R(x, \lambda)} \tag{19.2}$$

Outlier detection is another important preprocessing step. The hyperspectral sensors may have some defect pixels which are known and return invalid (e.g. constant) intensity values. But also over- and underexposed pixels with intensities near the extrema of the dynamic range have to be marked as invalid. To be able to use formula (19.1), the intensity has to be linearly dependent from exposure time. Hence, depending on the sensor characteristics, upper and lower thresholds exist, which define the valid intensity range. All other pixel values in I are marked as invalid and ignored in later steps.

Registration

If the probe is measured with different sensors (e.g. at different wave length ranges), the multispectral images have to be registered to be able to compute correlations between these ranges. This is done via a semi-automatic algorithm written in MATLAB. First, the user marks some corresponding object points in the multispectral images. Because the spectrum ranges of the sensors do not necessarily overlap, the intensity values can't be directly compared. Therefore, the two images are first converted to edge-images using a sobel filter. If E_x is the edge-image resulting from using a vertical sobel filter and E_y from using a horizontal sobel filter, the orientation independent gradient magnitude image is computed by:

$$E = \sqrt{E_x^2 + E_y^2} \qquad (19.3)$$

For every band of the multispectral images a corresponding edge-image is computed and afterwards the edge-images are averaged. The two resulting grayscaled images are normalized to the interval [0,1] because different materials can induce small differences in one spectrum but big difference in the other. The transformation matrix between the two hyperspectral images is computed with MATLAB by maximizing the cross correlation value of the grayscale edge-images. Because we deal only with line scan sensors the search space of the tranformation matrices can be reduced to affine transformations.

Segmentation

The resulting image of a measurement typically contains objects of the same material or different materials as shown in Fig. 19.4. The objects are segmented using a multimodal segmentation algorithm based on the algorithm described by Boykov and Funca-Lea [14]. All bands of the registered images are compound into a single stacked image. The algorithm works as follows:

- The user marks pixels which defintely belong to the background and pixels which belong to the foreground
- An energy minimization algorithm computes a foreground/background separation of the pixels in the image
- To remove very small foreground objects, a pixel is only marked as foreground if the pixels in the neighborhood are also foreground pixels. The neighborhood is defined by a mask with variable size.
- The foreground/background separation is used to number the objects in the image by computing the connected components of the foreground pixels.
- The user has the possibility to manually change the object numbering or assign objects to the background.

The foreground/background separation problem can be described as the MAP (maximum a posteriori) solution x^* of a markov random field:

$$p(x|y = \hat{y}) = p(x|\hat{y}) = \frac{p(\hat{y}|x)p(x)}{p(\hat{y})} \tag{19.4}$$

$$x^* = \max_x p(x|\hat{y})p(x) \tag{19.5}$$

$x = (x_0, \ldots, x_n)$ is a random vector which contains for every pixel a labeling $x_i \in \{Foreground, Background\}$. $\hat{y} = (\hat{y}_0, \ldots, \hat{y}_n)$ is the observed data. y_i is the spectrum of pixel i. $p(\hat{y})$ is a constant and can be discarded when computing the MAP. We use a 4-connected graph for the markov random field. Hence (19.4) can be factorized as:

$$p(x|\hat{y}) = \frac{1}{Z} \prod_i \psi(\hat{y}_i, x_i) \prod_{i,j \in \mathcal{N}} \phi(x_i, x_j) \cdot \frac{1}{p(\hat{y})} \tag{19.6}$$

The set $\mathcal{N}$ contains all edges of the graph, Z a normalization constant, and ϕ, ψ are interaction potentials. Applying log on both sides we obtain:

$$x^* = \max_x(\log p(x|\hat{y})) = \min_x(-\log p(x|\hat{y})) \qquad (19.7)$$

$$= \sum_i \underbrace{-\log \psi(\hat{y}_i, x_i)}_{=:E_d(x_i, \hat{y}_i)} + \sum_{i,j \in \mathcal{N}} \underbrace{-\log \phi(x_i, x_j)}_{=:E_s(x_i, x_j)} \qquad (19.8)$$

The data energy potential $E_d(x_i, \hat{y}_i)$ characterizes the compliance of the labeling of a pixel to its observed spectrum. If an arbitrary pixel in the image has a foreground label associated, then it should have a similar spectrum to the points, which were manually marked as foreground. The similarity of a pixel's spectrum to the spectra of the marked pixels is computed via k-NN search in $\mathbb{R}^s$ where s is the number of bands. The spectrum of every pixel x_i corresponds to a point $S(x_i)$ in $\mathbb{R}^s$ which is obtained from the intensity values of every band. For every pixel in the image the $k = 50$ marked pixels are searched, whose spectra match best i.e. have the smallest euclidean distance. $E_d(x_i = l, \hat{y}_i)$ is then set to the number of pixels whose label is l divided by k while $l \in \{Foreground, Background\}$. Instead of using the original spectra $S(x_i)$, the normalized spectra $\tilde{S}(x_i) = S(x_i)/||S(x_i)||$ are used. The cumulative intensity is discarded. This is needed because a human individual often marks pixels, which can be clearly recognized as foreground or background. Pixels at the border of the object are usually not marked, because their intensities are low due to poor illumination, unless an integrating sphere is used. By dividing by the cumulative intensity, all pixels of the same material have spectra which are very near in $\mathbb{R}^s$ independent of the surface orientation and therefore the cumulative intensity at those pixels.

The smooth potential $E_s(x_i, x_j)$ has to be a metric. The smooth potential has the following form:

$$E_s(x_i = l_i, x_j = l_j) = \begin{cases} 0 & \text{, if } l_i = l_j \\ \frac{\alpha ||S(x_i) - S(x_j)||^2}{2\sigma^2} & \text{, otherwise.} \end{cases} \qquad (19.9)$$

The term $||S(x_i) - S(x_j)||^2/2\sigma^2$ is derived from the logarithm of a normal distribution and σ is the sensor noise which is set to $1/256$. This value is derived from the quantization error of a 8 bit sensor. σ could also be assessed from the sensor specification. In contrast to the computation of E_d, the original spectra are used here. α is set to $1/5000$ to clearly prefer a low data potential over a low smooth potential because it proved to be more robust if hyperspectral images with many bands are used. x^* is computed using the graph-cut algorithm with α-expansion described in [15–17], which can be applied because E_s is a metric.

3.2 Data storage

Our main goal for the database is to develop a long term storage and sharing platform for spectral signatures of materials. A key feature is to store the full measurement raw data to work with arbitrary analysis software directly on it.

To avoid storing a large amount of raw pixel data in the relational database, causing it to grow fast and loose performance [18], we deciced to use a hybrid approach to store multispectral image data and metadata, shown in Fig. 19.2. While keeping measurement data in com-

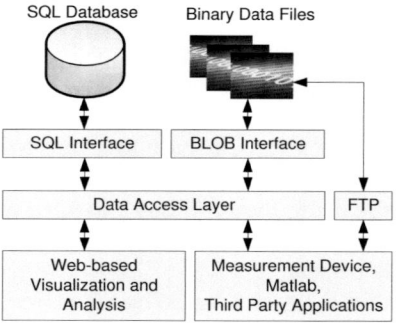

Figure 19.2: System overview of data storage and access.

pact binary files as created by the measuring device and accessing it with a fast binary data access library we store data that benefits from SQL Server query optimiziation and constraint checking in a relational database.

Compared to storing the measurement data and metadata in a filesystem structure, our approach of storing measurement data and metadata has several advantages:

- Increased flexibility using a data access layer. The data access layer allows changes to the database or the binary files without requiring changes on the client side.

- Improved access rights handling. Access rights to the data can be handled inside the data access layer. File system level permission handling is no longer required. In addition, database access can be regulated in fine detail.

- Metadata is stored in a relational database. Measurement metadata is stored in a relational database for improved query performance and data integrity checking. The metadata consists of 4 main groups of data:
  - Measurement related data e.g. materials, material groups, system operator, measurement device, project
  - Image related data e.g. object segmentation, file type, scaling information, color space.
  - Hardware related data e.g. spectrometer characteristics, white balance information, illumination parameters
  - Project related data e.g. projects, sites, operators, access rights

3.3 Data visualization and analysis

Another key feature of our application is the web-based visualization and analysis of multispectral measurement data. Besides a standard web browser no client side software installation is required to be able to browse the mulispectral image data and the metadata in the database. Standard analysis functionality includes e.g. intensity distributions or histograms of different materials, different material conditions or different measurements of a single material. Measurement series can be compared and the results are visualized as 2D-charts (Fig. 19.3). The web-based visualization is also capable of displaying the raw image data acquired by the camera as shown in Fig. 19.4. An intuitive slider control panel allows to quickly access a particular wavelength image

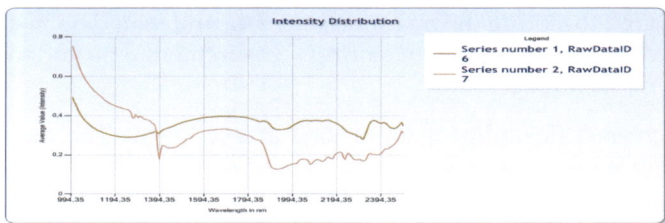

Figure 19.3: Intensity distribution for two different materials in the NIR and SWIR spectrum.

and data. The user can choose between a preview of the original image or showing only the labeled objects, hiding background and other objects. An additional feature shown in Fig. 19.4 is the possibility to create an RGB false color coded image by assigning intensity values of particular wavelengths to the R-,G- and B-channel of the resulting image thus allowing to better visualize spectral behaviour of the material. Based on our new mass storage infrastructure, the web-based visualiza-

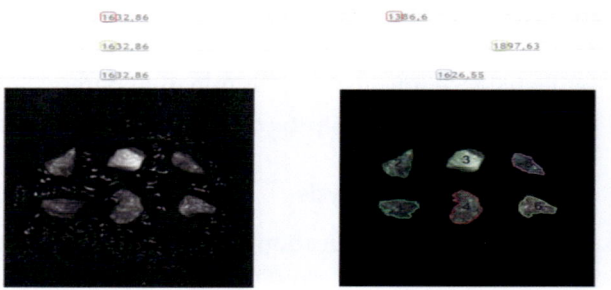

Figure 19.4: (Left) Preview of an intensity image for a selected wavelength including background and surrounding objects. (Right) False-Color display of labeled objects only with an overlay of object borders and object numbers.

tion and analysis allows fluent browsing through the database content and fast image and data preview while keeping load on database and webserver hardware as low as possible. The application is implemented using ASP.Net MVC.

4 Summary and outlook

We proposed a workflow and an infrastructure to acquire, enrich, store, analyze and retrieve multi- and hyperspectral measurement data. A working prototype implementation was presented. We're currently investigating how to improve binary data storage performance by using an object database.

Acknowledgements

Some of the software has been implemented as part of the student project ViMuDat. The authors thank the students Eva Wolkwitz, Angie Neumann, Niko Fellner, Marcus Gall, Anton Chalakov and Vivek Sharma for their valuable contributions.

References

1. W. K. Michener, J. W. Brunt, J. J. Helly, T. B. Kirchner, and S. G. Stafford, "Nongeospatial metadata for the ecological sciences," *ECOLOGICAL APPLICATIONS*, vol. 7, no. 1, pp. 330–342, 1997.

2. A. Baldridge, S. Hook, C. Grove, and G. Rivera, "The aster spectral library version 2.0," *Remote Sensing of Environment*, vol. 113, no. 4, pp. 711–715, 2009.

3. R. N. Clark, G. A. Swayze, R. Wise, E. Livo, T. Hoefen, R. Kokaly, and S. J. Sutley, "Usgs digital spectral library splib06a: U.s. geological survey, digital data series 231," Denver and CO and USA, 2007.

4. J. G. Ferwerda, "A free online reference library for hyperspectral reflectance signatures: A web-based interface for reference spectra of natural surfaces facilitates data sharing and increases access to reference material for classification," *SPIE Newsroom*, 2006.

5. A. Hüni, J. Nieke, J. Schopfer, M. Kneubühler, and K. I. Itten, "The spectral database specchio for improved long-term usability and data sharing," *Computers & Geosciences*, vol. 35, no. 3, pp. 557–565, 2009.

6. Vegetation Spectral Library, "Vegetation spectral library." [Online]. Available: http://spectrallibrary.utep.edu/

7. J. G. Ruby and R. L. Fischer, "Spectral signatures database for remote sensing applications," in *Imaging Spectrometry VIII*, ser. Proceedings of SPIE, S. S. Shen, Ed.   Seattle and WA and USA: SPIE, 2002, vol. 4816, pp. 156–163.

8. K. Pfitzner, R. Bartolo, Byan B., and A. Bollhöefer, "Issues to consider when designing a spectral library database," in *Spatial intelligence, innovation and praxis*, Spatial Sciences Institute, Ed., Melbourne, 2005.

9. K. Pfitzner, A. Bollhöfer, and G. Carr, "A standard design for collecting vegetation reference spectra: Implementation and implications for data sharing: Journal of spatial science," *Journal of Spatial Science*, vol. 51, no. 2, pp. 79–92, 2006.

10. Exelis Visual Information Solutions, "Envi." [Online]. Available: http://www.exelisvis.com/ProductsServices/ENVI.aspx

11. J. Jordan and E. Angelopoulou, "Gerbil - a novel software framework for visualization and analysis in the multispectral domain," in *Proceedings of the Vision, Modeling, and Visualization Workshop 2010*, R. Koch, A. Kolb, and C. Rezek-Salama, Eds.   Eurographics Association, 2010, pp. 259–266.

12. E. Arzuaga-Cruz, L. Jimenez-Rodriguez, M. Velez-Reyes, D. Kaeli, E. Rodriguez-Diaz, H. Velazquez-Santana, A. Castrodad-Carrau, L. Santos-Campis, and C. Santiago, "A matlab toolbox for hyperspectral image analysis," in *Proceedings of the Geoscience and Remote Sensing Symposium, 2004. IGARSS '04.*, vol. 7, 2004, pp. 4839–4842.

13. W. Kessler, *Multivariate Datenanalyse : für die Pharma-, Bio- und Prozessanalytik; ein Lehrbuch*.   Weinheim: Wiley-VCH, 2007.

14. Y. Boykov and G. Funka-Lea, "Graph cuts and efficient n-d image segmentation," *Int. J. Comput. Vision*, vol. 70, no. 2, pp. 109–131, Nov. 2006. [Online]. Available: http://dx.doi.org/10.1007/s11263-006-7934-5

15. Y. Boykov, O. Veksler, and R. Zabih, "Fast approximate energy minimization via graph cuts," *IEEE Transactions on Pattern Analysis and Machine Intelligence*, vol. 20, no. 11, pp. 1222–1239, 2001.

16. V. Kolmogorov and R. Zabih, "What energy functions can be minimized via graph cuts?" *IEEE Transactions on Pattern Analysis and Machine Intelligence*, vol. 26, pp. 147–159, 2004.

17. Y. Boykov and V. Kolmogorov, "An experimental comparison of min-cut/max- flow algorithms for energy minimization in vision," *Pattern Analysis and Machine Intelligence, IEEE Transactions on*, vol. 26, no. 9, pp. 1124–1137, sept. 2004.

18. R. Sears, C. van Ingen, and J. Gray, "To blob or not to blob: Large object storage in a database or a filesystem?"   17.06.2006. [Online]. Available: http://research.microsoft.com/pubs/64525/tr-2006-45.pdf

Potential of NIR hyperspectral imaging in the minerals industry

Christian Schropp[1], Henning Knapp[1] and Kilian Neubert[1]

RWTH Aachen, Aufbereitung mineralischer Rohstoffe,
Lochnerstraße 4-20, D-52064 Aachen

Abstract Material characterization by Near Infrared Hyperspectral Imaging (NIR HSI) is based on specific absorption features of different minerals. These absorption features are caused by the movement of molecular bondings of NIR active minerals on the material surface. Therefore, pollutions, such as dust and water, may influence the measurement outcome. An insufficient spatial resolution of the measurement can additionally falsify the hyperspectral image, because of mixed spectra effects at grain boundaries caused by the simultaneous collection of two or more spectra from unequal minerals. In order to compare NIR HSI to conventional analytical methods the above mentioned characteristics have to be investigated to reveal the potential of NIR HSI. The present paper describes investigation conducted on copper porphyry ore derived from the Kajaran copper mine, Armenia. During an extensive feasibility study rock samples are characterized by different measurement techniques. Two major analysis technologies are used for characterization including Mineral Liberation Analysis (MLA) and NIR HSI by using the Hyperspectral Imager SisuCHEMA (SPECIM) and Spotlight 400 FTIR Imaging System from Perkin Elmer. On basis of test-results derived from the feasibility study advantages and disadvantages of NIR HSI, in comparison to conventional measurement techniques in the minerals industry are discussed.

1 Introduction

To build up a process in the mineral processing industry, material characterisation is indispensable. Material characterisation is necessary to obtain all necessary material specifications to choose the optimum sorting criteria. Nowadays several analytical techniques are used for elemental (e.g. XRF (X-ray fluorescence)) or mineral component detection (e.g. MLA). Sensors used for material characterization cover most of the electromagnetic spectrum (EM).

The non-destructive Near Infrared Spectroscopy (NIRS), as a surface measurement technique allows the determination of molecular compositions and quantitative mixtures of a sample at any state. In addition to that NIRS sources are not hazardous to health in contrast to other methods [1]. Necessary sample preparation prior to analysis is reduced or can even be neglected. NIRS is a rapidly operating measurement technique which is used for mineral analysis in different fields of applications.

Former investigations have shown that NIRS can be applied for sensor-based sorting in the raw material industry. The principle of sensor-based sorting includes the singularly detection of particle properties by a sensor with subsequently mechanical separation in two or more fractions [2]. NIRS is an emerging sensor technology for sorting applications by using spectral differences in the NIR region as sorting criteria. In the borate and talc industry first NIR sorters have already been implemented. Investigations on the potential of NIR sorting in the minerals industry are on-going. Further sensor technologies applied for sensor-based sorting include optical, electromagnetic, XRF, XRT (X-ray transmission) to name a few [3].

Application fields for NIRS in the minerals industry further include the on-line moisture analysis of bulk streams. Experiences in remote sensing, including spectral interpretation, can even be applied for analysis at smaller spatial resolutions down to microscope usage. The narrow pixel size of NIR HSI allows the characterization of mineral distribution of particles at rock sample surfaces [4]. The crystal structure, in addition to the molecular composition of a sample, has major influence on the measured spectra. Therefore minerals with identical chemical composition, but differentiating crystal structures can be distinguished (e.g. Calcite [$CaCO_3$] & Aragonite [$CaCO_3$]). These advantages, among others show the large potential of NIR HSI for the minerals industry. The following investigation is used to evaluate the potential of applying NIR HSI for the characterization of a copper porphyry ore type. The major goal of the present investigation is a comparison of NIR HSI with

NIR point-measurements and MLA. The comparison is completed on basis of literature research and practical test-works. Second aim of the investigation is the determination of influences of the water content on the sample surface and impacts of spatial resolution variations on the NIR HSI measurement outcome. Results of the investigation are given in the following chapters.

2 NIR point measurement

In the first phase of the test-work each particle is measured by NIR point-measurements to evaluate the applicability of point-measurements for differentiating of particles. Each particle is therefore measured ten times by the NIR spectrometer.

The desktop NIR spectrometer used for analysis is a Fourier Transform Infrared (FTIR) spectrometer from the $TENSOR^{TM}$ series, Tensor 27 from Bruker Optics. FTIR spectra in a range of 1000-2632 nm were recorded for analysis. Exemplary measurement results are shown in Figs. 20.1 and 20.2. Detected NIR-spectra are illustrated by applying varying colours to each spectrum.

Measurements show that spectral differences between the particles

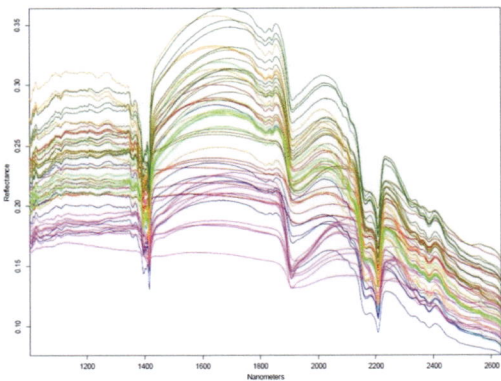

Figure 20.1: Examples of spectra of one of the groups based on spectral response [5].

are to minor in order to distinguish between each sample, based on NIR point-measurements. As a result from this investigation it was evaluated that the dissemination of valuable contaminants within the samples is to fine for the use of NIR point-measurement spectroscopy. Therefore the applicability of NIR HSI is evaluated.

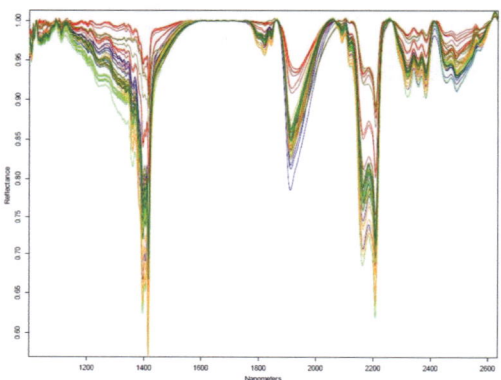

Figure 20.2: Examples of baseline corrected spectra of one of the groups based on spectral response [5].

NIR HSI in contrast to NIR-point measurement adds an additional venue coordinate to the measurements outcome, by using the ability of pattern recognition. Spatial and spectral resolution is much higher in case of NIR HSI in contrast to NIR point-measurements, which increases the level of detail. Therefore, the measurement enables the detection of small, minor constituents in the sample. Furthermore the impact of illumination complications is decreased [6].

3 SisuCHEMA hyperspectral imaging measurements

All NIR HSI measurements for this feasibility study were conducted at Specim Spectral Imagine Ltd. in Oulu Finland. The spectral imaging system used for analysis is the SisuCHEMA SWIR workstation shown in Fig. 20.3. The SisuCHEMA is a high speed imaging system which operates at wavelengths between 900- and 2500 nm. Features of the system include a spatial resolution of 320 pixels with a scalable pixel size of 31- to 625 microns. Samples are placed on a mobile platform which moves the sample through the detection area during measurement. All settings used for analysis are listed in Fig. 20.4.

Figure 20.3: SisuCHEMA SWIR [7].

pixel size	625 μm	312 μm	156 μm	31 μm

Figure 20.4: Used pixel sizes with the SisuCHEMA [8].

Each particle is measured at pixel sizes of 625-, 312-, 156-, and 31 μm. The UmBio Evince software is used for data processing and can display the results derived from SisuCHEMA NIR HSI as false colour pictures. These pictures are subsequently analysed in regard to mineral liberation to evaluate the influence of spatial resolution on the measurements outcome.

Additional to that influences of surface water on the measurements outcome are evaluated by applying three different moisture contents ("dry", "slightly wet", "wet") to each particle. For this measurement a fixed spatial resolution of 31 μm was used.

3.1 Influence of spatial resolution on NIR HSI

Evaluation of hyperspectral images derived from measurement of sample surfaces shows that a reduced spatial resolution increases the effect of spectral mixing at grain boundaries which is a logical result. Additional to that a lower spatial resolution could lead to an incorrect interpretation of mineral distribution for hyperspectral images of the sample surface. Two separate grains could be displayed as one particle, therefore incorrect interpretation is the consequence.

Figure 20.5 illustrates hyperspectral images derived from NIR HSI at varying spatial resolutions. It can be observed that the level of detail increases with higher spatial resolutions. The top-left picture illustrates a particle measured at the highest resolution with pixel sizes of 31 μm. Following pictures illustrate the same section at varying spatial resolutions from 156 μm up to 625 μm with the lowest level of detail. It can be observed that besides drying the samples surface, the minimum particle size has to be identified in order to reduce effects of spectral mixing at the grain boundaries.

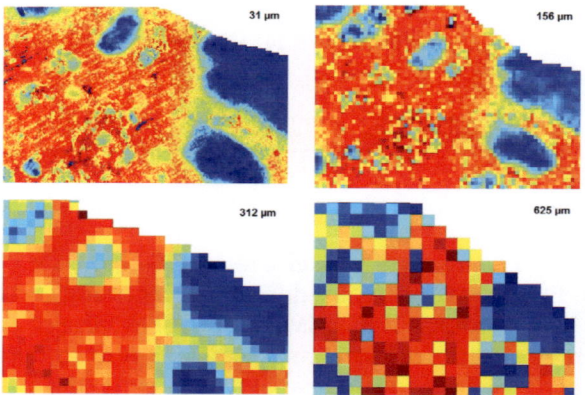

Figure 20.5: NIR-Hyperspectral Images by different spatial resolutions at pixel sizes between 31 μm and 625 μm. The blue areas contain mainly dolomite and halloysite. In contrast, quartz and feldspar are displayed red [8].

3.2 Influence of moisture content

Measurements with different moisture contents show that surface-water has a major influence on the detected NIR-spectra. Images obtained by NIR HSI become blurred at high moisture contents (Fig. 20.6). This effect is even more distinctive for NIR active minerals [5].

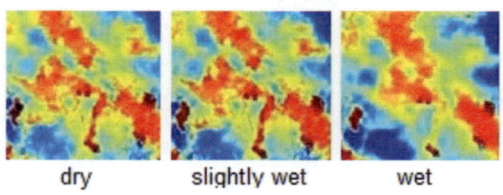

dry   slightly wet   wet

Figure 20.6: NIR-Hyperspectral Images at different moisture contents "dry", "slightly wet" and "wet". Halloysite and dolomite are displayed in red. The blue areas show quartz and feldspar [5].

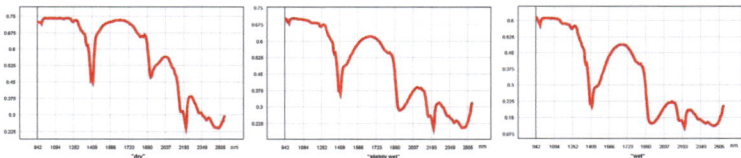

Figure 20.7: Average spectra of the measured area in Fig. 20.6 at different moisture contents on the sample surface [8].

Results additionally show that influences of surface-water on detected spectra increase with higher moisture contents (Figure 20.7). Measurable effects of surface water on measured spectra include smoother mineral boundaries shown at hyperspectral images making the identification of mineral distribution more difficult. Drying the sample surface is needed as sample preparation to decrease these influences.

4 Comparison of NIR hyperspectral imaging (Spotlight 400) and MLA measurements

MLA is the abbreviation for Mineral Liberation Analysis. The MLA is capable of measuring mineral components on sample surfaces. An MLA device consists of a Scanning Electron Microscope (SEM) and a multiple energy dispersive X-ray diffraction detector. Mineralogy software is used for data processing. Sample preparation for MLA-measurements includes different stages. Prior to each measurement samples have to be cut in order to fit in the MLA sample holder. Subsequently each sample is betted in epoxy resin and the substantiated surface is grinded and polished.

Parameters used for MLA analysis include a magnification of 175 and a resolution of 20 μm between each measurement point. The duration for MLA analysis (depending on applied spatial resolution and measured area) plus sample preparation time amounts to several hours per sample. Figure 20.8 shows four exemplary results of different samples derived from MLA measurement.

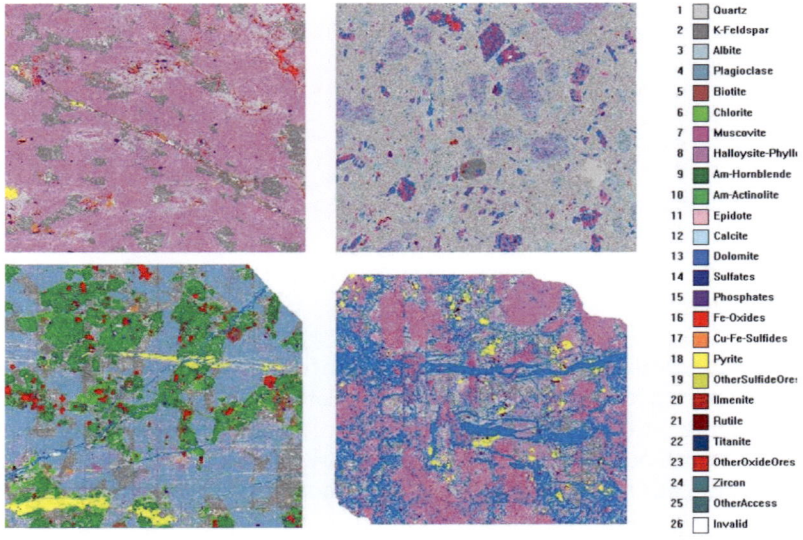

Figure 20.8: Distribution of mineral components obtained from the MLA measurements [8].

For the comparison between MLA and NIR HSI the same particles used for MLA are measured by NIR HSI measurements on the Spotlight 400 FTIR Imaging System [9]. During NIR HSI measurement each particle is measured at the same area which was previously measured by

MLA. A pixel resolution of 25 μm is used for NIR HSI test work. Figure 20.9 shows an exemplary NIR HSI measurement result after data processing such as noise reduction and baseline correction. Because no data base is available it is not possible to identify minerals directly with NIR HSI. Therefore, MLA results have to be used to identify minerals in the NIR HSI Image. Figure 20.9 illustrates exemplary spectra for dolomite, halloysite, feldspar and pyrite, derived from NIR HSI measurement. It can be seen that NIR inactive pyrite shows low absorption features and no spectral response, whereas spectra for NIR active dolomite shows characteristic spectra. In most cases halloysite and feldspar is finely distributed and intergrown with other contaminants such as quartz.

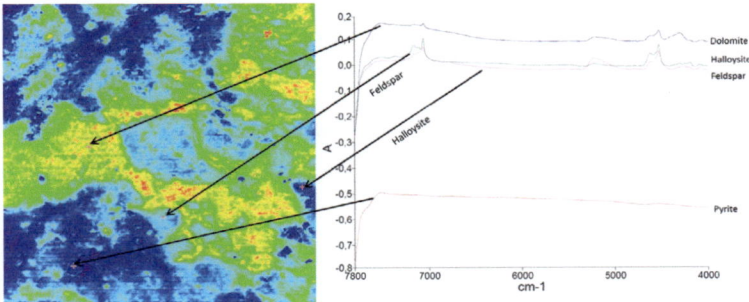

Figure 20.9: Example: NIR HSI Image with spectra of the some main minerals of the sample.

In Fig. 20.10 a monochromatic RGB (left), MLA (middle) and NIR HSI Image (right) derived from NIR HSI and MLA measurement are shown. Pictures from the different measurement techniques are derived from same sections of a particle. Based on the measurements outcome it can be seen that the level of detail of the NIR HSI image is lower compared to results from MLA measurement. Besides the level of detail it can be stated that NIR HSI enables a determination of mineral component distribution.

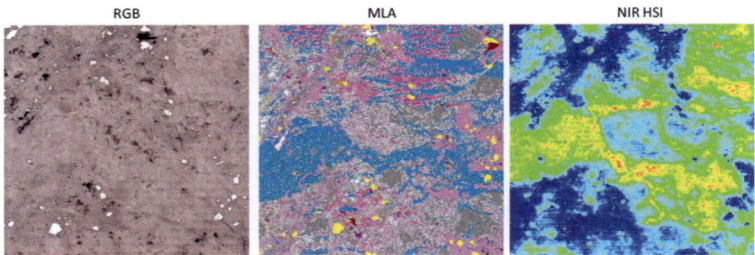

Figure 20.10: Example: Comparison between monochromatic RGB, MLA, and NIR HSI image of the same sample area.

5 Conclusion

The above described investigation has shown the general applicability of NIR HSI for the determination of mineral distributions on sample surfaces. NIR HSI however cannot be used without prior generation of a mineral data base. During this investigation MLA measurement is used for the identification of mineral components in the NIR HSI Image. Future investigation could enable the establishment of an NIR spectrum data based on NIR HSI test work.

Furthermore it has shown that surface moisture-content, as well as the applied spatial resolution have substantial influence on the measurements outcome. Surface moisture leads to blurred hyperspectral images due to the influence of water on the detected NIR-spectra. In addition to influences of surface water an insufficient spatial resolution leads to a wrong interpretation of the hyperspectral image.

Due to the promising results derived from the test-work, further applications for NIR HSI for process control in the minerals industry are imaginable, besides the laboratory usage. NIR HSI is not yet applied in sensor-based sorting due to long measurement time, in contrast to NIR-line scan sensors. Further improvements in data-processing speed however could make applications in the field of sensor-based sorting feasible.

Summing up it can be stated that NIR HSI seems to be a good alternative to conventional analytical methods. NIR HSI may become a major measurement instrument for analytical applications in the minerals industry. Further investigations will be conducted to evaluate the full potential of NIR HSI for applications in the minerals industry.

References

1. C. Sherman, "Infrared Spectroscopy," in *Handbook of instrumental techniques for analytical chemistry*, F. Settle, Ed.   Prentice Hall, 1997.

2. F. Riedel and H. Wotruba, "Review of sorting Technologies," in *AIMS Project P902 "Dry Sorting Processing Review"*, P. Martens, Ed., 2005.

3. M. Robben, H. Wotruba, and J. Heizmann, "Sensor-based separation of carbonates," in *XXVI International Mineral Processing Congress*, 2012.

4. G. Bonifazi, D. Cesare, and S. Serranti, "Hyperspectral imaging applied to minerals processing: Procedures, architectures and analytical strategies," in *XXVI International Mineral Processing Congress (IMPC 2012)*, vol. 276, 2012.

5. M. Robben and C. Schropp, "Feasibility study on the use of NIR Sorting in the process of Kajaran copper ore ," 2012, final project report.

6. D. J. F. September, "Detection and Quantification of Spice Adulteration by Near Infrared Hyperspectral Imaging," 2011, Masterthesis, Stellenbosch University.

7. Specim, 2011. [Online]. Available: http://www.specim.fi/files/pdf/sisu/datasheets/SisuCHEMA_1_2011.pdf

8. C. Schropp, "Spectral Imaging in the Mineral Processing," 2012, Masterthesis, RWTH Aachen.

9. Perkin Elmer, 2009. [Online]. Available: http://shop.perkinelmer.de/content/RelatedMaterials/Brochures/bro_spotlight-400.pdf

Luminescence- and reflection spectroscopy for automatic classification of various minerals

J. Hofer[1,2], R. Huber[1], G. Weingrill[3] and K. Gatterer[2]

[1] Binder + Co GmbH,
Grazer Strasse 19 - 25, A-8200 Gleisdorf
[2] Graz University of Technology,
Institute of Physical and Theoretical Chemistry,
Stremayrgasse 9, A-8010 Graz
[3] Montanuniversität Leoben,
Chair of Minerals Processing,
Franz-Josef-Strasse 18, A-8700 Leoben

Abstract Fundamental studies for sensor based sorting on several industrially relevant minerals and a lead containing glass sample are presented. The examined minerals were: Talc, Magnesite, Calcite, Fluorite, Scheelite and Chalcedony. The methods of investigation were UV-VIS-NIR reflection spectrometry between 200 - 2500 nm and UV induced solid state fluorescence measurements with excitation between 200 - 380 nm and emission detection between 400 - 900 nm. A common quenching mechanism for UV-induced fluorescence is discussed. Artefacts and sources of error for solid state luminescence measurements are mentioned.

1 Introduction

Sensor based sorting is a growing area of beneficiation of secondary and primary resources. There are several optical properties that can be used to obtain discriminators for different material classes [1]. An overview was given in literature and is reproduced in Table 1.1. This contribution will only cover UV-VIS-NIR reflection spectroscopy and UV excited fluorescence of minerals and glasses. Those two types of spectra often show features, which can be used for sorting purposes. UV-induced fluorescence is an optical property, which is not so well established for optical sorting until now. However, light induced fluorescence in minerals is known since the time of the ancient Greek philosophers. The first records of mineral fluorescence go back to writings by Herodotus, Aristotle, Theophrastus, Strabo and Pliny. It was defined as a glow of nonthermal origin. A. Magnus described the thermoluminescence of heated diamond in 1280. From 17th to 19th century many observations on natural phosphors were made. First scientific contributions to luminescence were made by G. Stokes (1852), E. Becquerel (1859) and E. Wiedeman (1888) who proposed the term "luminescence" and gave a definition [2]. The most important contributions on mineral fluorescence in 20th and 21th century were made by Marfunin [3, 4], Gorobets and Rogojine [5] and Gaft et al [6]. A good introduction to the field of luminescent inorganic materials is provided from Jüstel et al [7]. First results in the area of mineral sorting via UV induced fluorescence were published last year in the framework of a cooperation of the R & D department of Binder + Co, Austria, the Chair of Mineral Processing at the Montanuniversität Leoben, Austria, and the Institute of Physical and Theoretical Chemistry at the Graz University of Technology, Austria [8]. The sorting of lead containing glasses by UV induced fluorescence is a process which is already established by Binder + Co since a few years and the fundamental processes are well understood [9]. In general UV-VIS reflection spectra of solids consist of electronic transitions of transition- and rare-earth metal ions having unfilled d- and f-electronic shells, respectively, and can be interpreted using quantum mechanical models like ligand field theory, Tanabe-Sugano and configuration coordinate diagrams [10]. These electronic transitions occur between 200 and 800 nm. In the NIR range between 800 and 2500 nm combinations and overtones of fundamental vibrations of functional groups in minerals can be observed and are interpreted using the harmonic oscillator model. Slight deviations between calculated and observed energies for these overtones are expected because of the anharmonicity of the vibrations. Energies for the fundamental vibrations used to calculate of overtones and combinations can be found in the literature [11]. For the interpretation of solid state luminescence an understanding of the luminescence mechanisms is required. For a radiative transition an electron has to be in an excited state, from which it relaxes to its ground state under emission of a photon. Phosphors consist of a crystalline host lattice or a supercooled melt (for glasses). A host lattice always carries defects and impurity ions. These defects are highly important for luminescent processes. Non-radiative vibrational transitions, which only generate heat

Table 21.1: Optical properties used for mineral sorting [1].

Radiation	Sensor Technology	Material property	Sorter application
Gamma-radiation	radiometry	natural gamma radiation	radioactive ores
X-Ray	XRT (X-ray transmission)	atomic density	base and heavy metal ores, precious metal ores, industrial minerals, coal, diamonds, scrap metals
X-Ray	XRF (R-ray fluorescence)	visible fluorescence under X-rays	diamonds
UV-VIS	Color (CCD color camera)	reflection, absorption, transmission	base metal ores, precious metal ores, industrial minerals, diamonds, glass
VIS-NIR	Photometry	monochromatic reflection, absorption	base metal ores, industrial minerals, plastic, paper, cardboard
NIR	NIR-sensors (semiconductors)	reflection, absorption	base metal ores, industrial minerals, plastic, paper, cardboard
IR	Infrared cameras	heat conductivity, heat dissipation	base metal sulfide ores, precious metal ores, industrial minerals, graphite, coal
Radio waves and AC	Electromagnetic sensor	conductivity, permeability	base metal sulfide ores, scrap metals

UV = ultraviolett; VIS = visible light; NIR = near infrared light, IR = infrared, AC = alternating current instead of light, are competing with radiative transitions. Luminescence processes are subdivided according to the life time of the excited state. The threshold is 10^{-8} s to distinguish between short-time fluorescence and long-time phosphorescence.

A systematization of luminescent minerals was made by Gorobets and Rogojine in 2001, it provides a system of hierarchical order in three levels, which allows predictions of luminescence centers in minerals with known formula and structure [5]. A luminescent mineral has to satisfy the following three conditions [12]:

1. A suitable type of crystal lattice favorable for emission centers is formed.

2. The content of photoluminescent centers is high enough (usually $> 0{,}01$ w%)

3. The amount of iron or other quenchers is small enough (around $0{,}5 - 1$ w%). Iron is a principal quenching element in nature.

A subdivision of luminescence into five types is possible: **1) Center luminescence** is generated by an optical center, e.g., a transition metal ion like Mn^{2+}, a rare-earth ion like Eu^{2+} or a s^2-ion like Pb^{2+}. **2) Charge-Transfer luminescence** where a transition takes place between electronic states of different ions, e.g., in WO_4^{2-}, MoO_4^{2-}, VO_4^{2-} „ NbO_4^{2-} and TaO_4^{2-}. **3) Luminescence involving impurity levels** for semiconductors with certain dopants e.g. Mg^{2+} or Si^{4+} in GaN or defects. **4) Persistent luminescence**, where energy is stored in the host lattice by trapping free charge carriers. **5) Sensitization of Luminescent Centers** where an energy transfer from a non-luminescent ion to an activator takes place [7].

From a technologists point of view the features in a reflection spectrum are simply the sum of all possible features of the materials components. For luminescence spectra, however, more effects concerning the composition and interactions of components are possible. Notably, concentration quenching, inner filtering and energy transfer can occur. Concentration quenching means that, e.g., for a lead containing glass the luminescence intensity increases with the lead content up to a certain concentration and decreases again for higher lead concentrations. Fortunately those samples can be detected by their UV-cut off or reflection properties. The UV cut-off process is implemented in glass sorting systems by Binder + Co [13].

2 Experimental setup

2.1 Sample preparation

All samples were cut with a cutting machine (Einhell, BT-TC 600 Blue) mounted with a diamond circular saw (Baier's Enkel, cutting wheel F2). Then the samples were wet polished with diamond abrasive paper. The examined powders were used as received from the supplier. Powder samples were measured in the powder sample holder with a Quartz-glass window provided from Perkin Elmer.

2.2 Reflection measurements

The reflection measurements were carried out using a Lambda 950 Reflection spectrometer from Perkin Elmer. A 150 mm integrating spectralon-sphere with a double detector system (photomultiplier tube and an InGaAs-semiconductor detector) was used. Data recording was made using the UV-WinLab Software from Perkin Elmer. Automatic spectralon correction was performed by the software.

2.3 Luminescence measurements

The luminescence measurements were carried out using a LS 55 luminescence spectrometer from Perkin Elmer mounted with a red sensitive photomultiplier tube R955 from Hamamatsu. All samples were clamped into the measurement chamber with the original solid sample holder from Perkin Elmer.

All spectra were recorded with the BL-Studio from Biolight. All spectra were automatically excitation corrected via the internal Rhodamin6G standard. The spectra were not corrected for detector sensitivity and can be regarded as technical spectra.

3 Results and discussion

3.1 Reflection measurements

The examined sample set is depicted in Fig. 21.1.

Figure 21.1: Sample set for reflection measurements: a) Chalcedony, b) Magnesite, c) Calcite, d) Fluorite, e) Talc, f) Scheelite ore, g) Scheelite tailings [14].

The reflection spectra of Talc, Calcite, Fluorite and Magnesite are given together with the assignment of their spectral features as representative examples (see Fig. 21.2). For sorting applications the setting of discriminators is desired. The absolute reflectance of the mineral samples depends strongly on the positioning, surface condition, etc. To get rid of such artefacts the first and second derivatives can be calculated and compared.

The original data and the derivatives are shown in Fig. 21.3. The data depicted in Fig. 21.3 allow decisions about proper optical configurations of sensor based sorters. It is not only necessary to find spectral features, which allow the distinguishing of several mineral classes. It is also of interest to increase recognition efficiency and speed, which is often achieved by sensor fusion. This means that several recognition systems are linked together, e.g., shape analysis via CCD and NIR-sensors. Economic reasons and sensor-stability make detection systems in the VIS-range more desirable then NIR systems.

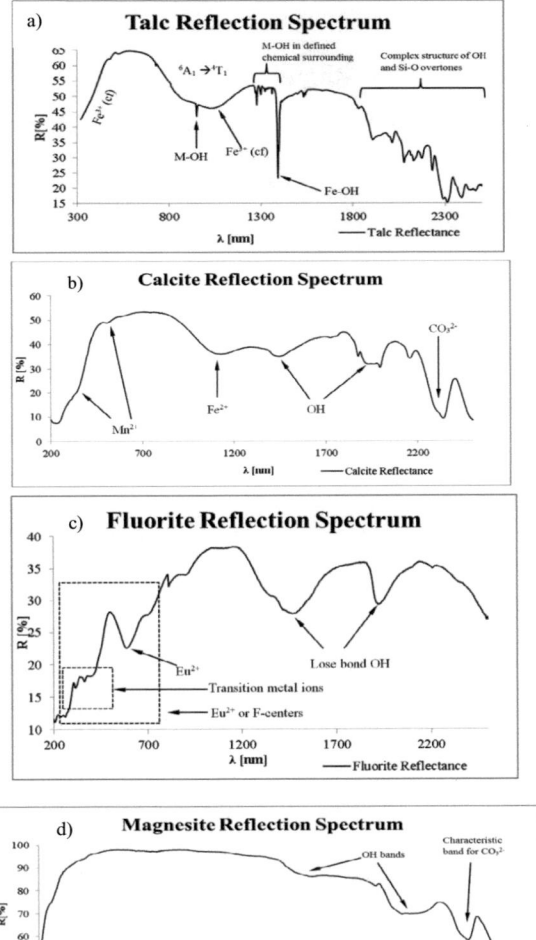

Figure 21.2: Interpretation of reflection spectra for a) Talc, b) Calcite, c) Fluorite, d) Magnesite [14].

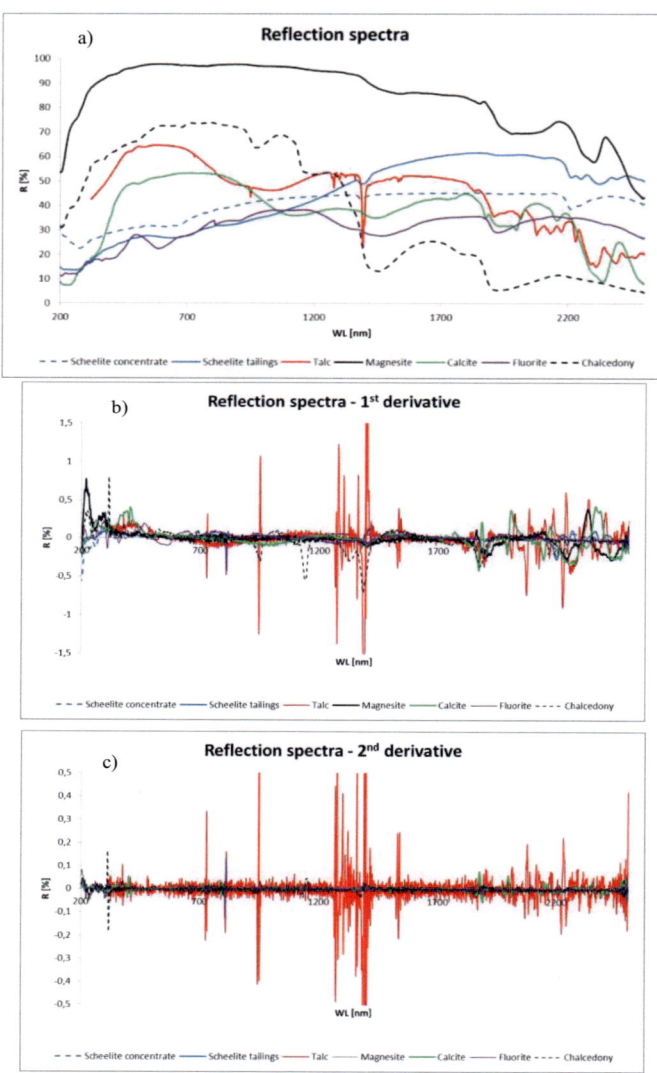

Figure 21.3: Reflection spectra a) original data, b) 1st derivative, c) 2nd derivative [14].

In nearly every NIR-spectrum of industrial minerals more or less sharp water-features around 1400 nm and 1900 nm and a decrease of the reflection intensity towards 2500 nm can be observed. The gaseous water molecule shows a symmetric OH-stretch at 2738 nm and an asymmetric stretch vibration around 2663 nm. The H-O-H bending mode is located in the MIR around 6270 nm. When a mineral contains a certain amount of water, both features at 1400 nm (overtone of the OH-stretches) and 1900 (combinations of H-O-H bend and OH-stretches) nm are present. When there is no water in or on a mineral no 1900 nm band will occur and a 1400 nm feature indicates only hydroxyl. A hydroxyl moiety has only a stretching mode, whose energy is highly dependent on its bonding partner. In minerals this stretching can be found between 2670 - 3450 nm. Since an OH can occur on multiple crystallographic sites and is usually attached to a metal ion, there can be a combination of metal-OH bend and OH stretch around 2200 - 2300 nm. For the carbonate group doublet-features around 2500 - 2550 nm and 2300 - 2350 nm are expected. Three weaker bands are reported around 2120 - 2160 nm and 1850 - 1870 nm. In general the energy and thereby the position in the spectrum of OH-moieties and CO_3-groups is very dependent on the group they are attached to [15]. As a rule of the thumb for OH-group features it could be said, that the lower the degree of freedom of an OH-moiety in a crystal, the sharper the peak which is observed. For loosely bond OH-groups or capillary water or surface water broad features are to be expected.

3.2 Luminescence measurements

The Scheelite concentrate- and tailing-samples were obtained from an industrial flotation process of an Austrian supplier. A piece of polycrystalline silicon from the semiconductor industry was used as a blank standard for the measurements.

The LS 55 has a pulsed Xe-flash lamp as excitation source. The pulsation of the source is coupled to the line frequency and has a full width at half maximum of 10^{-6} s. It was necessary to adjust the pulse to pause ratio so that the pause did not fall into a time slot were the sample was still emitting photons. This would have caused erroneous dark current compensation of the PMT. The measurement logic of the LS 55 is depicted in Fig. 21.4.

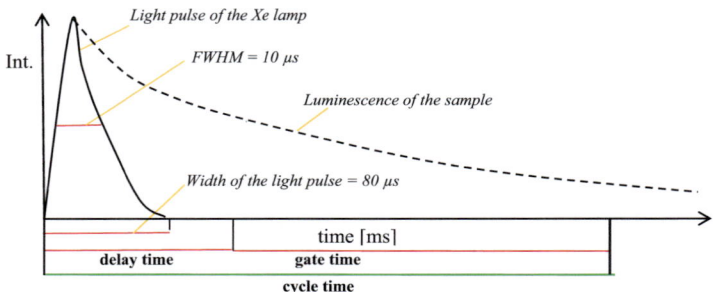

Figure 21.4: Measurement logic of the LS 55 (not to scale) [14].

The monochromator system of the LS 55 consists of a grid monochromator in the excitation channel and a grid monochromator in the emission channel. So artefacts from second and third order diffraction of excitation light and short wave luminescence are to be expected. To get rid of these artefacts additional cut off filters were used in the emission channel. An example for the second order biased emission spectra are given in Fig. 21.5.

Since the system has a two monochromators and a light source that provides illumination from a range of 200 – 400 nm, emission spectra and excitation spectra can be recorded. This makes the device more versatile than a device that works with laser excitation. A confinement of the LS 55 is that the minimal delay time after an excitation pulse is 0.01 ms. Thus decay time measurements for many of the short-lived activators are not possible.

In general excitation and absorption spectra give similar information of the material. But for samples which are not transparent to UV radiation, e.g., certain glasses the UV cut-off of the host material can conceal the excitation of an activator. In such cases the excitation spectrum reveals the absorption of the activator, while the absorption of the host material itself can be found by standard absorption/transmission measurements.

The investigated samples are depicted under daylight as well as under UV light in Fig. 21.6. The luminescence spectra for the samples

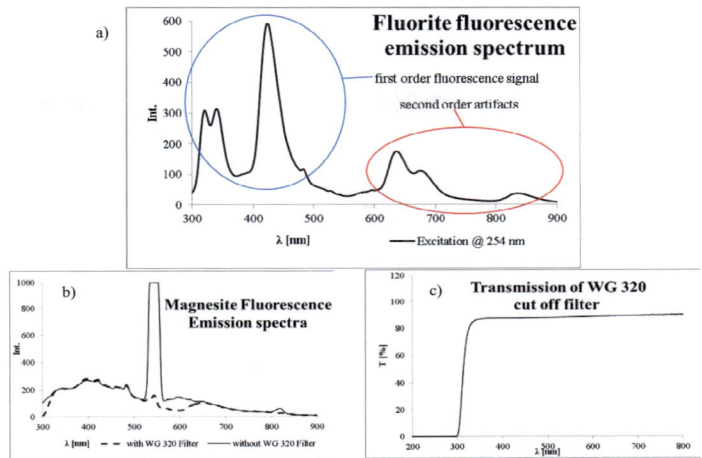

Figure 21.5: Spectra biased by second order artefacts a) a Fluorite Emission spectrum, b) a Magnesite emission spectrum after 266 nm excitation with and without a proper filter, c) transmission characteristic of the filter used [14].

are depicted in Fig. 21.7. In Fig. 21.7 the comment "fluorescence" and "phosphorescence" are linked to the settings of the spectrofluorimeter. "Fluorescence" is used for short-term luminescence measurements and "Phosphorescence" is used for long-term luminescence measurements.

When nothing is known about a sample the 3D-plot option in the software can used to automatically record several emission spectra for different excitation wave lengths. An example for a 3 dimensional plot for the Calcite sample is presented in Fig. 21.8. Unfortunately this measurement technique is more time consuming, than the traditional 2-dimensional measurements.

The Fluorite-Emission at 400 nm is assigned to traces of Eu^{2+}, the most common activator, which can be found in Fluorite. The green colour of the Fluorite sample indicates traces of Sm^{2+}, Dy^{2+} or Tm^{2+}, which could be responsible for the double peak feature between 300 - 400nm. The Fluorite system is frequently a multi-activator system, which has been extensively studied. Fluorites with Sm^{2+}, Dy^{2+}, Tm^{2+}, Nd^{3+}, Er^{3+}, Tm^{3+} and Ho^{3+} were used as laser materials [16].

Figure 21.6: Sample set for luminescence measurements: a) a piece of Scheelite ore, Scheelite concentrate, Scheelite tailing (left to right) in daylight, b) same samples under 254 nm light, c) same samples under 366 nm, d) Calcite, Chalcedony, Magnesite, Fluorite, lead containing glass and highly pure silicon (left to right) in daylight, e) same samples under 254 nm illumination [14].

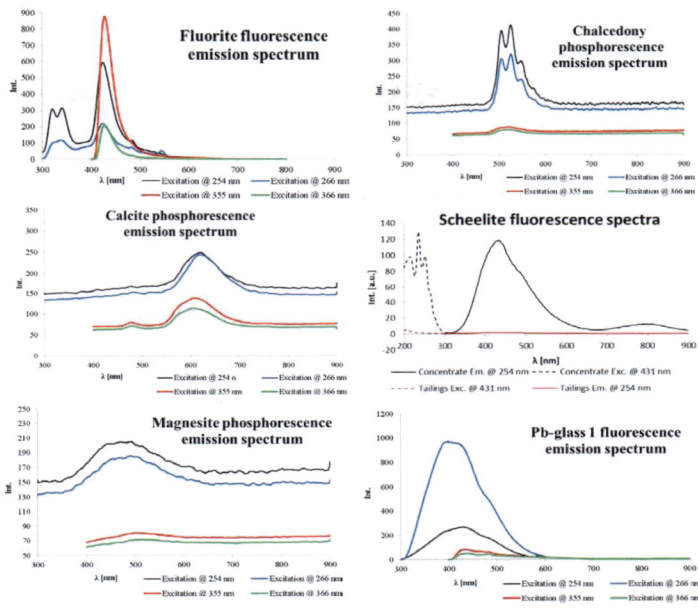

Figure 21.7: Emission spectra for the mineral and glass samples [14].

The Chalcedony sample shows a feature in the green region of the VIS between 500 - 600 nm that is characteristic for traces of Uranyl, UO_2^{2+}. This group is responsible for the green, yellow and orange colours of Uranium minerals. The characteristic structure in the emission spectrum is due to vibronic transitions of this molecule [17].

The red glow of the Calcite sample can be assigned to traces of Mn^{2+}. The emission is generated by a d $\rightarrow$ d transition with the term symbols $^4A_{1g} \rightarrow {}^6A_{1g}$. The optical properties of Mn^{2+} are highly dependent on its environment. For example in solution it appears colorless, in $CaCO_3$ it yields red fluorescence and in Zn_2SiO_4:Mn^{2+} it causes green emission [5,18].

The intensive white glow of Scheelite is related to a charge transfer-transition in the tungstate group, therefore an intrinsic fluorescence of the mineral is encountered. The charge transfer involves a transition of electrons from the oxygen ions to the empty d levels of the tungsten ion and backwards [19]. The bluish luminescence of Magnesite may be caused by oxygen around the carbonate-groups [20].

The intensive short-lived luminescence of the lead glass sample is caused by the s^2-ion Pb^{2+}. The luminescence is due to the lone pair $ns^2 \leftarrow ns^1np^1$ transition [19].

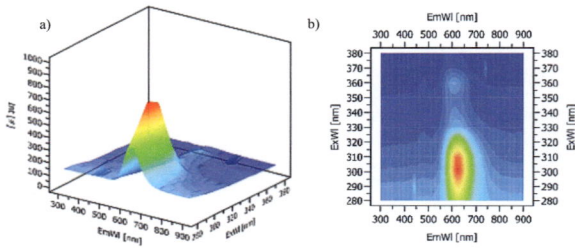

Figure 21.8: 3-D emission spectrum at different excitation wavelengths for the Calcite sample a) side view, b) top view [14].

As it was stated in the introduction iron is a common fluorescence quencher that can be found in many minerals. This is of special interest for the chalcedony sample. Many Chalcedony samples are coated by a brownish skin which is in many cases iron-oxide (see Fig. 21.9). The comparison of reflection spectra (see Fig. 21.10) of the brownish skin and the break planes shows that the brown part absorbs in the UV-VIS-range of the spectrum.

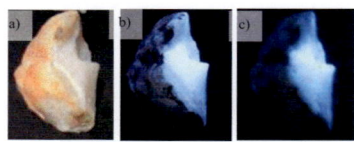

Figure 21.9: Chalcedony sample with brownish skin: a) under daylight, b) under 254 nm illumination and c) under 366 nm illumination.

This "quenching" by iron is an absorption process that is related to a charge transfer transition of Fe^{3+}, whose absorption maxima lays in the UV region and stretches far into the VIS range. Charge transfer quenching can also occur with Fe^{2+}, Co^{2+} and Ni^{3+} ions, but is not so strongly

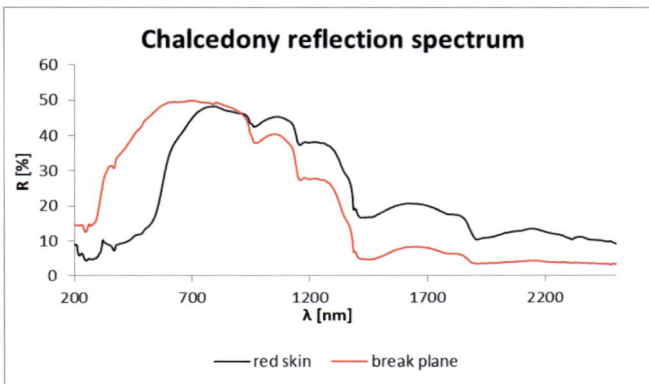

Figure 21.10: Reflection spectra of the red skin of Chalcedony and its breaking planes.

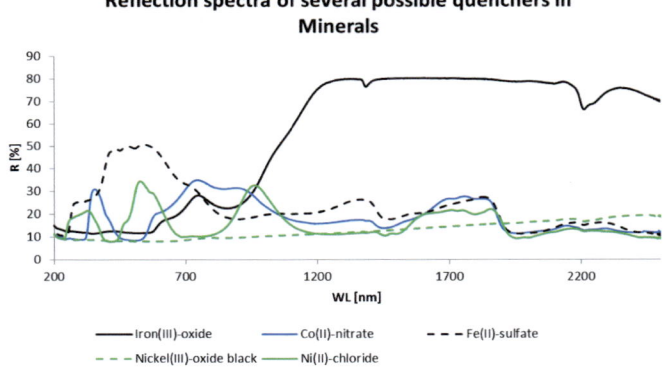

Figure 21.11: Reflection spectra of possible quenchers in minerals.

observed as with Fe^{3+}. The Fe^{3+} content in a material drastically reduces the glow of every activator in a crystal [21]. To verify that the strong absorption in the VIS range of the Chalcedony skin is due to Fe^{3+} the reflection spectra of some pure transition metal compounds were investigated (see Fig. 21.11). All the examined compounds were of analytical grade.

In fact, the Fe^{3+} absorption covers the whole VIS range and corroborates the statement that it seems to be the most important and strongest quencher encountered in naturally occurring minerals.

4 Conclusion

Like all samples that come from nature and are not manufactured in a laboratory minerals have many impurities, dopants and trace contaminations. Often these traces are responsible for distinct features in fluorescence and reflection spectra. For fundamental studies for sensor based sorting of minerals, glasses and other materials an investigation of samples from an actual deposit is necessary. The decision which sensor system, what type of optics and/or sensor fusion should be used is based on efficiency and economic considerations. It could be shown, that with the presented methods distinguishing between different material classes and interpretation of spectral features is possible.

Acknowledgements

The authors wish to thank Prof. Dr. Helmut Flachberger from Montanuniversität Leoben, Chair of Mineral Processing for his continuous support throughout the project.

We also wish to thank the FFG (Österreichische Forschungsförderungsgesellschaft) for funding of the project.

References

1. H. Wotruba and H. Harbeck, "Sensor-based sorting," *Ullmann's Encyclopedia of Industrial Chemistry*, vol. 32, pp. 396 – 404, 2012.

2. A. S. Marfunin, "Spectroscopy, luminescence and radiation centers in minerals," *Springer: Berlin-Heidelberg-New York*, pp. 143 – 146, 1979.

3. ——, "Physics of minerals and inorganic materials," *Springer: Berlin-Heidelberg-New York*, 1979a.

4. ——, "Spectroscopy, luminescence and radiation centers in minerals," 1979b.

5. S. Gorobets, B. and R. Rogojine, A., *Luminescent Spectra of Minerals: A Reference Book.*   RPC VIMS: Moscow, 2002.

6. M. Gaft, R. Reisfeld, and G. Panczer, *Modern Luminescence Spectroscopy of Minerals and Material.*   Springer: Berlin - Heidelberg, 2005.

7. M. S. Jüstel, T., H. Winkler, and W. Adam, "Luminescent materials," *Ullmann's Encyclopedia of Industrial Chemistry*, 2012.

8. R. Huber, "Sorting based on uv-absorption and -fluorescence," *Sensor Based Sorting-Proceedings*, 2011.

9. M. Kieler, "Optische erkennung bleioxidhaltiger gläser in recyclingglasscherben," *Master Thesis at the Graz University of Technology*, 2010.

10. N. Figgis, B., *Ligand Field Theory and Its Applications.*   Wiley-VCH: New York, 2000.

11. K. Nakamoto, *Infrared and Raman Spectra of Inorganic and Coordination Compounds*, 4th ed.   Wiley-Interscience: New York-Chichester- Brisbane - Toronto - Singapore, 1986.

12. S. Gorobets, B., M. Portnov, A., and A. Rogozhin, A., *Rad. Meas.*, vol. 4, pp. 485 – 491, 1995.

13. G. Ohnewein, "Verwendbarkeit des uv-cut-off-verfahrens als optisches sortierkriterium im altglasaufbereitungsprozess," *Master Thesis at the FH JOANNEUM Gesellschaft mbH Graz*, 2006.

14. J. Hofer, "Fluorescence- and reflection spectroscopy of industrially relevant minerals for automatic sensor based sorting applications," *Master Thesis at the Graz University of Technology*, 2012.

15. N. Clark, R., *"Spectroscopy of Rocks and Minerals and Principles of Spectroscopy"* in *Manual of Remote Sensing.*   John Wiley and Sons: New York, 1999.

16. A. S. Marfunin, "Spectroscopy, luminescence and radiation centers in minerals," *Springer: Berlin-Heidelberg-New York*, pp. 209 – 210, 1979.

17. ——, "Spectroscopy, luminescence and radiation centers in minerals," pp. 212 – 215, 1979.

18. S. Marfunin, A., "Spectroscopy, luminescence and radiation centers in minerals," *Springer: Berlin-Heidelberg-New York*, pp. 150 – 153, 1979.

19. "Luminescent materials," *Ullmann's Encyclopedia of Industrial Chemistry*, p. 13, 2012.

20. "http://www.fluomin.org/, looked up on 3.1.2012."

21. S. Marfunin, A., "Spectroscopy, luminescence and radiation centers in minerals," *Springer: Berlin-Heidelberg-New York*, p. 175, 1979,.

X-ray transmission sorting of tungsten ore

M. R. Robben[1], H. Knapp[1], M. Dehler[2] and H. Wotruba[1]

[1] RWTH Aachen, Lehr- und Forschungsgebiet Aufbereitung mineralischer
Rohstoffe (AMR),
Lochnerstraße 4-20, Haus C, D-52064 Aachen
[2] Tomra Sorting Solutions, Mining,
Feldstrasse 128, D-22880 Wedel (Hamburg)

Abstract The Deutsche Rohstoff AG, TOMRA Sorting Solutions|mining and the RWTH Aachen University have performed a study on the applicability of sensor-based sorting in the process of tungsten ore for the Wolfram Camp Mine in Australia. The aim of this project was pre-concentrating of tungsten ore by removal of barren material. The pre-concentration can lead to energy and water savings, decrease of reagent input in downstream processes and increase minerals reserve utilization by lowering the cut-off grade. A comprehensive research programme concluded that the best suited sensor-technology for this material was X-Ray Transmission (XRT). The XRT sensor provides a highly efficient system for classifying and sorting different materials based on their atomic density. XRT sorting is already applied as well in the recycling as in the minerals industry. The results of the test runs have shown that XRT sorting can effectively remove and reduce barren material and that it is an effective technology for the pre-concentration of tungsten ore.

1 Introduction

One of the challenges for the minerals industry is the economization of the most important resources energy and water. Other challenges like increasing demand for resources, decreasing ore grades, reducing accessibility to resources and meeting the sustainable development also need to be faced. This requires research and implementation of innovative, dry and energy efficient technologies. Sensor-technology in connection with intelligent data processing systems is playing a key role facing those challenges. The recognition of diagnostic material properties and machine control by innovate sensor-technologies cause higher automation levels, higher recovery and better quality (purity) of resources [1,2].

X-ray sensor-technologies are well developed and already wide applied covering all steps in the resource process chain from exploration through grade control to process control and product quality assurance. X-ray sensor-technologies are key technologies for characterizing elements and crystalline phases of material.

X-ray Transmission (XRT) can recently also be applied as a scanning method for sensor-based sorting (SBS). SBS involves the detection of single particles and the rejection of those single particles out of a material flow that do not warrant further treatment. This way SBS can help to face the above described challenges. Most of the solutions are based on the fact that SBS is a dry and energy efficient sorting technology which allows a pre-concentration step (waste removal at an earlier stage) [3]. Pre-concentrating increases the plant efficiency, because gangue material is rejected prior to the mineral processing plant and therefore improves the downstream processes. Pre-concentration can tip the balance for otherwise nonviable resources. This way potential reserves can be turned into reserves, the cut-off grade reduced and the reserves and life time of the mine increased [4]. The benefits of pre-concentration are well documented in the literature (e.g. [5]). By pre-concentration close to the mining face, the capacity required for transport is decreased. The removal of gangue from the ROM (run-of-mine) ore enables an increase in the ore throughput rate and therefore a better utilization of the installed processing unit with decreased specific costs and increased productivity. This means for the milling process an increase in capacity and reduction in the Bond Work Index, wearing and energy requirements. Furthermore by pre-concentration the quantity of the material is reduced but the grade of the ore increased. With the smaller quantity, but higher grade of concentrate feed, other savings can be achieved, such as reagent costs, costs for water, tailings dewatering and disposal of fine tailings. Pre-concentration can also open up opportunities for the introduction of alternative mining methods. Low-cost mining methods that are associated with a higher percentage of gangue can be used due to effective pre-concentration [2].

In this paper, the XRT sorting technology and the results of a number of test runs conducted on tungsten ore, from Wolfram Camp Mine, are described. The aim of the test work was pre-concentration of the ore.

2 The functional principle of XRT-sorting

Sensor-based sorting is introduced as an umbrella term for all applications where particles in a material flow are singularly detected and evaluated by a sensor-technology and then rejected by a mechanical process [4]. A wide variety of sensors are currently available within the electromagnetic spectrum, which can be utilised individually or in combination to identify properties such as conductivity, response to optical and near-infrared light. Sensor-based sorters can be implemented in different mineral processing stages to fulfil various tasks [6,7], which is in more detail described later in this article. Typically sorters can process materials within the size range $-300mm + 6mm$ at a throughput of around 150 tons per hour. Smaller size ranges can be processed for specialised applications, but at reduced throughput.

The functional principle of SBS can be divided in five sub-processes; material preparation, material presentation, material sensing, data processing and material separation. The critical stage of examining the particle and determining whether material is valuable or barren, is done by a combination of sensor and data processing unit. A valve bank with high pressure jets makes the physical separation possible.

The XRT sensor in sorting works according to the airport baggage security inspection applications. The sensor system has been developed further suitably adapted to minerals sorting. A radiation source, an electrical X-ray source with the energy range between 90 and $200keV$ (depending on the application), is placed on top of the unit, as indicated in Fig. 22.1. The radiation penetrates the particles that are presented on a conveyor belt running at $3m/s$ or on a chute. The residual radiation is registered by the detector, a line scan camera with a spatial resolution of approximately $1mm$, beneath the travelling path (Fig. 22.1). The sensor consists of an array of scintillation crystals that capture the number of counts on each element for the array. Figure 22.1 shows the schematic setup of a belt-type XRT-based sorter.

X-rays are transmitted through material at varying degrees, depending on the atomic density of the material and the thickness of the ma-

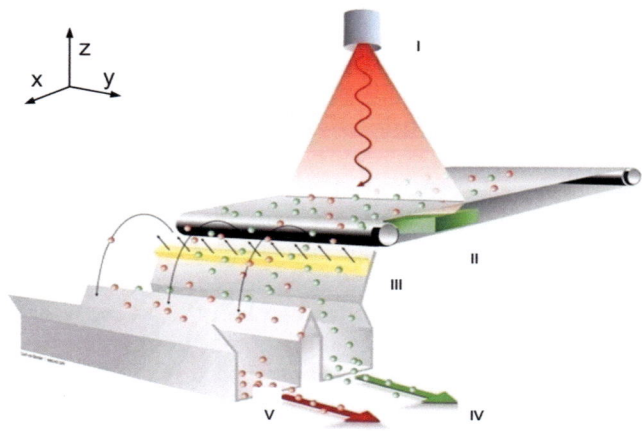

Figure 22.1: Schematic set-up of XRT sorting system. I) X-ray source/tube, II) X-ray detector, III) Valve bank with high pressure jets, IV) Ejected fraction, V) Rejected fraction [3].

terial. In other words, material absorbs a proportion of the radiation resulting in a reduction in the intensity of the X-ray. The detected intensity is an exponential function of the thickness of the irradiated material. As long as variations in particle thickness are restricted and the difference in atomic density is large enough, the use of a single energy wave to classify the material is accurate enough. By conditioning the material, the influence of particle thickness can partly be levelled out. The feed material needs to be prepared by screening this way that the ratio between the largest and the smallest particle is around 3 or 4, also due to mechanical restrictions of the sorter.

Observing the effects of two or more different wavelengths would eliminate the effects of particle thickness completely. Dual energy XRT involves the use of a high energy and low energy X-ray beam (or two detectors one with a filter and the other one without). In Fig. 22.2, the difference between single and dual energy X-ray detection is presented.

If the influence of particle thickness can be levelled out, the sorting criteria or discrimination is thus only based on the atomic density of

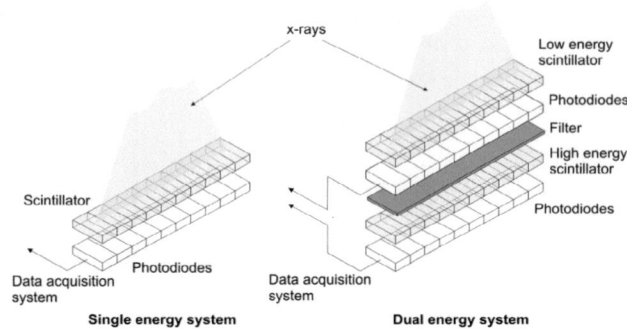

Figure 22.2: Single-energy vs. Dual-energy X-ray sensing principle [8].

the particle. In the below mentioned application example only a single energy X-ray wave is applied.

The X-rays penetrating the material are converted into digital image data. An image of the object is generated in a "line by line" fashion, similar to optical sorting. A typical example of such and image is presented in Fig. 22.4. Images, with different shades of grey, provide a great deal of information regarding the density of the objects i.e. an object of low density appears brighter than a denser object. The analysis of images in order to facilitate separation is conducted using different algorithms. It is for example possible to eject objects based on their percentage of high density material. Suitable values for the minimum percentage of high density material in one object are usually determined through process optimization based on final product specifications.

Information regarding particle shape, size and texture is also used for evaluation. The decision to accept or reject a particle and the position of particles on the conveyor belt is passed from the data processing system to the control unit of the valve bank (Fig. 22.1). The sorter's control unit activates the respective high pressure jets. This burst of compressed air diverts the direction of flow of selected individual particles so that they get separated to the reject-fraction (Fig. 22.1). The amount of rejected material has therefore a direct relation to the compressed air consumption; the more rejected particles, the higher the usage.

It can be concluded that the XRT sensor provides a highly efficient sensor system for classifying and sorting different materials based on their atomic density.

3 Potential of XRT-sorting

As mentioned, a multitude of different sensors is applicable for sensor-based sorting. The choice is generally driven by the mineralogy of a given ore. Optical sensors are the most common sensor type, and have been very successfully used in the industrial minerals industry [2]. In 2007 the RWTH Aachen University started research on the applicability of near-infrared spectroscopy (NIRS) sorting in the minerals industry. This sensing technology has high potential and the first sorters are implemented [2].

One of the advantages over surface sensing technologies like optical and NIRS, is that XRT-sorting is insensitive to surface conditions, because instead of surface layer, particle volume is detected. This means that no surface conditioning like washing/scrubbing is necessary and XRT-sorting can therefore be operated completely dry. Additionally the composition of the surface does not have to be representative for the composition of the whole particle. The images produced provide information on the internal structure, texture and shape of the particle.

The absence of water in the process does not only result in highly reduced effort during the licensing procedure, or to the absence of a tailings pond and costly dewatering process and therefore reducing disposal costs, environmental and footprint of the plant, but also decreases the amount of units and space needed for the plant. It finally leads to high flexibility where whole plant setups can be moved to a new position within days when applying a modular plant design [3]. Dry processing is of course also advantageous in climatic dry regions.

The space saving design of the plant with only four units enables the flexible application of XRT-sorting in the optimum position in the process chain – ideally in close proximity to the mining face. The four main units needed are crusher, screen, XRT-sorter and compressor. The environmental impact can be significantly decreased when applying XRT-sorting close to the mining operation. The reductions of carbon emissions in the transport process as well as in the comminution process do not only limit the environmental impact but also lead to high specific cost reductions [3].

SBS is an innovative technology, which, as mentioned before, can be implemented in different mineral processing stages to fulfil various tasks. SBS can, for example, be implemented in the processes as a pre-concentration or waste removal step for coarse size particles (up to 300 mm), for ore type diversion into different processing streams, (final) product quality improvement, marginal dump retreatment and waste dump retreatment. SBS can turn waste dumps and diluted mining blocks into reserves. As mentioned in the introduction, the implementation can also cause a decrease in specific operating costs of mill and mine when for example replacing selective mining by bulk mining methods with subsequent sorting. SBS can be implemented for simple sorting tasks where hand-sorting was used before, with the advantages that they are more stable, based on objective sorting criteria, higher security standards, applicable for smaller size ranges with higher throughput and lower operational costs. Additional it is possible to combine different sensors contrary to traditional unit operations, in this way multiple sorting criteria can be used in one processing step [2].

The economic evaluations show that the capital costs of XRT-sorting installations are at least 25% cheaper and the operating cost low in comparison to competing technologies like dense-medium-separation. Harbeck [9] indicates that operating speeds of the XRT sorting units are comparable to standard optical sorting units.

SBS is nowadays a proven technology that has been successfully implemented in recycling and mineral processing industry. This limits the technical risk for new applications. XRT systems are for example applied to the aluminium heavy metal separation in the metal scrap industry and the estimation of calorific value of packed mixed and sorting of shredder residue. The use of XRT sorting is also successfully demonstrated for number of mineral applications as well. For example, an XRT-sorter is implemented at a tungsten mine, owned by the company Wolfram Bergbau und Hütten AG, near Mittersill, Austria. This mine is only still in operation because XRT sorting is lowering the cut-off point. The sorting is based on the difference in densities of scheelite ($6.0g/cm^3$)

and the tailings ($2.8g/cm^3$) [10]. Another successful application is large diamond recovery from primary kimberlitic run-of-mine (ROM) before crushing stages. Other research examples with a positive outcome are separation of metal sulphides from gangue (e.g. [9]), sorting of nickel sulphide ores (e.g. [11, 12]), sorting of copper sulphide ore [13], pre-concentration of gold ores (e.g. [3]), de-shaling and de-stoning of coal and the separation of different coal qualities [3, 8, 14].

The potential of any ore sorting venture is highly dependent on the liberation of the material to be examined. It is therefore important to evaluate the validity of sorting on a case by case basis. Because the sorting criterion is based on atomic density the reliability of the applicability is high, for the life of mine but also for other deposits.

4 Tungsten sorting

In collaboration with the Deutsche Rohstoff AG and CommodasUltrasort, RWTH Aachen University has performed a feasibility study on the applicability of SBS as pre-concentration step in the process of tungsten ore for the Wolfram Camp Mine in Australia. The aim of this project was pre-concentration by removal of barren material. The pre-concentration of the tungsten ore cannot only lead to energy and water savings but also to a decrease of reagent input in downstream processes and increase mineral reserve utilization by lowering the cut-off grade.

A pre-screened sample suite of around $340kg$ from the mine site was available in two different size fractions $16 - 50mm$ and $10 - 20mm$. This sample suite was taken after the secondary crusher in the process of Wolfram Camp Mine. The sample was handled dry.

Out of this sample suite a training set of 20 single samples was used for preliminary laboratory test work to test the applicability of NIRS and optical sorting and to train the XRT sorter and to possibly build up a sorting algorithm (Fig. 22.3). Of all 20 samples, chemical information was available.

To test the applicability of optical sorting, pictures and false colour figures were made. The figures were treated with special developed sorting analyzing-software tool from CommodasUltrasort to simulate the sorting test. Optical sorting is technical feasible if detectable differences in colour, brightness, transparency, form or texture are present

Figure 22.3: Picture of the training set (left).

between ore and waste material. No correlation between the occurring different colour classes (dark grey, light grey and orange) and the tungsten content exist for this sample suite.

To test the applicability of NIRS sorting, the 20 samples were measured with a desktop spectrometer. The spectra of product and waste were compared and different spectral processing steps were conducted. Spectral differences in the near-infrared region of the electromagnetic spectrum make material sortable with NIRS sorters. No reproducible spectral differences between the product and the other samples exist for this sample suite.

Another outcome of the comparison of the X-ray fluorescence surface analysing measurements and the chemical analyses of milled samples was that surface measurements are not convenient for this sample. The tungsten content measurement on the surface did not correlate with the tungsten measurement of the crushed sample. This means that the surface is not representative for the whole particle.

The same 20 samples were also used to train the XRT-sorter. Figure 22.4 displays line scan images of tungsten bearing and tungsten barren material. The images appear to be bright where density is low and it appears to be dark where the density is high. The atomic density of tungsten bearing minerals is depicted as a dark grey in the X-ray image (speckled appearance in the images). Figure 22.4 also illustrates clearly that the sample suite can be sorted in ore bearing and waste material with the XRT line-scan camera.

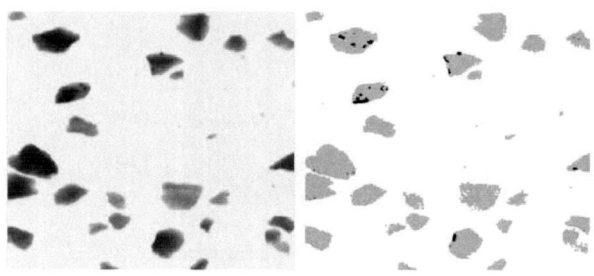

Figure 22.4: Left: Line scan images of tungsten bearing and tungsten barren material. Right: Contrast filter based on different densities.

The conclusion of this comprehensive research programme was that the best suited detection technology for sensor-based sorting of this ore is XRT. The outcome of this test work is encouraging. However, it is recognized that a more detailed examination on a bulk sample is required to determine the performance of this technology. Laboratory scale test work cannot provide data regarding the performance of the sorting process, such as product purity and associated mass yields.

5 Sorting test work

Because a sorting algorithm was successfully established, bulk sorting tests are run on a CommodasUltrasort Pro Secondary XRT belt 1200 sorter, which can handle the required size range at a throughput of around 40 to $50t/h$. A $55kW$ compressor with an operating pressure of 8 bar is used. For adjusting the sorting algorithms, the XRT pictures are uploaded into specialized software where simulations and the applications of filters and object detection are possible. A contrast filter is used for the sorting of the sample suite. The filter enhances the contrast between colour differences in pixels. In Fig. 22.4 the result of this can be seen. The sorting program can be adjusted by defining various percentages of inclusions. The setting of the sorter was changed three times. The first time the sorter opens the high pressure jets if at least 0.5% of the pixels in one particle are dark (tungsten), the second time with 1% and the third time if 2% are dark. Those percentages are labelled as "sensitivity" in Table 22.1. Table 22.1 shows the test run on the XRT sorter.

During the analyses of the training set it became clear that in every waste rock particle at least a small amount (average 0.0105%) of tungsten was present. This means that with a single particle sorting technology only a certain amount of the tungsten can be recovered (the recoverable recovery). The "recoverable recovery" takes into account the average grade of tungsten in the waste rock samples. This grade is calculated for the sorting test as well (table 22.1).

Table 22.1: Sorting results of bulk tests.

Size fraction	Selectivity/Setting	Recovery (%)	Rec.Rec (%)	Masspull to waste (%)
$10 - 20mm$	0.5	75	83	82
	1	68	82	93
	2	54	64	95
$16 - 50mm$	0.5	83	89	72
	1	59	72	76

Samples from each run are taken for assay. The results clearly show that XRT sorting can effectively remove and reduce barren material and that X-ray transmission is an effective technology for the preconcentration of tungsten ore. With an increase of sensitivity the recovery decreases and the masspull increases. This is a positive development.

The product of every test is re-sorted to decrease the difference between detection and sorting. A two step sorting does not change the recovery much (the recovery at the second step is around 95%), but it increases the masspull to waste again.

It can be concluded that the sorter application is ideally suited for coarse tungsten beneficiation. A pilot plant is currently operated in production mode to prove its robustness and reliability in a real operational environment.

6 Conclusions and recommendations

The use of dry and energy efficient methods will be more important in the future. Sensor-based sorting, including XRT sorting, is already gaining more and more significance in the minerals industry. XRT-sorting is applicable for a large variety of sorting tasks. While being technically feasible, XRT-sorting is offering side effects that underline its sustainability. It is a dry separation technology that needs little energy when compared to other coarse particle separation technologies. This also means that it needs little infrastructure and can be applied in semi-mobile separation units that can be erected in strategic locations close to the mining face, minimizing mass movement and costs and avoid unnecessary crushing of barren material while increasing downstream productivity [3].

This article describes a successful application of XRT-sorting in tungsten processing. The XRT sorting technology has good potential to become a fundamental component of future processing of tungsten ore. A pilot plant for the pre-concentration of tungsten ore is currently operated in production mode to prove its robustness and reliability in a real operation environment.

Until today, sensor-based sorting machines have only been used as separation units. The potential that lies in the huge amount of data generated is not yet unfolded. Sensor-based sorters cannot only be integrated online into mine-wide information systems to improve downstream processes, but can also be used as analytical tools for sample assaying. The possibility to scan high amounts of mass in real time improves the correctness and representativeness of the data generated when comparing to conventional sample taking, splitting and essaying procedures [3].

XRT-sorting is believed to be a powerful addition to the portfolio of processing machinery and therefore must be considered in early test work and plant planning stages.

Acknowledgements

We would like to thank DRAG for financial assistances and for their co-operation during the test work. We would like to thank TOMRA Sorting Solutions|mining as well for their cooperation and expertise and for the use of their facilities and equipment.

References

1. M. Robben, M. Gaastra, C. Kleine, A. Maul, F. Mavroudis, K. Raulf, and M. Warcholik, "Intelligente sensorsysteme," *AT International*, vol. 4, no. 52, pp. 40–53, 2011.

2. T. Pretz, H. Wotruba, and K. Nienhaus, Eds., *Applications of Sensor-based Sorting in the Raw Material Industry.*   Aachen, Germany: Shaker Verlag, 2011.

3. C. Kleine, M. Robben, and H. Wotruba, "Theory and operational experience of x-ray transmission sorting in the minerals industry," in *Proceedings of Physical Separation 2011 CD*, Falmouth, UK, June 2011.

4. H. Wotruba, "Sensor sorting technology- is the minerals industry missing a chance?" in *XXIII International Mineral Processing Congress*, Istanbul, Turkey, 2006, plenary lecture.

5. J. D. Salter and N. P. Wyatt, "Sorting machines in the minerals industry: Problems or opportunities?" in *Proc. XVII International Mineral Processing Congress*, vol. 5, Dresden, Germany, 1991.

6. F. Riedel and H. Wotruba, "Dry processing review," AMIRA International, Tech. Rep., November 2005, review of Sorting technologies, Chapter 5., Project P902.

7. H. Wotruba and T. Pretz, "State of the art in sensor-based sorting," in *Sensor Based Sorting*, Aachen, Germany, 2008.

8. L. v. Ketelhodt and C. Bergmann, "Dual energy x-ray transmission sorting of coal," *The Journal oft he Southern African Institute of Mining and Metallurgy*, no. 110, 2010.

9. H. Harbeck, "Classification of minerals with the use of x-ray transmission," in *Colloquim Sensorgestützte Sortierung*, Stolberg, Germany, 2004.

10. A. Mosser and H. Gruber, "Operational experience with xrt-sorting for pre-concentration of tungsten ore," in *Proceedings- Sensor Based Sorting*, Aachen, Germany, 2010.

11. F. Riedel, "Sortierung von disseminerten sulphiderzen mittels rontgentransmission und elektromagnetischen sensoren," in *Sensor Based Sorting Colloquiem*, Aachen, Germany, March 2006.

12. A. Allen and H. Gordon, "X-ray sorting and other technologies for upgrading nickel ore," in *ALTA 2009 Nickel-Cobalt, Copper and Uranium Conference*, Perth, Australia, May 2009.

13. L. v. Ketelhodt, "Sensor based sorting:- new developments," in *Mintek 75th Anniversary Conference*, Dresden, Germany, June 2009.

14. T. P. R. De Jong, "De-xrt sorting of coal," in *Sensor Based Sorting Conference*, Aachen, Germany, 2006.

Quantitative sorting using dual energy X-ray transmission imaging

Markus Firsching[1], Jörg Mühlbauer[1], Andreas Mäurer[2],
Frank Nachtrab[1] and Norman Uhlmann[1]

[1] Fraunhofer IIS, Development Center X-Ray Technology EZRT,
Dr-Mack-Straße 81, D-90762 Fürth
[2] Fraunhofer IVV, Process Engineering and Packaging,
Giggenhauser Straße 35, D-85354 Freising

Abstract Dual energy techniques are well-known methods in X-ray transmission imaging. However they are not commonly used in a quantitative manner in sorting applications. We introduce a method called Basis Material Decomposition (BMD) that allows the determination of the fraction of mass of different, a priori known materials using two X-ray spectra and/or spectral detector efficiencies for dual energy X-ray imaging. The method exploits the dependency of the X-ray attenuation on density and atomic number of the object and the energy of the X-rays. One example is the quantitative sorting of pollutants from valuable material, e.g. halogens as bromine from plastics to enhance their recovery rate significantly. A possible application in mining is the detection and sorting of diamonds from the host ore kimberlite, allowing diamonds to be detected even if they are covered in mud or dust or completely enclosed in the ore. We present measurements from a lab setup and discuss how this approach can provide benefits in an industrial environment in the near future.

1 Introduction

Dual energy X-ray imaging is a method to obtain quantitative information from X-ray images for material characterization. To get this information, either two sets of images with different spectra need to be acquired or a detector system providing two energy channels needs to be used.

In X-ray imaging, two independent quantities of the object define the attenuation of X-rays: The atomic number and the areal density of the object to be penetrated. For a homogenous object, the areal density is the product of density and thickness; in general it is the projection of the density along the X-ray path. In radiographic images, the product of attenuation coefficient (which is material specific) and density are integrated along the X-ray path through the object. Thus they cannot be distinguished in a projection image without further knowledge. However, the attenuation coefficient depends on the energy of the X-rays. Therefore information on the type of material becomes available, if an object is imaged using different X-ray spectra or using an energy resolving detector. Such Dual Energy techniques have been known since the mid-70s [1] and are well established in medical imaging and qualitative applications as security scanning, but have not yet been commonly used in quantitative sorting applications or non-destructive testing.

In such a case, Basis Material Decomposition by dual energy imaging is a very powerful tool to overcome the limitations of standard radioscopy, as it provides quantitative information for given constituents, i.e. the areal density of the basis materials. These can be used to derive quantities as concentration or the total amount of each basis material can be calculated. Furthermore, it implicitly contains a beam-hardening correction that reduces the artifacts resulting from the thickness dependence of other dual energy techniques.

2 The method of basis material decomposition

The energy-dependent extinction $K(E)$ of a compound material is a linear combination of the attenuation coefficients $\mu_j(E)$ of the constituents (basis materials, indexed with j) weighted with their respective concentration.

$$K(E) = \sum \mu_j(E) a_j$$

where a_j is the areal density of material j. According to Lambert-Beer's law, the attenuated intensity I behind the object is

$$I = \int S(E) D(E) \, e^{-K(E)} dE$$

where $S(E)$ is the source spectrum and $D(E)$ is the spectral detector efficiency. Given that the spectral characteristics of the imaging system and the attenuation coefficents of the basis material $\mu_j(E)$ are known, it is feasible to obtain areal densities of the corresponding basis materials by either energy resolved measurement or two measurements with different X-ray spectra [2]. The spectral characteristics of the imaging system can either be measured or simulated from a physical model and the attenuation coefficients of the basis materials can be looked up from respective tables if the occuring materials are known.

3 Applications

3.1 Brominated plastics

For demonstration of the method, a typical waste sorting application was chosen: discrimination between regular plastics acrylonitrile butadiene styrene (ABS) and polystyrene (PS) and those containing brominated flame retardants with a bromine content up to 10%. In recycling of these products bromine is considerd as a contamination. For this example shredded bulk material will be considered, e.g. from the housings of consumer eletronics. Those pieces of plastic that exceed a given bromine content need to be sorted out.

Exemplarily, four pieces of plastic, ABS and PS, both pure and brominated, were imaged at different X-ray spectra. One of the standard radiographic images can be seen in Fig. 23.1. From these images, it is impossible to decide whether a part contains bromine or not, because it is impossible to distinguish whether higher absorption is caused by a higher bromine content or from greater thickness.

By using carbon and bromine as basis materials, the method allows to identify those parts containing bromine, which must be separated before recirculation of the remaining plastics. The bromine concentration image (Fig. 23.2) clearly shows the possibility to distinguish bromine free from bromine containing plastics. The bromine free parts almost vanish in the background of this image, because of their nonexistent bromine concentration.

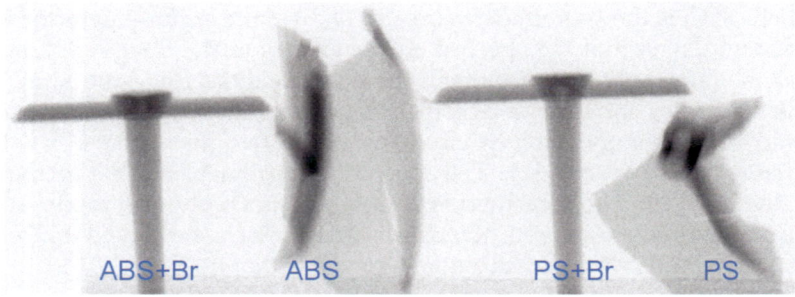

Figure 23.1: X-ray transmission image: brominated (ABS+Br, PS+Br) and bromine free (ABS, PS) plastics are not distinguishable from each other.

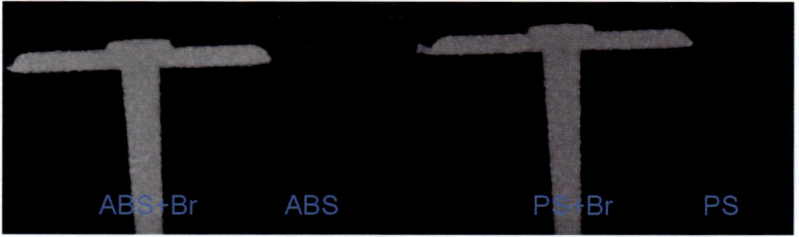

Figure 23.2: The resulting image of the bromine concentration of each particle. The plastics containing bromine can be distinguished from the others clearly.

3.2 Diamond detection

An other example is the detection and sorting diamonds from the host ore kimberlite. State-of-the-art technology use the X-ray exitation of fluorescence in the visible and UV range of electromagnetic radiation. Thus, only diamonds on the surface can be detected. Diamonds embedded in kimberlite or covered with dust and mud cannot be detected using that method.

This example is containing a diamond embedded in granulated kimberlite. It can be seen in Fig. 23.3: Two images at two different spectra are shown (80 kV and 120 kV). The diamond is not visible in either image. The resulting BMD images (Fig. 23.4) are shown in color. Black and blue denote no or low material, green indicates high content of the

Figure 23.3: The two images show the example of the diamond embedded in granulated kimberlite at two different spectra (80 kV and 120 kV).

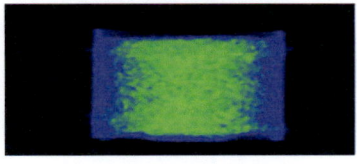
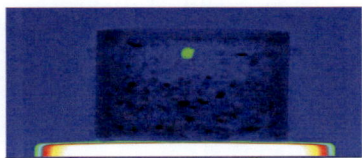

Figure 23.4: The resulting BMD images, calculated from the images in Fig. 23.3, are shown in color. The left image represents the kimberlite content. The right image represents the carbon content and the diamond can be seen clearly.

respective basis material. The left image represents the carbon content and the diamond can be seen clearly.

4 Results

The applied dual energy analysis (Basis Material Decomposition) led to a positive separation of the respective basis materials in both cases. As shown above, both settings, diamond/kimberlite and plastics with-/without brominated flame retardants, reveal that the contrast in conventional acquisition (single spectrum) is very low or even nonexistent, making differentiation and recognition respectively hardly possible, especially for objects with varying thickness. Thereby a separation of the given materials is not possible using conventional methods while BMD has proven to be a powerful method in quantitative X-ray imaging.

It was possible to reliably detect a concentration of 5-10% of brominated flame retardand in plastics as ABS and PS. For the detection and sorting of diamonds in kimberlite, BMD allows to detect diamonds even if they are completely enclosed.

5 Summary and outlook

The method of Basis Material Decomposition is demonstrated to be a powerful method in quantitative X-ray imaging. In the application of sorting plastics with and without brominated flame retardants, it would be possible by BMD to systematically enrich the plastics fraction to a certain bromine content by monitoring and registering the bromine content of every single piece of the shredded plastic particle. This would give the opportunity to meet statutory limits safely while utilizing them most effectively. In a mining application, the introduced method allows to detect the diamonds in an earlier step of the chain of the crushing processes with decreasing grain size and thus can prevent large and very valuable diamonds to be crushed into small and less valuable parts in the following stage.

The Areas of application include, but are not limited to: mining, recycling, food industries etc. Currently an evaluation and comparison with other dual energy methods are being done. Different setups of demonstrators for industrial sorting applications are currently under construction. The analysis software containing the BMD algorithm will be trimmed for sorting application needs regarding processing speed and real time capabilities and will provide the flexibility for adaption to other areas of application, e.g. the food industry. The first tests in a lab setup are very promising, next step is the application to industrial conditions and investigations concering performance and stability under those conditions.

References

1. R. E. Alvarez and A. Macovski, "Energy-selective reconstructions in x-ray computerized tomography," *Physics in Medicine and Biology*, vol. 21, no. 05, pp. 733–744, 1976.

2. M. Firsching, F. Nachtrab, N. Uhlmann, and R. Hanke, "Multi-energy x-ray imaging as a quantitative method for materials characterization," *Advanced Materials*, vol. 23, no. 22-23, pp. 2655–2656, 2011. [Online]. Available: http://dx.doi.org/10.1002/adma.201004111

Polymer identification with terahertz technology

Anja Maul[1] and Michael Nagel[2]

[1] RWTH Aachen, Department for Processing and Recycling (I.A.R.),
Wüllnerstr. 2, D-52056 Aachen, Germany
[2] AMO GmbH
Otto-Blumenthal-Straße 25, D-52074 Aachen, Germany

Abstract The spectral range of Terahertz-radiation (THz) is currently not fully utilized in industrial applications. The area of secondary raw material (generated waste) characterisation is a field where the technology is currently not applied at all. To transfer the THz-technology towards the raw material sector, the RWTH Aachen and company AMO GmbH cooperate to harness the advantages of THz-technology for material characterization. This paper presents an overview of current fields of application and summarizes the results and projections for an advanced polymer characterization with the help of THz-technology.

1 Introduction or the physics behind "T-rays"

THz-waves or T-rays lie within a relatively unexplored area of the electromagnetic spectrum, which also has been referred to as "terahertz gap" in the past. The waves are located between the infrared and microwave region of the spectrum and therefore lie between optical and electromagnetic ranges, as shown in figure 24.1. The technologies based on "THz" combine electronic and photonic applications. The "gap" is attributed to a lack of efficient sources being able to generate frequencies in the 10^{12} range. Thus the field is, due to its recent emergence, rich in open scientific questions, the technology is yet relatively immature, but rapidly developing [2, p. 1509].

The use of THz-radiation has many advantages. The THz-radiation has no ionizing effect and is not affected by influences due to differences

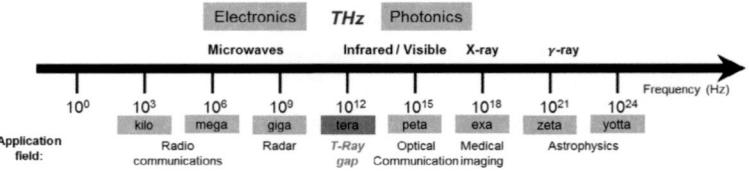

Figure 24.1: Electromagnetic spectrum with "T-ray" gap; based on [1].

in colour; thus dark material can be identified as well as light coloured materials.

One main benefit arising from THz-imaging techniques is the possibility of gathering additional information. During regular image processing or conventional imaging applying visible light, each pixel contains only information on amplitudes, since photo-sensors are only capable of detecting amplitude changes. THz-imaging instead can provide functional images where each pixel contains spectral information. This is typically achieved by terahertz pulsed imaging (TPI) systems that use a pump-probe configuration so that both amplitude and phase information can be gathered [2].

The gathering of imaging or spectroscopic data in the THz range is possible via active or passive methods. The passive measurement uses the T-ray emission at a certain temperature. The active measurement uses the absorption or reflection on objects when exposed to T-rays. The passive method provides information of the thermal properties of objects, their "body" or "internal temperature". This can be mapped as contrast in the imaging data. As an example, the signature of a hot cup of coffee is visible in high intensity, those of a cold metal blade on the other hand appears only at a low intensity [3].

2 Area of application

The generation and detection of THz-radiation is still cost-intense, therefore it is only applied in certain industries. Current applications are, for example, quality control of high-priced products in the food and medicine sector. Many materials are hereby identified by a fingerprint-method based on a characteristic absorption patterns in the terahertz range.

The most common application for THz-technology lies in safety or security applications. The so-called "full-body scanners" used for passenger controlling at airports work at the lower THz range [4]. THz imaging and spectroscopy works contact-free and without use of ionizing radiation [5, p. 71]. With this surveillance device it is possible to detect hidden weapons or explosives at a high reliability without manual frisking of passengers [3]. In order to examine an object in the THz range, to be able to generate imaging or spectroscopy data, either passive THz-radiation, emitted at a certain temperature or active radiation irradiated by THz sources is detected. Full-body scanners apply as well active as passive THz-radiation. During passive sensing methods the differences in thermal imaging of objects due to their internal temperature provides a visible contrast. For the scanned passenger a passive sensing means that the contour of the body is not visible as a sharp image and therefore the resulting image is more polite and accepted by individual persons [3, p. 296].

3 Transferring THz towards raw materials

The raw materials industry increasingly faces new challenges, like growing industrial nations, improved living standard and up-keeping economic power, to provide a secured and sufficient raw material-supply. The growing demand for raw materials leads to the necessity of satisfying the demand for primary raw materials as well as for high-quality and pure secondary raw materials from waste streams by recycling processes. This demand can only be reached by advanced processing and sorting technologies. As the following example shows:

There are many materials which cannot or only with difficulties be identified with established sensor-based sorting techniques. One example are dark-coloured materials, especially dark or black-coloured polymers. Due to the lack of sufficient reflection in the visible spectrum detection with, for example, Near-Infrared sensing for the detection of dark polymers is not possible. The THz-technology holds the potential to achieve a technical solution for this yet unsolved problem. Furthermore it might not only allow the determination of the type of polymers, but also the identification of used additives. The detection might prevent further downcycling in closed-loop recycling processes. One central question resulting here from is whether, measurement methods based on THz-technology can be applied for distinguishing different polymer types and their additives.

4 Test measurements

To reveal the many advantages of THz technology for the raw material sector, researchers of the RWTH Aachen research group 'SiR' (Sensor Technology in the raw materials industry) initiated a project with AMO GmbH.

The aim of this research cooperation is to evolve a THz-sensing system for raw material identification, especially polymer identification. At the time there is no information available on the applicability of this technology in the raw material industry. The first lab measurements conducted by AMO GmbH and the SiR-group clearly show the potential and possibilities for this new field of application.

The test measurements have been conducted in terms of proof-of-principle for the implementation of THz-technology into the raw material industry. The main focus of the first measurements has been set on the identification of different coloured polymer types - some of them being subject of the mentioned lack of sorting technologies. The measurements were carried out at the local AMO GmbH which is specialized in the development of custom-designed sensor heads and near-field probes for the THz-range.

A waveguide-based probing configuration depicted in Fig. 24.2 and developed by AMO has been applied for this study. The set-up is based on a classic optical pump/probe scheme which is widely used for THz time-domain spectroscopy [6]. A pulsed laser system with a centre wavelength of $810 \, nm$, $150 \, fs$ pulse duration and a pulse repetition rate of $78 \, MHz$ is used as the optical signal source. The laser beam is split into a pump and a probe beam. For THz generation the pump beam is focussed on a photoconductive THz emitter structure which is held in direct contact with a THz slit-waveguide (SWG) [7] with a length of $76 \, mm$. This type of waveguide is characterized by low attenuation and very low dispersion and the lowest-order propagating field mode, illustrated in Fig. 24.2 (a), is well confined to the slit region. The main

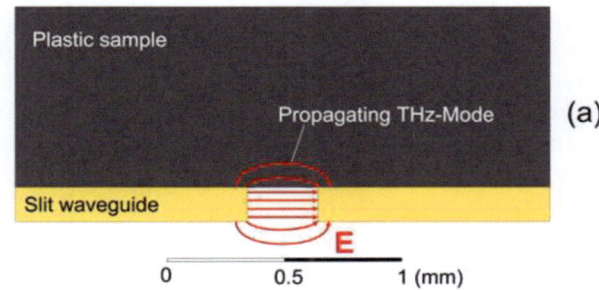

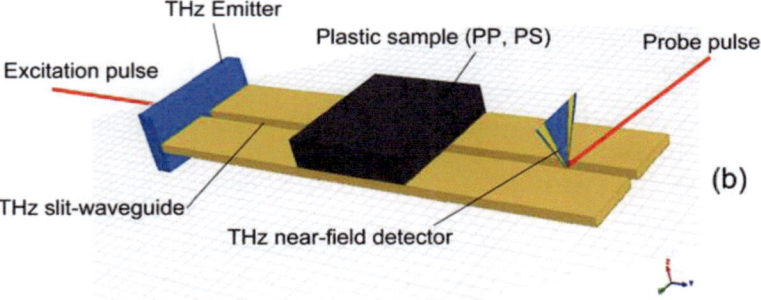

Figure 24.2: (a) Cross-section view of the THz slit-waveguide with sample material and the field distribution of the main propagation mode. (b) Schematic illustration of the applied measurement configuration.

function of the SWG is to control and enhance the THz field interaction to the sample structures placed on it. The waveguide slit has a width of 300 μm and a height of 150 μm. Each optical excitation pulse at the emitter generates a THz pulse which is propagating along the SWG. A photo-conductive near-field (NF) probe-tip [8] is placed in the slit in a longitudinal distance of 10 mm from the open end of the waveguide. The NF probe contains an ultra-fast photoswitch which is "opened" for a very short duration (approx. 200 fs) every time a probe pulse impinges. The time delay **t** between the emitter and the probe pulse is controlled by an opto-mechanical delay stage. In this way the THz pulse propagating along the SWG can be sampled in the time-domain and the average photocurrent $\mathbf{I}_{pc}(t)$ measured at the NF probe is proportional to the adjacent THz field amplitude $\mathbf{E}_{THz}(t)$. As shown in Fig. 24.2 (a) and (b), the sample under test is placed on the SWG between the emitter and the detector. Hence, a part of the transmitted THz field is penetrating a part of the sample volume which in return (depending on its dielectric properties) is causing a material specific modification of the transmitted signal [9].

The considered sample materials consist of the polymer types: polypropylene (PP) and polystyrene (PS). Both polymer types are provided in two different colours, so that estimations can be made whether different colours show characteristic differences in the detected signals. The samples are analysed regarding their different THz-transmission properties. In order to ensure a direct relation of transmission changes to differences in dielectric sample properties in this simple first configuration all samples were cut in to comparable sized pieces of ca. 17 mm x 10 mm x 2 − 3 mm length. Samples were measured along the length directions of 10 mm (in the following denoted by index 1) and 17 mm (index 2) lying flat.

The results of the measurements are summarized in the following figures (Figs. 24.3 and 24.4). In both figures the blue line determines the reference value, the THz-pulse without sample. Figure 24.3 shows the results for the measurements with polystyrene (PS) samples (PS black 1/2, PS clear 1/2). The second figure displays the results of measurements with polypropylene samples (PP black 1/2, PP grey 1/2) [9].

5 Results

At first view, the time evolution of the transmitted signals appears to be relatively complex which is caused by an instantaneous generation of three modes at the sample forefront. Each mode has a different sample interaction behaviour and propagation speed. The modes are clearly separable by comparison of the different propagation lengths. The transmission signals proved to be very robust against slight sample displacements and rotations. Characteristic differences in the transmission properties of the two polymer types PP and PS are clearly visible

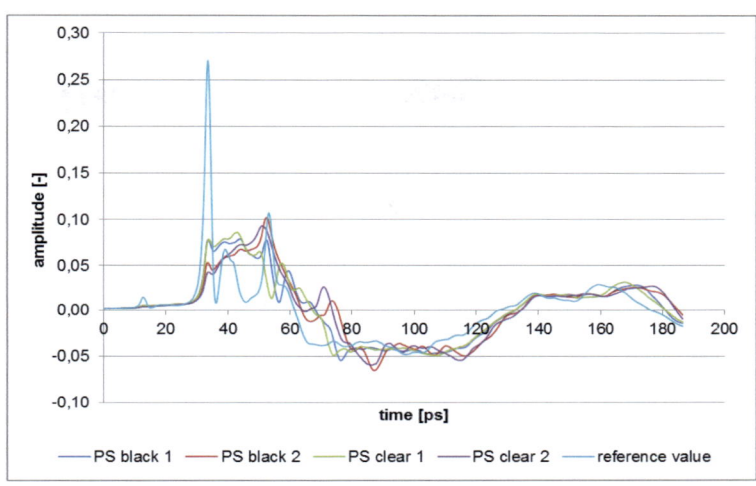

Figure 24.3: Measurement of different PS samples, source: [10]. *With friendly permission of AMO GmbH.*

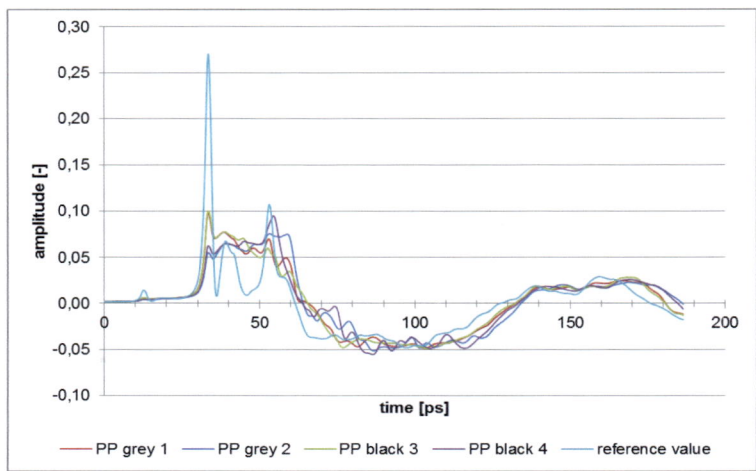

Figure 24.4: Measurement of different PP samples, source: [10]. *With friendly permission of AMO GmbH.*

from the data. Significant transmission differences are also observed for the different colour grades of each polymer type. The results reveal that the PS samples can be clearly distinguished from PP because of a lower refraction index in the THz range [9].

In conclusion, we have shown that there is a possibility of identifying critical types of polymers with THz probing technology. The application of this approach to arbitrarily shaped samples will require a measurement of the size of the sample or a design modification of the waveguide structure with suppressed sensitivity to this parameter. Detection of sample sizes could be achieved by implementing a 3D measurement system using laser triangulation techniques prior to the THz measurement.

The results show that application of THz probing in the raw material industry is very promising and surely worth further research. The topic of material recognition, especially recognition of dark materials (e.g. from shredded cars), is still an unsolved problem. Terahertz technology might become an important part of the technical solution in the nearby future.

6 Summary and outlook

But, even if the results show a high potential some restraints have to be taken into consideration. In the waste sector every technology underlies the "human factor": every detected material underlies a certain anthropogenic influence. So it is urgent, that this influences in materials have to be erased by a high number of measured objects. Therefore to evolve the THz-technology into the waste sector, large amounts of single objects have to be measured to generate a data base for further statistical analysis. At the moment measurements are still too time and cost intense to generate the required amount of data, due to the lack of cheap and sufficiently powerful THz-devices. But the already visible high potential for the raw material industry is a very strong argument to start dealing with Terahertz-technology.

At the moment there is no deeper knowledge available on the applicability of this technology into the raw material industry. The first lab measurements clearly show potential for further research and applicability for raw materials. But it is urgently required to increase the effort in research and development for implementing this technology into the raw material sector.

References

1. B. Ferguson and X.-C. Zhang, "Materials for terahertz science and technology," *nature materials*, vol. 1, no. September, pp. 26–33, 2002.

2. D. Abbott and X.-C. Zhang, "Special issue on t-ray imaging, sensing, and retection," *Proceedings of the IEEE*, vol. 95, no. 8, pp. 1509–1513, 2007.

3. M. Theuer, D. Molter, M. Rahm, and R. Beigang, "Zwischen mikrowellen und infrarot. terahertz-wellen," *Physik in unserer Zeit*, vol. 40, no. 6, pp. 296–302, 2009.

4. Tauer and Hinkov, "Terahertz-strahlung: Neue perspektiven in der messtechnik," *GIT Labor-Fachzeitschrift*, no. 2, pp. 101–103, 2006.

5. C. Jördens, S. Wietzke, M. Salhi, R. Wilk, and M. Koch, "Potenziale der bildgebenden terahertz-spektroskopie (potentials terahertz imaging)," *tm - Technisches Messen*, vol. 75, no. 1, pp. 71–76, 2008.

6. D. Grischkowsky, S. Keiding, M. Vanexter, and C. Fattinger, "Far-infrared time-domain spectroscopy with terahertz beams of dielectrics and semiconductors," *Journal of the Optical Society of America B-Optical Physics*, vol. 7, no. 10, pp. 2006–2015, 1990.

7. M. Wächter, M. Nagel, and H. Kurz, "Metallic slit waveguide for dispersion-free low-loss terahertz signal transmission," *Applied Physics Letter*, vol. 90, no. 6, 2007.

8. M. Wächter, M. Nagel, and H. Kurz, "Tapered photoconductive terahertz field probe tip with subwavelength spatial resolution," *Applied Physics Letter*, vol. 95, no. 4, 2009.

9. A. Maul, M. Gaastra, F. Mavroudis, and M. Nagel, "Detection of raw materials with terahertz-technology," in *Sensor Based Sorting 2012*, T. Pretz and H. Wotruba, Eds., vol. 128.   Clausthal-Zellerfeld: GDMB Informationsgesellschaft, 2012, pp. 1–9.

10. M. Nagel, "Feasability of thz-measurement methods for identification of polymer types: short description of measurment method and achieved results," Aachen, 14.02.2012.

Characterisation of materials in the millimeter wave frequency region for industrial applications

Matthias Demming, Dirk Nüßler, Christian Krebs and Jasmin Klimek

Fraunhofer Institute for High Frequency Physics and Radar Techniques FHR
Fraunhoferstraße 20, D-53343 Wachtberg

Abstract The millimeter wave region up to the lower THz region offers a good penetration ability for many dielectric materials which are in use today. Especially for the quality control of foods within its package, impurities can be clearly identified as long as the package is free from any metallic material. Another field of interest is the quality of welded-, brazed- and soldered joints. The present paper describes the detection and characterization of different materials under test by two different measurement systems. An vector network analyzer and a "Stand Alone MilliMeter wave Imager" called SAMMI developed by Fraunhofer FHR. For the characterization the different materials will be detect with a clustering algorithm in connection with the optimization of the measured data with regard to the problem of ambiguous phase values, called Phase Unwrapping. The permittivity of the different clusters are determined by a reconstruction algorithm.

1 Introduction

Today the non-destructive material analysis plays a major role in several applications, e.g. the quality control of industrial production lines, security applications etc. For those applications a new sensor concept working in the millimeter wave range offers an alternative to present systems, which are based on X-Ray or optical sensors. The advantage is the information about the internal structure of the device under test (DUT), which cannot be collected in the same quality by a system with optical sensors. The frequencies of interest are in the millimeter wave region starting at 30 GHz and ending around 800 GHz. This frequency range offers a better measurement capabilities than IR or optical spectrometers. Due to the shorter wavelengths compared to classical radar applications a better spatial resolution can be obtained. For the calculation of the material parameters we need the physical dimensions of the object and the runtime of the signal inside the device under test (DUT). For multilayer structures a range resolution is necessary, the range resolution can be realized through a pulsed system or the phase measurement with broadband frequency modulated continuous wave (FMCW) or stepped frequency continuous wave (SFCW) system.

The characterization of materials is a critical task for every operational system. For systems in industrial production lines belt systems between 60m/min and 300m/min are typical. A cheap, efficient and fast millimeter wave inspection system could be not realized with a vector network analyzer and a reconstruction for every pixel. Therefore a cheap inspection system called SAMMI was developed to solve these problems in three steps. The first step contains the elimination of ambiguities in the measured phase values, so called Phase Unwrapping, to ensure a precise clustering of the material parameters. In a second step the different materials of the DUT are classified by a cluster algorithm in matters of the measured amplitude and unwrapped phase values. The cluster algorithm allows a graphic presentation of the DUT where the different materials are explicitly distinguishable. In the last step the permittivity of the material is determined for each cluster, i.e. for each material, by a reconstruction algorithm. In this Paper the same steps are performed with a vector network analyzer and compared with the results of SAMMI.

2 Meausurement system

The first very simple measurement system is a mechanical xyz-scanner with a network analyzer (PNA E8361C) from Agilent (Fig. 25.1 on the left) [1]. This system is called materialscanner. The PNA allows the analysis of amplitude and phase information of the DUT with a SFCW mode. With several modules this system allows a frequency range from 10 MHz to 325 GHz. With the three connected linear motors it is possible to scan a three-dimensional area. The second system is called SAMMI

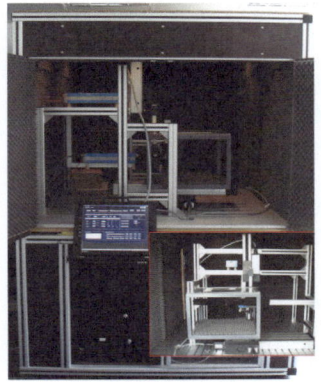 

Figure 25.1: On the left is shown the materialscanner with the xvz-motors. SAMMI is shown on the right.

(Fig. 25.1 on the right) and is a continuous wave system at the frequency of 78 GHz.

SAMMI was developed at the Fraunhofer-Institute for High Frequency Physics and Radar Techniques FHR and allows the analysis of amplitude and phase information of the DUT. SAMMI has rotating plates on which dielectric antennas are attached, which sampled a DUT in transmission. An endless belt ensures a continuous flow of material and a DIN A4 sheet is scanned within 20 s. SAMMI has the size of an average laser printer, whereby it is easy to transport. The big advantage of SAMMI is the construction off low cost materials whereby the whole system has a low price in comparison with a vector network analyzer. Due to their low loss at higher frequencies compared to common waveguides two dielectric waveguide tips act as antennas in both systems. Another advantage of dielectric waveguides is their high flexibility, which allows changing simply between the transmission and reflection configuration.

To detect the thickness of the DUT a light-section sensor (C4-1280CS) from Automation Technology are used for both systems.

3 Device under test und measurement method

The measured DUTs are two different plastics which have both the same width and height from 100 mm and differ only in the thickness and the permittivity. The first DUT is PVC (polyvinyl chloride) with a thickness of 7 mm and a permittivity of 3 to 3.5. The second DUT is POM (polyoxymethylene) with a thickness of 4 mm. It is the lower DUT at all amplitude and phase images of this paper. In general has POM a permittivity of 2.9 to 3.8. The two materials were chosen by means of their similar permittivity to show whether they can be distinguished by the clustering algorithm. All samples have a planar structure. To compare the results of both systems the same measurement method is choosen. This means a transmission measurement at a frequency of 78 GHz at SAMMI and a transmission measurement at the frequency range from 75 GHz to 110 GHz at the materialscanner.

4 Simplified signal processing for material characterization

4.1 2D phase unwrapping

In general phase unwrapping describes the elimination of ambiguities in the measured phase values, which are wrapped into the interval $(-\pi,\pi]$, i.e. the phase is known except for multiples of 2π. The two-dimensional phase unwrapping is divided into the path-following and the minimum-norm methods. In opposition to the minimum-norm algorithms, which regard the entire image, the path-following methods consider the image pixel by pixel guided by a certain path. A classical path following method is the quality guided algorithm which is guided by so called quality maps, i.e. matrices whose entries describe the quality of the recorded phase values. As a measure the variance of the phase gradients is used. Another possible measure is the correlation of the phase values [2]. Due to the error rate of the quality guided algorithm for noisy data a modified quality guided method [3] is used here. The modification consists in the valuation of the adjusted phase values after each step and the correction of possible errors to avoid their propagation. The algorithm is subdivided into two main steps, the unwrapping of the recorded phase value and the evaluation of the result by means of a certain quality criterion.

1. The modified unwrapping algorithm starts as the original one at a pixel of high quality in a homogeneous region. For each pixel the adjusted phase is determined by the information of its eight neighbours in a region of 5×5 pixels around the considered phase value, where only those pixels are taken into account which are already unwrapped [3].

2. As criterion for the quality of the adjusted phase value the deviation between the result and an estimate for the unwrapped phase value is established [3]. If the deviation is lower than a certain threshold, the adjusted phase value, calculated in step one, will be hold. Otherwise the determined phase will be discarded and the unwrapping continues at another pixel, i.e. the algorithm starts again at step one.

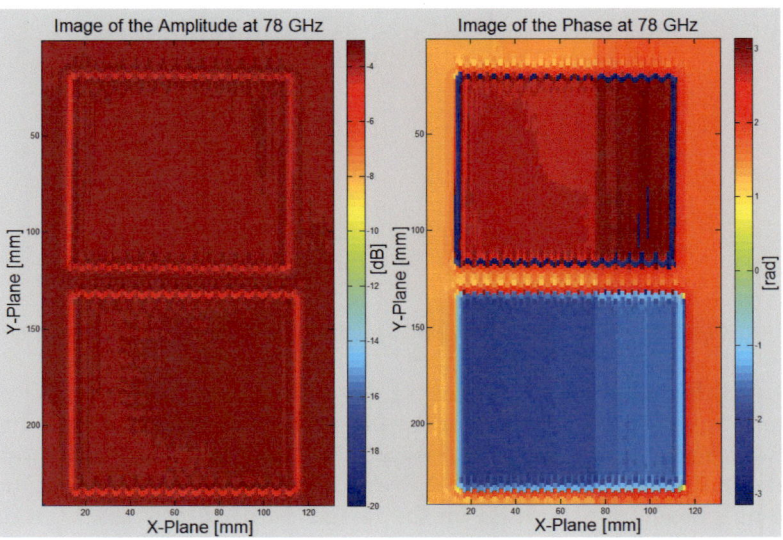

Figure 25.2: Raw data (amplitude and the wrapped phase) from the materialscanner.

Figure 25.2 shows the measured raw amplitude and raw phase from the materialscanner at 78 GHz with the phase values wrapped into the interval $(-\pi,\pi]$. The phase shifts are mainly distinguishable at the upper DUT (PVC) and at the outlines of the DUTs, i.e. there are jumps from $-\pi$ to π between two adjoining pixels. Figure 25.3 shows the unwrapped continuous phase, which is no longer bound to the interval $(-\pi,\pi]$. It is in evidence that the phase jumps within the DUTs have been eliminated. Based on the images of the materialscanner it is visual distinguishable that there are two different DUTs within the image.

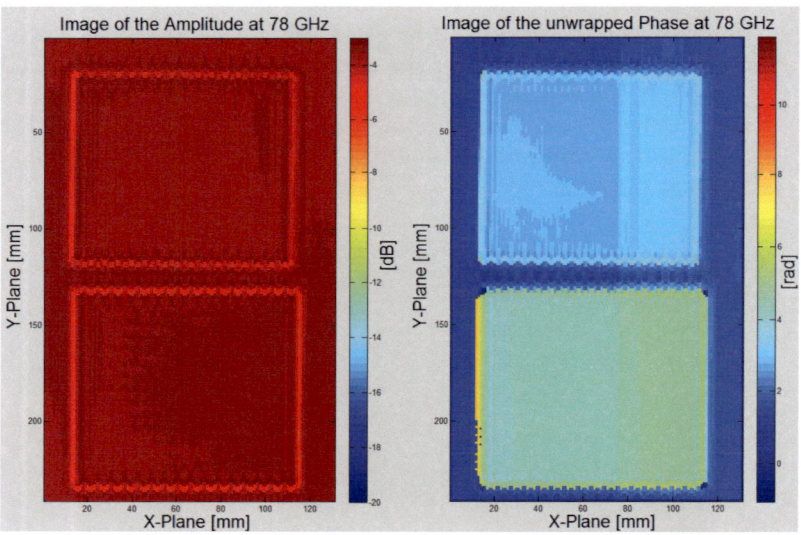

Figure 25.3: Amplitude and the unwrapped phase from the materialscanner.

SAMMI has a pre-processing of the raw data which includes the phase unwrapping. The aim of the pre-processing is a faster data handling for real time application. Figure 25.4 shows the measured amplitude and phase from SAMMI at 78 GHz. This image shows that their are no phase jumps. Based on the images of SAMMI it is visual distinguishable that there are two different DUTs within the image. One current drawback of the preprocessing can be seen at the bottom DUT. A part of the edge of the DUT assumed to the background and hence the DUT it is not rectangular.

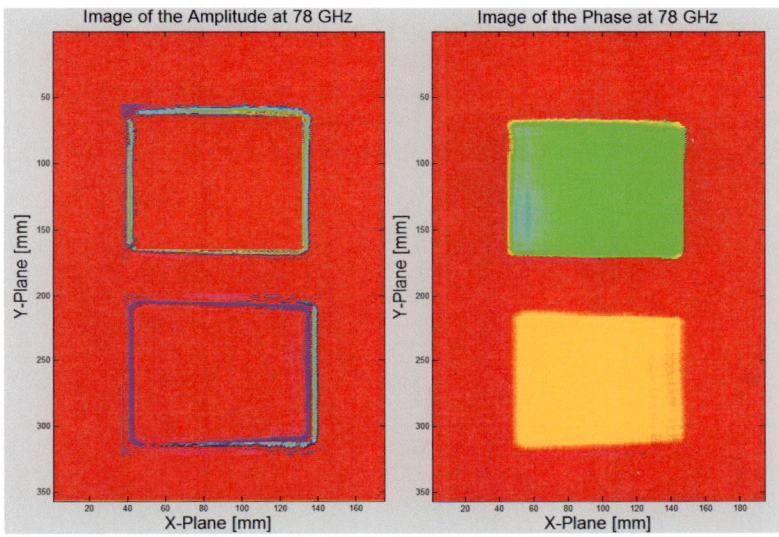

Figure 25.4: Pre-processed raw data (amplitude and the unwrapped phase) from SAMMI.

4.2 Clustering algorithm

The aim of cluster analysis is to identify groups of objects in a certain dataset, which are similar to each other but different from individuals in other groups. However, a cluster algorithm should capture the nature structure of a data set. There are various ways in which clusters can be realized. One of the most straightforward methods is the hierarchical clustering algorithm, which will be described here briefly. Hierarchical clustering can be either agglomerative or divisive.

Agglomerative hierarchical clustering begins with each object of the data-set as an own cluster. Similar clusters are merged after successive steps into subclusters based on chosen linkage functions. The algorithm ends with all objects in one cluster. The divisive clustering method starts with each object in one cluster and ends up with each as an own cluster. However, it is the opposite way of the agglomerative method. Linkage functions are used to determine in which order clusters may merge. E.g. two clusters can be merged to one cluster if its elements are the most similar objects (single linkage) or if their objects are the elements which are most dissimilar (complete linkage). More linkage methods are listed in [4]. The key of this algorithm is the calculation of the so called proximity matrix between two clusters [5]. As basis for the clustering algorithm the unwrapped phase and the amplitude of the objects is regarded (Figs. 25.3 and 25.4).

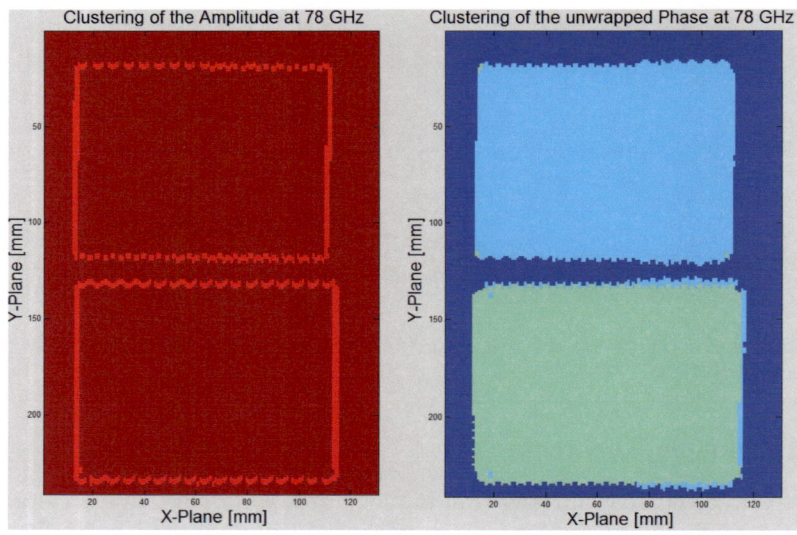

Figure 25.5: Result of the cluster process for the images of the material scanner.

Using the agglomerative clustering algorithm, the result of the cluster process for the images of the material scanner is illustrated in Fig. 25.5. The result for the images of SAMMI is illustrated in Fig. 25.6. For merging the clusters, Ward's method [6] was used. This method uses an analysis of variance approach to evaluate the distances between clusters. Ward's algorithm attempts to minimize the sum of squares of any two clusters that can be formed at each step. The aim is to create clusters of similar sizes. To determine the number of groups in the current dataset, Mojena's stopping rule was applied [7]. The number of clusters is 3.

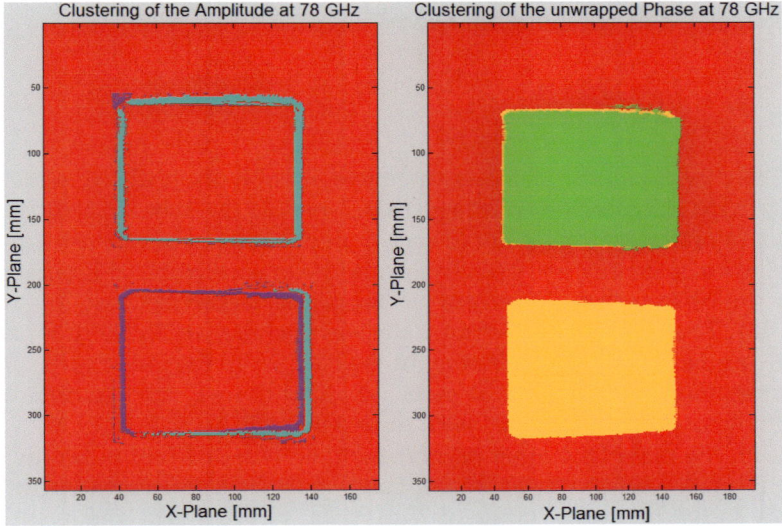

Figure 25.6: Result of the cluster process for the images of the SAMMI.

Comparing the clustered image of the amplitude and of the unwrapped phase, it can be seen, that on the amplitude image only the outlines of the DUTs are detected by the materialscanner and SAMMI. The differences in the amplitude are too similar. For this reason the results are regarded not further. In the clustered images of the unwrapped phase of the materialscanner and of SAMMI are mainly three clusters, i.e. the background, the PVC and the POM sample are clearly reproduced in spite of their similar permittivity.

4.3 Reconstruction of the permittivity

The permittivity is calculated from the time difference between a test section with and without a sample. The time difference is caused by the permittivity of the material which slows down the electromagnetic wave inside the material. This difference is expressed in the frequency domain by a phase difference which can be measured. If the phase difference and the thickness of the material is known, the permittivity can be calculated by using the equation 25.1.

$$\varepsilon_r = \left(\left(\frac{\Delta\varphi \, c_0}{\omega \, d_{DUT}} \right) + 1 \right)^2 \tag{25.1}$$

The cluster algorithm shows that there are only three different materials in the clustered phase image, therefore only the material characteristics of one measuring point of each material need to be reconstructed. For this reason only one pixel in the middle of each material is enough. For the background the reconstruction is not needed because it is not a DUT. The light-section sensor detects a thickness of 3.95 mm for the POM and a thickness of 6.98 mm for the PVC. With the phase value and the measured thickness of the pixel the permittivity of the two different materials can be determined with the equation 25.1.

With the materialscanner will be calculate two different permittivity per DUT. A permittivity at the frequency at 78 GHz and a mean permittivity in the frequency range of 75 GHz up to 110 GHz. The result of the mean permittivity is for PVC 2.92 and for POM 2.84. At a frequency of 78 GHz the permittivity of PVC is 2.92 and of POM 2.83. SAMMI reconstructed a permittivity of 2.94 for PVC and a permittivity of 2.88 for POM. The reconstructed permittivity of SAMMI and the materialscanner are similar and corresponds almost exactly with the theoretical permittivity of the both DUTs.

5 Conclusion

In conclusion a compared between a vector network analyzer and SAMMI for a procedure of non-destructive detection and characterisation of materials was presented. It was shown that SAMMI is a cheap, efficient and fast millimeter wave inspection system which delivers nearly the same quality as a expensive vector network analyzer. Different materials can be distinguished by SAMMI by an clustering algorithm, based on the phase information of a transmission measurement. Previously the phase ambiguities were eliminated by a phase unwrapping algorithm. It was shown that the clustering algorithm detected all samples in each case as one cluster. Based on the classification of the clustering algorithm the permittivity of the different clusters were reconstructed by a reconstruction algorithm. The reconstruction results showed that the permittivity nearly match with the theoretical values.

References

1. J. Rubart, R. Brauns, D. Nüßler, and C. Krebs, "High resolution measurements to determine the permittivity in artificial structures," in *Int. Conf. on Infrared, Millimeter and THz Waves*, Rome, Italy, 2010.

2. D. Ghiglia and M. Pritt, Eds., *Two-Dimensional Phase Unwrapping: Theory, Algorithms and Software.*   New York, USA: John Wiley and Sons, 1998.

3. W. Xu and I. Cumming, "A region-growing algorithm for insar phase unwrapping," *IEEE Transactions on Geoscience and Remote Sensing*, vol. 37, no. 1, pp. 124–134, 1999.

4. P. Tan, M. Steinbach, and V. Kumar, Eds., *Introduction to Data Mining.* München, Germany: Addison-Wesley, 2005.

5. L. Kaufman and P. Rousseeuw, Eds., *Finding Groups in Data - An Introduction to Cluster Analysis.*   München, Germany: Addison-Wesley, 2005.

6. J. Ward, "Hierarchical grouping to optimize an objective function," *Journal of the American Statistical Association*, vol. 58, no. 301, pp. 236–244, 1963.

7. R. Mojena, "Hierarchical grouping methods and stopping rules: an evaluation," *The Computer Journal*, vol. 20, no. 4, pp. 359–363, 1977.